Salesforce.com®

6th edition

by Liz Kao and Jon Paz

Salesforce.com® For Dummies®, 6th Edition

Published by: **John Wiley & Sons, Inc.**, 111 River Street, Hoboken, NJ 07030-5774, www.wiley.com

Copyright © 2016 by John Wiley & Sons, Inc., Hoboken, New Jersey

Published simultaneously in Canada

For general information on our other products and services, please contact our Customer Care Department within the U.S. at 877-762-2974, outside the U.S. at 317-572-3993, or fax 317-572-4002. For technical support, please visit www.wiley.com/techsupport.

Wiley publishes in a variety of print and electronic formats and by print-on-demand. Some material included with standard print versions of this book may not be included in e-books or in print-on-demand. If this book refers to media such as a CD or DVD that is not included in the version you purchased, you may download this material at http://booksupport.wiley.com. For more information about Wiley products, visit www.wiley.com.

Library of Congress Control Number: 2016935333

ISBN 978-1-119-23931-4 (pbk); ISBN 978-1-119-23932-1 (ebk); ISBN 978-1-119-23933-8 (ebk)

Manufactured in the United States of America

10 9 8 7 6 5 4

Contents at a Glance

Table of Contents

Introduction

*S*alesforce.com For Dummies, 6th Edition, is for users of Salesforce, including those users who have the Unlimited, Enterprise, or Professional Edition. It's for Salesforce users who want to quickly know how to use this web-based application, running "in the cloud" — also known as Software-as-a-Service (SaaS) — for sales, marketing, and customer service.

About This Book

Don't use this book to find out how Salesforce works. Use this book to find out how you can manage your customers and your teams and close more business by using Salesforce:

- **If you're a sales rep,** this book shows you how to use Salesforce to manage your leads, accounts, contacts, and opportunities. Spend less time doing administrative work and more time focused on making money.

- **If you're a sales manager,** this book shows you how to use Salesforce to track team activities and pipeline, shorten the ramp-up time on new hires, and pinpoint key deals that require your involvement.

- **If you're in channel sales,** this book shows you how to track your relationships with companies that are — or will be — your partners and all the deals they work for you.

- **If you're a partner,** this book shows you the world of Salesforce and how you can improve your deal pipeline and win rate with your vendor.

- **If you're in marketing,** this book shows you how to use Salesforce to make an immediate and measurable impact on your sales organization. We cover how to manage campaigns and track leads to fill your funnel.

- **If you're in customer service,** this book shows you how to manage customer issues, from creation to resolution. Support managers will see how to improve agent productivity and customer self-sufficiency.

- **If you sit on the executive team,** this book shows you how to use Salesforce for internal collaboration and to measure your overall business.

>> **If you're an administrator or involved in your company's customer relationship management (CRM) initiative,** this book gives you practical knowledge for customizing, configuring, maintaining, and successfully implementing your solution.

We show you everything you need to know to manage the life cycle of your customer relationships in Salesforce, from qualifying leads to closing opportunities to handling service agent inquiries. Along the way, we share a laugh or two. And this book can expose you to useful features and functionality that you might not have even known existed!

Note: Not all portions of this book necessarily apply to your edition of Salesforce. Different editions have varying degrees of features and functionality. We make sure to point out the differences where relevant.

This book has been revised to reflect the latest Salesforce.com product and feature offerings as of the Spring 2016 release. Salesforce is an Internet-based service where new releases occur simultaneously for all customers, about three times a year, without your having to lift a finger (okay, except to just log in). Because of this model, Salesforce.com can release new versions of its product faster than many traditional software vendors — and faster than we can write! We did our best to update this book to the current version of the product, but please bear in mind that new versions of Salesforce are always in the works.

Keep in mind that references to the product use the word *Salesforce,* and references to the company that makes the family of products, or the family of products as a whole, use the term *Salesforce.com.* That's a tiny detail, but we didn't want you to think our eagle eyes had glossed over it!

Finally, within this book, you may note that some web addresses break across two lines of text. If you're reading this book in print and want to visit one of these web pages, simply key in the web address exactly as it's noted in the text, pretending as though the line break doesn't exist. If you're reading this as an e-book, you've got it easy — just click the web address to be taken directly to the web page.

Foolish Assumptions

Please forgive us, but we make one or two foolish assumptions about you, the reader. We assume the following:

>> You have access to a high-speed Internet connection, have used a web browser, and have access to the most up-to-date version of your chosen

browser. If we assumed incorrectly, you have much more pressing problems than understanding the effective use of Salesforce.

>> You have a Salesforce account and some interest in knowing how to use it, beyond the mere curiosity of reading our riveting prose.

>> You have some business experience — at least enough to understand that winning deals is good, and losing deals is bad.

>> You have at least a vague idea of what a database is, including basic concepts such as fields, records, files, and folders. (Imagine an organized filing cabinet and all its contents.)

Icons Used in This Book

To help you get the most out of this book, we place icons here and there that highlight important points. Here's what the icons mean:

TIP

Next to the Tip icon, you can find shortcuts, tricks, and best practices to use Salesforce more effectively or productively.

WARNING

Pay extra attention when you see a Warning icon. It means that you might be about to do something that you'll regret later.

REMEMBER

When we explain a juicy little fact that bears remembering, we mark it with a Remember icon. When you see this icon, prick up your ears. You can pick up something that could be of wide or frequent use as you work with Salesforce.

TECHNICAL STUFF

When we're forced to describe something geeky, a Technical Stuff icon appears in the margin. You don't have to read what's beside this icon if you don't want to, although some readers might find the technical detail helpful.

Beyond the Book

In addition to what you're reading right now, this product also comes with a free access-anywhere Cheat Sheet that tells you how to perform your day-to-day functions in Salesforce. To get this Cheat Sheet, simply go to www.dummies.com and type **Salesforce.com For Dummies Cheat Sheet** in the Search box.

Where to Go from Here

If you're just getting started with Salesforce, you may want to turn the page and start reading. If you're an administrator and have a deadline, you may want to jump to Part 6. If you're a manager, try reading about reports and dashboards in Part 7. Sales reps and service reps should start in on Parts 8 and 4, respectively. Regardless of what you choose, we're sure that you'll find what you're looking for!

1

Introducing Salesforce

Chapter 1

Customer Relationship Management at a Glance

You may not realize it yet, but every time you log in to Salesforce, you're accessing an extremely powerful lever of change for you, your group, and your company.

Sounds like a tall order, but consider this: What value do you put on your customer relationships? Your partner relationships? If you're a sales rep, it's your livelihood. And if you're in management, you have fewer assets more valuable than your existing partner and customer base. What if you had a tool that could truly help you manage your partners and customers?

That's where customer relationship management software comes in. *Customer relationship management* (CRM) is an umbrella term for the parts of your business that are "front office," also known as those that have direct interactions with your customers and prospective customers. The CRM life cycle encompasses business processes and associated applications that help businesses better track their leads, manage customers, track opportunities, resolve cases, and more.

The more you and your team adopt a CRM system into your work, and you determine how you want your business process to be reflected within the technology, the more information you'll have at your fingertips to deepen customer relationships and improve your overall business.

In this chapter, we establish a common understanding of the CRM life cycle. Then we describe areas where a CRM system can improve your business.

Introducing the Customer Relationship Management life cycle

Within the world of CRM exist additional processes focused on specific areas of the life cycle. You may hear the phrases *marketing automation, sales force automation,* and *service and support.* These are front-office areas of your business that vendors (like Salesforce.com!) work on to make your front-office teams more efficient and productive.

Understanding your customer's customer

How can you sell to and retain customers if you don't understand their needs, key contacts, and what account activities and transactions have taken place? A CRM system allows you to track all your important customer interactions and data so that you can develop solutions that deliver real value to your customers, which in turn should mean higher customer satisfaction with *their* customers. Whether people are in marketing, sales, or customer support, they should all have the ability to access the same source of truth about your customer. After all, how can your company serve its customers well if you're not familiar with how your products and services help improve your customers' customers' (no, that's not a typo) experience?

Centralizing customer information under one roof

How much time have you wasted tracking down a customer contact or an address that you know exists within the walls of your company? What about trying to find out which sales rep owns the relationship with a subsidiary of a global customer? A good CRM system lets you quickly centralize and organize your accounts and contacts so that you can capitalize on that information when you need to.

Looking to Customer Relationship Management to Solve Critical Business Challenges

We could write another book telling you all the great things you can do with Salesforce, but you can get the big picture about CRM systems' benefits from this chapter. We focus here on the most common business challenges that we hear from sales, marketing, and support executives — and how a CRM system can overcome them.

Expanding the funnel

Inputs and outputs, right? The more leads you generate and pursue, the greater the chance that your revenue will grow. So, the big question is, "How do I make the machine work?" A CRM application helps you plan, manage, measure, and improve lead generation, qualification, and conversion. You can see how much business you or your team generates, the sources of that business, and who in your team is making it happen.

Consolidating your pipeline

Pipeline reports give companies insight into future sales, yet we've worked with companies in which generating the weekly pipeline could take more than a day of cat herding and guesswork. Reps waste time updating spreadsheets. Managers waste time chasing reps and scrubbing data. Bosses waste time tearing their hair out because the information is old by the time they get it. The prevalence of cloud computing makes this traditional method of siloed data collection obsolete (or pretty darn inefficient). A good CRM system helps you shorten or eliminate all that pulling and pasting of data across multiple sources. As long as reps manage all their opportunities in one place that's always available, managers can generate updated pipeline reports with the click of a button.

Collaborating effectively with your colleagues

Remember when you were the new person at the company, and you had to find out who knew everything about a particular customer, process, or product? Even at smaller companies, it takes time to discover who possesses that extra bit of historical knowledge that could help you close that important deal or resolve a support issue. Other times, you may be so busy that you're out of the loop on certain key company updates, even when departments try to keep you informed. What if you could harness the insights from others within the company, yet not be overwhelmed by information overload? A CRM system should provide a means for employee communication that increases internal awareness and collaboration on the business issues that matter the most to you, so you're always up to date and never caught unawares.

Working as a team

How many times have you thought that your own co-workers got in the way of selling? Oftentimes, the challenge isn't the people, or even the technology, but standardizing processes and clarifying roles and responsibilities. A CRM system will let you define teams and processes for sales, marketing, and customer service so that the left hand knows what the right hand is doing. It should also be flexible enough to change all those team members the next time a reorg happens. Although a CRM system doesn't solve corporate alignment issues, the tool should drive and manage better team collaboration.

Extending your sales force with partners

In many industries, selling directly is a thing of the past. To gain leverage and cover more territory, many companies work through partners. CRM systems should let your channel team track and associate partners' deals and get better insight about who their top partners are. Partners now can strengthen their relationships with their vendors by collaborating more easily on joint sales and marketing efforts.

Beating the competition

How much money have you lost to competitors? How many times did you lose a deal only to discover, after the fact, that it went to your archenemy? If you know who you're up against, you can probably better position yourself to win the opportunity. CRM systems let you and your teams track competition on deals, collect competitive intelligence, and develop action plans to wear down your foes.

Improving the customer experience

As a salesperson, have you ever walked into a customer's office expecting a bed of roses only to be hit with a landmine because of an unresolved customer issue? And if you work in customer support, how much time do you waste on trying to identify the customers and reviewing the context of previous support interactions? A CRM system should let you efficiently capture, manage, and resolve a high volume of customer issues that come in from a variety of communication channels. The customer relationship doesn't end once they've bought your product — that's just the beginning. A CRM system should allow sales reps to have visibility into the health of their accounts, and service can stay well informed of sales and account activity.

Measuring the business

How can you improve what you can't measure? Simple, huh? If you use your CRM system correctly and regularly to manage customers, you have data to make informed decisions. That benefits everyone. If you're a rep, you know what you need to do to get the rewards you want. If you're a manager, you can pinpoint where to get involved to drive your numbers. A CRM system's reporting and dashboards should provide easy-to-use tools to measure and analyze your business.

Selecting Salesforce as Your Customer Relationship Management System

Salesforce wasn't the first CRM system to hit the market, but it's dramatically different from the other CRM systems you may have used (spreadsheets and sticky notes count as a system, too!). Unlike traditional CRM software, Salesforce is the first successful business application offered as an Internet service. You sign up and log in through a browser, and it's immediately available. We currently call this *cloud computing*, where the customers access "the cloud" (that is, the Internet) for their business needs, and are not required to install any traditional software on, presumably, Earth. As long as you have an Internet connection, you can be anywhere in the world and have access to the clouds.

You may already be at a company that uses cloud-based applications, as Salesforce.com's success has spawned a whole new marketplace full of business applications done "in the cloud." Or you may just be entering the workforce, but you're very familiar with the use of Internet-applications in your personal life (think Twitter, Instagram, or Facebook). If this is your first foray into cloud computing, you may be taking a first step by yourself or with the rest of your company. Don't worry — your company made the right choice by picking Salesforce.

Salesforce customers typically say that it's unique for three major reasons:

>> **It's fast.** When you sign on the dotted line, you want your CRM system up and running yesterday. Traditional CRM software can take more than a year to deploy; compare that to months or even weeks with Salesforce.

>> **It's easy.** End user adoption is critical to any application, and Salesforce wins the ease-of-use category hands down. You can spend more time putting it to use and less time figuring it out.

>> **It's effective.** Because it's easy to use and can be customized quickly to meet business needs, customers have proven that it has improved their bottom lines.

Salesforce's success has empowered a whole new generation of managers and administrators to become business operations gurus. Cloud computing's generally lower licensing costs, its ability to allow system configuration to happen with no prior programming experience, and its ability to make modifications quickly to the system mean that newer businesses can compete with slower, older, bigger competitors, but at a fraction of the cost.

In the next chapter, we cover more specifics about Salesforce.com's products.

Chapter 2

Discovering Salesforce.com's Products

N ow that you have a general idea about what Salesforce is, let's delve into the various products that Salesforce.com offers. Generally speaking, the products we cover here fall into the three major categories or departments traditionally used to understand customer relationship management (CRM): sales, marketing, and service.

You may not have thought about it yet, but if you think about the basic structure of CRM, it follows the customer journey from pre-sales to sales and finally post-sales. In other words, marketing departments market the business to spark interest in a customer base and attract potential leads for your sales teams. When those leads are good and qualified, the lead is handed off to sales to close a deal. After the sale, the customer interacts with customer support for service, questions, or feedback about the product sold.

When you step back and look at the big picture, this entire life cycle centers around the customer. As you can see, we're trying to sufficiently hammer home the fact that Salesforce.com and its products are all about enhancing the relationship between your business and your customer. Although it's important to see this big picture, Salesforce.com also recognizes that the devil is in the details, especially from your customers' perspective. Salesforce.com encourages its users to capture customer details and use them to improve this customer relationship.

In this chapter, we discuss three of Salesforce.com's products and show you how they can transform a relationship between an organization and its customer base. First, we show you how you can improve your selling with Sales Cloud. Then we talk about Marketing Cloud — how it improves lead quality and automates important marketing tasks. Then we look at customer support and the features of Service Cloud that streamline it. Finally, we wrap up the chapter by helping you decide which Salesforce edition is right for you.

Using Sales Cloud to Win More Deals

Sales Cloud helps companies increase their sales success in a number of ways that we describe in the next few pages. But first, it's important to note that any system you use is only as good as the data entered in it. This is an important point that cannot be emphasized enough throughout this book. If your data is stale and outdated or just plain incorrect, the entire infrastructure built around it is essentially worthless. And that's why user adoption is so important. With Salesforce, it's easy to put in place a number of guardrails to ensure that the integrity of your data isn't compromised. Assuming that data is up to date and accurate, Salesforce is a powerful sales machine that gives organizations all around the world insight into their businesses.

Making sales groups more effective

So, how does Salesforce do it? Let's look at a few ways Sales Cloud makes sales teams more efficient at their jobs.

Account management and contact management are the focal point of sales teams and the foundation of Salesforce.com's products. What would a CRM tool be if you couldn't use it to track your customers and the organizations they're a part of? Accounts are those organizations or businesses. Contacts are the individuals that belong to those Accounts. Salesforce lets you establish and differentiate between your customers, partners, competitors, and distributors effortlessly. It also shows you valuable information about these people and organizations in one place (again, assuming someone is inputting that data).

This allows any company using Salesforce to view customer details quickly and easily. Moreover, it ensures that any department within that company is looking at the same customer details, assuming you permit it. It's also built with the user in mind, providing a simple user interface so that inputting this crucial information isn't too cumbersome. Of course, it can get laborious over time if you aren't careful. But Salesforce gives administrators what they need to make entering or updating accounts and contacts easy.

Another way Salesforce boosts sales efficiency is by minimizing time spent trying to communicate across and within teams. Salesforce provides multiple tools for on-demand work collaboration, as well as quick communication. Many companies see a dramatic decline in emails after using Chatter. Tasks and events that are automatically created and synced to the digital calendars of sales teams also increase efficiency, forecasting, and opportunity management.

Improving sales productivity

Sales Cloud can be used to dramatically increase sales productivity for many organizations. Sales Cloud can increase forecasting accuracy, which has many obvious benefits. Tracking and managing leads, following up with them, and converting them with a single click of a button can help sales teams focus more on selling and less on entering data into a cumbersome Excel spreadsheet. Organizing massive amounts of data and presenting these results in a way that makes sense to users in real time is one of the most powerful weapons of Sales Cloud.

In essence, there really is no secret formula to how Salesforce boosts productivity and efficiency for sales teams. You can manage and view all customer information in one place, while updating contacts or following up with them (again, from the same single place), and track all this using powerful reporting to see trends over time and act accordingly. You can organize your tasks by priority, forecast more accurately, and respond to customers more quickly, thereby helping your business become a "customer company."

Generating Better Leads with Marketing Cloud

We could write a separate book about Salesforce Marketing Cloud and do a deep dive into the various features it offers, but you can get the big picture from this section. Marketing Cloud is really a suite of multiple product offerings, but in this section we focus on email campaigns, marketing automation, and lead management, and how Marketing Cloud can improve your organization's ability to execute on all of them.

Managing email campaigns with Marketing Cloud

How can you drive online commerce, as well as sell to and build customer relationships, without email? Email is the engine behind these forces. Marketing Cloud gives companies the tools to quickly create and automate attention-grabbing emails to customers throughout the customer life cycle. It's essentially a user interface for managing communications and content to a wide customer base. The platform maintains mailing lists and schedules and can modify email messages based on what recipients read, click, and forward. You can easily filter your subscriber base so that you're sending specific, targeted emails based on criteria or events of your choosing. You don't want certain customers to be bothered by email campaigns? No problem. All of this can be set up and monitored as you desire.

TIP

ExactTarget is the name Marketing Cloud used to go by, so if you see ExactTarget in documentation somewhere, don't get confused.

Improving marketing automation

How much time have you wasted tracking down customer activity, emailing potential buyers that weren't even interested, or trying to understand who clicked your links? *Marketing automation* is a general term for platforms that enable the automation of repetitive tasks, as they relate to marketing on multiple online channels. In other words, automating marketing communication. So, via multiple channels, a company that uses marketing automation is able to manage and automate the targeting, timing, and content of outbound messages. What's more, it can do this intelligently, using cues from prospective actions and behaviors on the customer side.

Think of this like responding to body language. In today's world, consumers do their homework and visit the websites of multiple competitors before deciding which product they want to buy. Email blasts are no longer acceptable means of capturing a large piece of the consumer pie. More personalized and sensitive communications must be sent out, based on various criteria such as the buyer's role in his or her organization or the buyer's purchase readiness. It's more important than ever to send the right message at the right time.

Marketing Cloud includes a host of features that assist in automating these marketing processes. Even better, Marketing Cloud is already part of the Salesforce network, meaning that you can leverage all the information in one database, instead of worrying about complex integration of various systems feeding into one another. Now it's easier than ever to manage these interactions and deploy online campaigns from a central platform.

Identifying qualified leads with Pardot

Leads are the lifeblood of your business. The more leads you generate and pursue, the greater the chance that your revenue will grow. We already know that with Salesforce, you can plan, manage, measure, and improve lead generation, qualification, and conversion. You can see how much business you or your team generates, the sources of that business, and who in your team is making it happen. What about the step preceding that, though? There's no use in filling your pipeline with leads that won't actually follow through. So, how do you make sure your leads are qualified?

Pardot, Salesforce's marketing automation tool, ensures that you fill your pipeline with the highest-quality leads. You can use the tool to create custom landing pages, lead capture forms, and targeted personalized emails. This helps your business shorten the sales cycle and close deals faster. You can set up personalized lead scoring based on criteria that you decide, to evaluate how qualified prospective buyers are. You can control which marketing content and messaging goes out to those leads based on that score criteria. Finally, you can add those leads that aren't quite ready to buy to your nurture campaigns, so that you can spend more time "nurturing" them into high-scoring leads that will more likely purchase your product. This, in turn, accelerates your pipeline and ensures that team effort is being spent where it will pay off most, all from a central place.

Providing Excellent Customer Service with Service Cloud

When the sale is closed, good companies don't say sayonara. An organization should still keep tabs on customers, or have relevant purchase history ready on the off chance that the customer will reach out with questions or issues. This is the foundation of customer support. Salesforce Service Cloud is a tool that helps call centers and customer service agents track customer interactions after point of sale.

This section provides an overview of what you can do with Service Cloud. For a lot more information, see *Salesforce Service Cloud For Dummies*, by Jon Paz and TJ Kelley (Wiley).

Managing customer interactions with cases

Remember when you used to call a toll-free number about a broken product that you bought? Maybe you emailed a support email address or filled out a web form. Whichever method you chose, chances are, you weren't at your happiest at that moment. And who can blame you? It's critical that customers receive world-class customer service from companies. Today, customers demand satisfaction more than ever before. If they aren't satisfied, they can easily turn to competitors, or even worse, create smear campaigns against a company with bad customer service on social media networks.

Have you ever heard a customer service representative say, "One second while I pull up your record"? Those records are what we call *cases* in Service Cloud. Cases are related to contact records, so when a customer calls in, an agent can quickly pull up her record and see not only her purchase history, but also a record of every issue and interaction that customer has had with your organization. Cases, and the ability to clearly see what's going on with customers, make both your customer service reps, as well as your customers themselves, much happier. Nobody wants to be transferred to another agent, only to have to repeat the issue for the third time.

Service Cloud uses case management to expedite and streamline customer service, creating a much more efficient experience for everyone involved and bringing your service organization into the 21st century.

Interacting with the customer across multiple channels

Service Cloud has an added benefit: the ability to interact with customers across multiple channels. Or perhaps it's better said differently: Service Cloud gives your customers the choice of how they want to connect with your company.

Not only can customers choose to contact you anytime, anywhere, and from any device, but they can also choose the medium through which they do so. Some customers are old-fashioned and prefer calling a toll-free number. Other customers dread long hold times and would rather chat with an agent online. Giving your customers the choice to contact you the way they see fit will do wonders for their perception of your company. Service Cloud gives you many different ways to do this, and it will pay off in terms of satisfaction, as well as reduced operational cost.

Deciding Which Salesforce Edition Is Best for You

If you already use Salesforce, this topic may be a moot point. At the very least, you know which version of Salesforce you have.

TIP

If you're not sure which edition you have, look at the top of your browser after you've logged into Salesforce.

All versions have the same consistent look and feel, but each varies by feature, functionality, and pricing. If you're considering using Salesforce, consult with an account executive for more details about edition differences, pricing, and upgrade paths. Here are four versions of Salesforce.com's service:

>> **IQ Starter:** This edition has replaced the Group and Contact Manager editions. It's a basic, out-of-the-box CRM system that offers basic account and contact management for up to five users.

>> **Professional:** A thorough CRM system for any size organization that's starting to nail down processes. Again, you can track the full sales life cycle from a new lead to a closed opportunity. Dashboards allow managers to track key metrics at a glance. Some optional features for businesses with more detailed process needs (such as managing marketing campaigns, creating contracts, tracking various products sold, or accessing Salesforce while offline) come at an extra cost.

>> **Enterprise:** More sales and service functionality for more complex organizations, including the ability to integrate with other systems within your company, and the ability to create custom solutions with code. This edition provides more value than if you were to pay extra for certain add-on features in more basic editions. If you absolutely need your business processes to look and act a specific way, this edition provides more ways to make that happen for you.

>> **Unlimited:** Even more customization capabilities for extending Salesforce to other business uses. You need a dedicated (and usually technical) administrator to take advantage of all the options that this edition delivers.

>> **Performance:** This edition offers bundled pricing for Sales and Service Cloud licensing. It has everything the Unlimited Edition provides, but also includes features such as Live Agent Chat, an integrated knowledge base, as well as additional sandboxes.

TECHNICAL STUFF

Salesforce.com also provides another edition, Developer Edition, which is a free instance of Salesforce with which developers can test and build third-party solutions. It has full functionality but a very limited license count and storage space.

Whichever edition you choose, the good news is that every edition of Salesforce is rich with features that can help companies of every size address their business challenges. You can choose a more basic edition today and upgrade later, as needed. Upgrades happen in the background and are easy, so you can focus on the business processes that drive the need for new functionality. And when Salesforce.com rolls out new releases of its service, it provides product enhancements for the different editions wherever relevant.

PROFESSIONAL OR ENTERPRISE EDITION?

Most companies tend to make a decision between using Professional or Enterprise Edition. Budget may be an issue, but the decision usually boils down to core business needs. Consider these questions:

- Does your company have different groups with distinct sales processes, customers, and products?
- Does your company have a lead-generation or service team that relies on a call script when initially speaking with prospects or customers?
- Does your company plan to integrate Salesforce with other applications?
- Does your company require complex data migration into Salesforce?
- Does your company need greater control over users, what they see, and what they can do?
- Does your company sell in defined teams with specific roles?
- Does your company require consistent, specific workflow or approval steps to further automate processes?

If the answer to any of these questions is a definitive "Yes," your company should probably at least evaluate Enterprise Edition, and possibly Performance Edition.

2

Understanding Salesforce Features

Chapter 3
Navigating Salesforce

I f an application isn't easy to use, you won't use it. Period. Salesforce succeeds not only because it offers a universe of integrated tools but also because users can pick it up within minutes. You navigate Salesforce much the same way you do other websites: by clicking text links and buttons.

Still, you have so many ways to navigate Salesforce that it makes sense to lay down the obvious (and not-so-obvious) best practices for getting around the application.

TIP

Even if you're familiar with Salesforce, you may want to scan this chapter because we cover terms that we use repeatedly throughout this book.

In this chapter, you can find out how to log in to Salesforce and use the home page to manage your activities, create records, and jump to other tabs. We briefly review the major functional areas and describe how to use the internal home pages. Finally, we introduce you to the optional Lightning Experience that ushers in a dramatically different look and feel for end-users.

Getting Familiar with Basic Salesforce Terms

Before we delve into the mechanics of navigating Salesforce, familiarize yourself with these basic terms:

» **Salesforce:** The secure website that your users log in to that contains your customer information. Salesforce.com, Inc., offers a family of products used by hundreds of thousands of customers, but each company's secure website is separate from the other websites and may look different in order to suit that company's unique needs. When we use the terms *Sales Cloud, Marketing Cloud* or *Service Cloud,* those are parts of Salesforce specifically meant for use by sales and marketing or by a support organization.

» **Home tab:** The main page that appears when you log in to Salesforce or click the Home tab.

» **Tabs:** Clickable words appear in a row across the top of any Salesforce page. When selected, a word is highlighted and looks like a tab. Each tab represents a major module in which your company needs to know some information. By clicking a tab, you go to a tab-specific home page. For example, if you click the Accounts tab, the Accounts home page appears.

» **Tab home pages:** These are the pages where you go to find, organize, and manage specific information related to a particular tab. For example, to access your opportunity records, you could go to the Opportunities home page.

» **Object:** Often used interchangeably with the name of a tab. Generally used by administrators when talking about creating custom apps. For example, you may tell a user to "click the Account tab," or you may hear your system administrator refer to the "Account object."

» **Apps:** Tabs that have been grouped together and given a name, providing you with the convenience of seeing only those tabs most relevant to you.

» **Record:** A record is a page in Salesforce made up of a bunch of fields that hold information to describe a specific object. For example, a contact record typically contains fields pertinent to a person, including name, title, phone number, and email address. A record is displayed on a detail page.

» **Detail page:** A web page that shows both the saved record and a set of related lists pertinent to the record.

» **Chatter feed:** If you have Chatter enabled (see Chapter 6), you'll see the center column of your logged-in Salesforce experience with a chronological list of updates made by you or other co-workers. This feed is a critical way for Salesforce users within your organization to communicate with each other.

REMEMBER

» **Search bar:** In the upper-left portion of your Salesforce page, a search field resides as another way you can quickly find companies or contacts. Search results returned can be customized to return only a certain type of record.

We often use the terms *record* and *detail page* interchangeably. From a detail page, you can perform and track a variety of tasks related to the specific record. For example, if you have and are looking at an Account detail page for Cisco, you see fields about the company and lists of other records related to Cisco.

» **Related lists:** Lists that comprise other records linked to the record that you're looking at. For example, the Account detail page for Acme may display related lists of contacts, opportunities, activities, and so on associated with that company.

» **Sidebar:** Located at the left margin of a Salesforce page, the sidebar displays messages and alerts, custom links, recent items, and a drop-down list that you can use to create new records.

Accessing Salesforce

You need to log in to your account to access your company's instance of Salesforce because every company's Salesforce website is different, and Salesforce.com goes to great lengths to protect your company's information.

Setting up a password

The first time you log in to the Salesforce service, you'll do so from an email you receive containing your Salesforce login information. To set your password, follow these steps:

1. **Open the email and click the link provided.**

   A page appears, prompting you to set a new password and security question.

2. **Complete the fields.**

   Be sure to select a question and provide an answer that can verify your identity if you forget your password. Use this password from now on unless your administrator resets the password.

3. **When you're done, click Save.**

   The Salesforce home page appears.

Logging in

You log in to Salesforce just as you would any other secure website.

To log in, open a browser and follow these steps:

1. **In your browser's address bar, type** `https://login.salesforce.com` **and then press Enter.**

   The Salesforce.com login page, shown in Figure 3-1, appears.

   TIP

   To save yourself steps when logging in, bookmark the login page in your favorite web browser.

FIGURE 3-1:
Logging in to
Salesforce.

2. **Enter your username and password, and then click the Log In button.**

   Your username is typically your corporate email address. Click the Remember Me check box if you want your computer to remember it. After you click Log In, you may be asked to register your mobile phone. This is an additional, optional security step. After this step, your main home page appears.

TECHNICAL STUFF

For security purposes, Salesforce notices when you're trying to log in to the website from a different computer or a different browser than the one you first used. If this happens, make sure that you have access to your email or mobile phone (remember when Salesforce asked you to register your mobile phone number?)

because Salesforce emails or text messages you a confirmation code to confirm that you are who you say you are.

Navigating the Home Page

Every time you log in to Salesforce, you begin at your home page. The look and feel of the elements on your home page are similar to other users' home pages, but the tasks and events that appear in the body of the page are specific to you.

Use the home page to manage your calendar and tasks, stay informed of the latest Chatter conversations, jump to other areas by clicking tabs, or access recent items by using the sidebar. If your company has customized the home page, you may also see key charts or graphs from your company's *dashboards* (visual snapshots of key performance metrics based on your custom report data).

Finding records with Search

At the top of every Salesforce page, you'll find the Global Search bar. You can find a majority of the information that you want by using Search. To search for information, follow these steps:

1. **At the top of Salesforce, enter keywords into the Search field and then click the Search button.**

A Search Results page appears, as shown in Figure 3-2. Salesforce organizes the search results in lists according to the major types of records, including accounts, contacts, leads, and opportunities.

FIGURE 3-2: Looking at a Search Results page.

2. **Scroll down the page. If you find a record that you want to look at, click a link in the Name column for the row that represents that record.**

The detail page appears, allowing you to review the record and its related lists.

3. **If you see too many results, you can limit them to items you own or search for an exact phrase by clicking Options to the right of the Search Again button on the Search Results page. You can also select a single type of record from the list in the sidebar.**

If you can't find what you're looking for, try adding the asterisk (*) wildcard before, after, or in the middle of your keywords to expand your search to words that start with, end with, or are similar to your keywords.

TIP

If you're focusing on a page (such as a list of search results or a report) and want to open one of the results in a new browser tab, instead of clicking the link, right-click that link and choose Open Link in New Tab from the contextual menu that appears.

Managing your calendar

The calendar section of the home page defaults to a calendar of the current month and your scheduled events for the next seven days. Like other calendar tools, the calendar allows you to drill down. Your scheduled events are based on events that you assigned to yourself or that other users have assigned to you.

From this calendar section (shown in Figure 3-3), you can do the following:

» **Schedule a new activity.** Click the New Event button, and a New Event page appears in Edit mode. (See Chapter 5 to see how to complete a new event record.)

» **View an event record.** If you see a listed event, click the link. A page appears with details on the activity.

» **Drill into your schedule.** Click a date on the calendar to drill into your schedule for a specific day. The Day View page appears.

» **Schedule a group activity.** Click the Multi User View icon (which looks like two little people). A page appears for the selected day that displays the availability of multiple users. From there, click the New Event button and follow the same instructions for scheduling a new event, as described in detail in Chapter 5.

FIGURE 3-3:
Looking over your
calendar options.

Tracking your tasks

On the home page, you see a section entitled My Tasks, which displays tasks that you created for yourself or that have been assigned to you.

A *task* is an activity that you need to do, and it can have a due date. Unlike an event, however, a task doesn't have a specific time and duration. For example, if you want to remind yourself to send a proposal, you typically create a task instead of scheduling an event. (See Chapter 5 for additional tips on managing tasks.)

From the My Tasks section (shown in Figure 3-4), you can do the following:

>> **Add a new task.** Click the New button, and a New Task page appears in Edit mode.

>> **Change task view.** Use the drop-down list at the top right of the My Tasks section to select from a list of common task views. For example, select Overdue to see your open tasks that are past their respective due dates.

>> **Review a task.** Click a link in the Subject column to review a task. A task record appears with details.

>> **Go to associated records.** Click links in the Name column, the Related To column, or the Account column.

>> **Complete the task and enter any details before saving.** Click the X link in the Complete column. You can also use this link to update a task, but if you haven't completed the task, remember to adjust the Status field before you save it.

>> **See more tasks.** If you have several tasks in your list, the View More link appears at the bottom of the My Tasks section on the home page. Click it to see more tasks on the list. The Day View appears, and the My Tasks section appears in the right column.

FIGURE 3-4:
Reviewing the My
Tasks section on
the home page.

My Tasks			New				All Open
Complete	Date	Status	Subject	Name	Related To	Account	
X		Not Started	Send proposal	Edna Frank		GenePoint	
X		Not Started	Schedule demo	Tim Barr		Grand Hotels & Resorts Ltd	

Using dashboard snapshots from the home page

If your company has customized your home page, you may also see and select up to three key charts or tables from your dashboards. *Dashboards* display important information from reports in Salesforce that can provide key performance indicators on the health of your business. Each dashboard chart or table is composed of at least one *component.* (See Chapter 24 for details on building dashboards that can measure and analyze your business.) As of this writing, dashboards are available in the Group, Professional, Enterprise, and Unlimited editions.

If you see a chart or table on your home page, you can also perform these actions from the Dashboard section:

» **Click a chart or table to drill into the detail.** A report page appears with the data that supports the graphic.

» **Choose a different dashboard.** Click the Customize Page button at the upper right of the section. The Customize Your Home Page page appears; here, you can select from available dashboards if you have the proper administrator permissions. Your home page displays a snapshot of only the three components along the top of any dashboard.

» **Refresh the dashboard snapshot.** Click the Refresh button at the top of the section. In the left of the section, a date and timestamp appear showing when your dashboard was last refreshed.

Accessing information with the sidebar

The sidebar is the column on the left that appears on just about every page of Salesforce except for dashboards and reports. On the home page, use the sidebar to quickly go back to pages you recently accessed, stay informed about important company messages, click links to useful websites, and create new records.

Creating new records

Use the compact Create New picklist on the sidebar to quickly create any new record.

Revisiting recent items

The Recent Items section displays up to ten records that you most recently clicked. Use the list to quickly get back to records that you've been working on, even if you logged out and logged back in. The recent items show an icon and the name or number of the record. These items include mostly the records that are organized under a tab heading, such as Accounts, Contacts, and so on. To visit the detail record of a recent item, simply click a listed link.

Getting more out of your home page sidebar

With the help of your administrator, you can offer other tools and information from the sidebar on the home page to improve productivity and drive overall adoption. Review the following tips, see Chapter 17 on customizing Salesforce, and consult with your administrator if Custom Components could help your organization:

» **Display company messages.** Your administrator can add a section to the home page that displays text to keep users informed of important announcements. For example, if you're in sales management, you may want to use the home page to alert reps to end-of-quarter goals or bonus incentives.

» **Emphasize important custom links.** If you rely on other websites to carry out part of your work, your administrator can help you post them for all your users or just ones that fit certain profiles. For example, if you have a company intranet, your company can add a custom component that is a link to that internal website, and insert it on the Salesforce home page.

TIP

If you'd rather not have the sidebar take up some of your browser window's horizontal real estate, Salesforce allows you to hide and expand the sidebar when you want. Your administrator can set up this option by choosing Setup➪Build➪Customize➪User Interface and clicking the Enable Collapsible Sidebar check box.

Navigating the Apps

Salesforce allows you to organize tabs into groups. These groups, also known as *apps*, help reduce screen clutter and give you quicker access to the tabs that you use the most. For example, a marketing manager may rarely use the Cases or Opportunities tabs but spend most of her time looking at Campaigns and Leads.

With the Salesforce.com Force.com platform, your company can now create custom apps for more specific uses within customer relationship management

(CRM) — or for anything else, for that matter. Sales reps can use an expense reporting app, and product managers can use a product release app to manage their product requirements. The mind-blowing part of all of this is that apps can be composed of standard tabs or *custom ones that you create.* Anyone in your company can benefit from sharing one set of data. And don't worry if you're not the most creative type. Salesforce.com has a bunch of prebuilt apps available (for free or for an additional charge), which we discuss in more detail in Chapter 19.

Discovering the app menu

In the upper-right corner of any Salesforce page, you can find the app menu (see Figure 3-5). The drop-down list allows you to switch between apps. You find some standard tab groupings, such as Sales and Call Center. Administrators can also add or create new apps to address what their specific users need to see. Don't worry if you choose an app and see new tabs. You can always go back to the drop-down list, select your previous app, and have your familiar tabs return.

FIGURE 3-5: Choosing apps by using the Force. com app menu.

Uncovering the App Launcher

From the app menu, selecting the App Launcher option takes you to the App Launcher page where all your apps are now displayed as clickable tiles, as shown in Figure 3-6. Clicking a tile is the same as selecting that app in the app menu, as described in the immediately prior section. Depending on what other systems your company has integrated with Salesforce, you may also see installed app icons for other applications used at your company, like Gmail or Concur.

Finding out about the tabs

In this section, we describe the major tabs in Salesforce and show you how to use the tab home pages to quickly access, manage, or organize information.

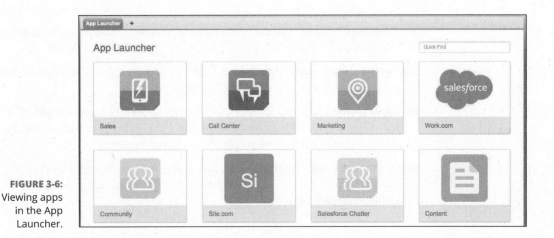

FIGURE 3-6: Viewing apps in the App Launcher.

Each tab within Salesforce represents a major module or data element in an interconnected database. That's as technical as we get.

In the following list, we briefly describe each of the standard tabs (as shown in Figure 3-7). We devote a chapter to each of the tabs mentioned here:

>> **Chatter (see Chapter 6):** Manage all aspects of your collaboration efforts here. From the Chatter home page, you can view all updates to your feed, as well as search for people and groups to follow. If you don't see this tab, you may not have Chatter enabled in your organization.

>> **Campaigns (see Chapter 15):** Specific marketing efforts that you manage to drive leads, build a brand, or stimulate demand.

>> **Leads (see Chapter 7):** *Suspects* (people and companies with whom you want to do business). But don't start grilling your lead about where she was on the morning of July 23, because the only clue you'll gather is the sound of a dial tone.

>> **Accounts (see Chapter 8):** Companies with whom you currently do or previously did business. You can track all types of accounts, including customers, prospects, former customers, partners, and competitors.

>> **Contacts (see Chapter 9):** Individuals associated with your accounts.

>> **Opportunities (see Chapter 10):** The deals that you pursue to track transactions or drive revenue for your company. Your open opportunities constitute your pipeline, and opportunities can contribute to your forecast.

>> **Products (see Chapter 11):** Your company's products and services, associated with the prices for which you offer them. You can aggregate different products and their prices to your opportunities.

- **>> Cases (see Chapter 13):** Customer inquiries that your support teams work on to manage and resolve.

- **>> Content (see Chapter 18):** The sales and marketing collateral and documents that you use as part of your selling or service processes.

- **>> Reports (see Chapter 23):** Data analyses for you and your entire organization. Salesforce provides a variety of best practices reports, and you can build custom reports on the fly to better measure your business.

- **>> Dashboards (see Chapter 24):** Graphs, charts, and tables based on your custom reports. You can use dashboards to visually measure and analyze key elements of your business.

FIGURE 3-7:
Navigating
through the tabs.

| Home | Chatter | Campaigns | Leads | Accounts | Contacts | Opportunities | Products | Cases | Content | Reports | Dashboards | + |

Discovering a tab home page

When you click a tab, the tab's interior home page appears. For example, if you click the Accounts tab, the Accounts home page appears. The tab's home page is where you can view, organize, track, and maintain all the records within that tab.

Do this right now: Click every tab visible to you.

The look and feel of the interior home pages never change, regardless of which tab you click (except for the Home, Reports, and Dashboards tabs). On the left, you have the sidebar with the Create New drop-down list, Recent Items, and (depending on your company and the tab) a Quick Create tool. In the body of the page, you have a View drop-down list, a Recent Items section related to whichever tab you're on (for example, Recent Accounts), and sections for popular Reports and Tools (see Figure 3-8).

Using the View drop-down list

Strategy and execution are all about focus. With custom list views, you can see and use lists to better focus on your business. A *list view* is a segment of the tab's records based on defined criteria. When you select a list view, a list of records appears based on your criteria.

FIGURE 3-8:
Deconstructing
the tab home
page.

On each tab, Salesforce provides a selection of popular default views to get you started. To try a list view (using Accounts as the example), follow these steps (which apply to all tabs):

1. **Click the Accounts tab.**

The Accounts home page appears (refer to Figure 3-8).

2. **Select My Accounts from the View drop-down list.**

A list page appears that displays a set of columns representing certain standard account fields and a list of your account records. If no account records appear, you don't own any in Salesforce.

3. **From the list page, you can perform a variety of functions:**

- *Re-sort the list.* Click a column header. For example, if you click the Account Name header, the list sorts alphabetically, as shown in Figure 3-9.

- *View records beginning with a certain letter.* Click that letter link above the list to view those records.

  If a user sorts by a column other than name, the letter search looks for values in that column starting with the selected letter. For example, if sorting by State, selecting C filters for accounts with states starting with C rather than account names starting with C.

- *Display fewer or more records on the page.* Use the Display Records per Page picklist on the bottom left of the page to show more or less records. Additionally, the Next Page link takes you to the next set of records.

- *View a specific record.* Click the link for that record in the Account Name column. The Account detail page appears, displaying the record and its related lists.

- *Update a specific record.* Click the Edit link at the beginning of its row. The account record appears in Edit mode.

- *Delete a record.* Click the Del link near the beginning of that record's row. A pop-up window appears, prompting you to click OK to accept the deletion. If you click OK, the list page reappears, minus the account that you just wiped out. Don't worry — in Chapter 5, in the "Resurrecting records from the Recycle Bin" section, we show you how to bring recently deleted records back to life.

- *Follow this record.* If you have Chatter enabled, you'll see a green circle with a white plus sign (+) in it to the right of the Del link. Clicking this plus sign changes the green circle to a blue checkmark that signifies that you are now following that record. Any updates, modifications, or discussions made on that record will show up in your Chatter feed so you can stay informed.

FIGURE 3-9: Re-sorting a list.

Building a custom list view

If you have a particular way that you like to look at records, you can build a custom list view. If you have the right permissions, you can share this view with other groups or your entire organization. (Or maybe you should just keep your views to yourself.)

To create a custom list view (using Contacts as the example), follow these steps (which apply to all tabs):

1. Click the Contacts tab.

The Contacts home page appears.

2. To the right of the View drop-down list, click the Create New View link.

A Create New View page appears.

3. **Name the view by typing a title in the View Name field.**

For example, if you want to create a list of your contacts that are senior executives, use a title like My Senior Execs.

4. **Select whether you want to search All Contacts or just My Contacts by selecting one of the two radio buttons.**

In this example, select the My Contacts radio button.

5. **Type the campaign name into the Campaign Name field.**

For this running example, assume that your marketing manager created campaigns. You may want to tie a campaign to filter your List View after identifying which contacts you want the view to search.

TIP

Tying a campaign to your List View filters your results to those contacts related to a specific marketing campaign. You must have the proper permissions in the Professional, Enterprise, and Unlimited editions for this capability.

6. **(Optional) Below the Filter by Additional Fields heading, enter search criteria.**

A basic criteria query is made up of three elements:

- *Field:* The leftmost box is a drop-down list of all the fields on the contact record. In this example, choose Title.

- *Operator:* The middle box is a drop-down list of operators for your search. That sounds complicated, but it's easier than you think. For this example, select the Contains option.

- *Value:* In the rightmost box, type the value that you want in the search. In this example, you might type **vp**, **vice president**, **ceo**, **cio**, or **cto**.

7. **Select the columns that you want to have displayed by selecting a value from the drop-down lists in some or all of the fields provided.**

Although Salesforce's preset views have common fields, such as Phone and Email, you can select any of up to 15 fields to display on your custom view page.

8. **Decide whether you want others to see your custom view.**

Administrators and certain users have this permission. Your decision is made simple if the step doesn't appear. Otherwise, select one of the three options. (Basically, the three radio buttons translate to none, all, or selective.) If you choose the third option, use the drop-down list to select a group and then click the arrows to move that group into the Shared To column.

9. **Click Save.**

A new list view appears based on your custom criteria. If you don't get all the results that you anticipate, double-check and refine the filter criteria. For example, if your list should include directors but doesn't, click the Edit link and update the view.

REMEMBER

As long as you save your custom list view, you can use it later from the Views menu. To reduce list view clutter, be considerate and lean toward saving list views that are visible only to yourself. Otherwise, you risk flooding your public list view with several similar-but-slightly-different views that aren't culled over time.

Reviewing the Recent Items section

On a tab's home page, just below the views, you see a Recent Items section. (The name of the item will match whatever type of record you're on. For example, Recent Accounts is the section name if you're on the Accounts tab.) This section comes with three or four relevant columns that you can modify. You can see as few as 10 items and as many as 25 items at a time by clicking the link at the bottom of the table.

To test the Recent Items section (by using Leads as the example), go to the Leads home page and follow these steps (which you can apply to all tabs):

1. **In the Recent Leads section, select an option from the drop-down list at the upper-right corner of the table.**

   The table reappears with changes based on what you select.

2. **Click a link in the table to go to a record.**

   The detail page appears, displaying the record and related lists.

3. **At any time, click the New button in the upper middle of the table to create a new lead record.**

   A New Lead page appears in Edit mode, ready and waiting. (See Chapter 7 to read more about the fields in the Lead record.)

Reviewing common reports

In the lower-left corner of a tab's home page, Salesforce displays a small selection of commonly used reports associated with that tab. You can click a link to go directly to the report or click the Go to Reports link, which takes you to the Reports home page.

Tooling through the Tools section

In the lower portion of a tab's home page, Salesforce provides a set of unique tools associated with a particular tab. Depending on which tab you're viewing, use these tools to help you manage and maintain records within that tab. For example, on the Accounts home page, in the Tools section, you can click the Merge Accounts link to merge duplicate accounts. See the related chapters later in this book for details on using specific tools.

Explaining the Lightning Experience

Late in 2015, Salesforce.com debuted a revamped user experience in Salesforce, called Lightning Experience. It was based on extensive user research and provides a look and feel that better prepares new users for an experience that's effective across multiple access methods. Salesforce users are no longer just using a computer and web browser to access their company's version of Salesforce. An increasingly mobile sales force now needs to get its work done while updating Salesforce from a smartphone or tablet, too.

In this section, we discuss how the Lightning Experience affects information in this book, and some fundamental updates in its new interface.

Approaching the Lightning Experience in this book

Thankfully, with the Lightning Experience, Salesforce.com realized that its existing customer base of hundreds of thousands of users needed to feel warm and fuzzy about the new user interface (UI) before choosing to adopt it. Salesforce users will remain on the UI referred to as Salesforce Classic, and have ample ways to test out whether the Lightning Experience is right for their organization before enabling it across the organization.

In this book, we continue to discuss the existing UI, which Salesforce.com refers to as Salesforce Classic, since the majority of Salesforce users are still on that UI. Our screenshots are taken in Salesforce Classic, unless otherwise noted. At the time of this publication, the Lightning Experience does not yet fully support all features and behaviors available in Salesforce Classic.

Existing customers can choose to enable and switch to the Lightning Experience when they're comfortable and ready. Even then, Salesforce.com allows a user to switch back and forth between the Salesforce Classic UI and the Lightning Experience UI.

TIP

Make sure you read the fine print in the Salesforce release notes (http://docs. releasenotes.salesforce.com) to thoroughly understand what features are and are not yet supported in the Lightning Experience. With three releases a year, the list of supported features will only grow. Also make sure you understand Lightning Experience's impact on your users by testing business processes out in a sandbox environment before turning this on.

Reviewing Lightning Experience fundamentals

In this section, we discuss the most visible changes between the Salesforce Classic UI and the Lightning Experience UI. Read on to get familiar with basic changes so you can start assessing where your organization may or may not yet be ready to make a change.

Summarizing the home page in the Lightning Experience

The home page in the Lightning Experience has been re-envisioned to empower a salesperson to more efficiently manage his day in Salesforce.

Make sure to familiarize yourself with the following home page concepts, as shown in Figure 3-10:

>> **Quarterly Performance chart:** Designed for people using opportunities to track their sales performance, this chart appears prominently on the home page. A rep can add her goal for the quarter and quickly see how close she is to hitting this quarter's target. Opportunities with close dates this quarter that are already closed or with probability of greater than 70 percent will show up here.

   The chart is also interactive. Hovering over it can reveal specific opportunities with close dates in this quarter. Clicking the corresponding blue dot opens a pop-up window with some additional opportunity details, so a sales rep can quickly prioritize her work.

>> **Assistant:** The right-hand column of your screen now displays a combination of overdue and open tasks with some details, as well as leads assigned to you and activities related to opportunities that should matter to you.

>> **Account Insights:** Below the Quarterly Performance chart is an area that has news about your accounts, its executives, and industries that your accounts are in. The news is curated from Data.com and other third parties.

>> **Top Deals:** This section shows a list of your biggest open opportunities.

REMEMBER

The importance of maintaining accurate and clean data in your company's Salesforce instance is reflected in these new features. Garbage data in results in garbage data out. It's never too late to instill a culture of data discipline in your organization, so your sales team can take advantage of clean data in outsmarting and being more productive than the competition's sales force.

FIGURE 3-10:
Presenting the
home page in the
Lightning
Experience.

Here are the key UI differences between the Lightning Experience and Salesforce Classic:

>> **Tabs have been replaced by a navigation bar.** Gone are the tabs across the top of page, which have been replaced by a collapsible navigation bar on the left, as shown in Figure 3-10. Words next to new icons are similar to tab names in the Salesforce Classic view. To maximize horizontal screen real estate, when you're used to identifying which icons represent which records, you can collapse the navigation bar by clicking the topmost icon, which looks like a set of three horizontal lines.

>> **The app menu has been replaced by the App Launcher.** Instead of going to a drop-down in the upper-right corner of the screen to switch between clusters of tabs as you do in Salesforce Classic, you click the icon that looks like a 3 x 3 grid of little squares, as shown in Figure 3-11. Hovering over that icon changes it from boring gray squares to colored ones. Clicking the icon results in the App Launcher page showing. Different from Salesforce Classic, if you click a tile, you're taken to a new page that shows all records (or "items") associated with that app. The page also specifies which objects are not yet supported in the Lightning Experience, which means if you click it, it'll go back to the Salesforce Classic UI.

FIGURE 3-11:
Accessing apps
using the App
Launcher.

>> **The Setup link has been replaced by a gear icon.** System administrators need to click the gear icon with a lightning bolt in it (shown in Figure 3-12), to get to their familiar Setup area, which is now called Setup Home.

SETUP

Setup Home

Developer Console

FIGURE 3-12:
Getting to the
Setup Home.

>> **Calendar, Chatter feed, Dashboard view, and My Tasks have been moved off the home page.** These sections of the old standard home page are no longer on the Lightning Experience home page. They're still accessible via the navigation bar on the left.

Getting to records in the Lightning Experience

To get to a record, find its equivalent object icon in the navigation bar and click the icon, as shown in Figure 3-13. If it's not there, use the App Launcher to click the corresponding app's tile, and then locate a specific object name to click. Clicking the object name from the navigation bar results in a page displaying a list view of the most recently viewed objects. You can then change this to a custom list view by clicking the little triangle to the right of the Recently Viewed picklist name. Select your record from the list of items returned.

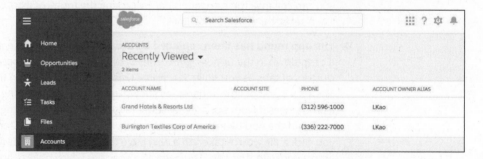

FIGURE 3-13:
Getting to the
Account record.

Navigating a record in the Lightning Experience

When you're looking at a record, realize that the Lightning Experience is meant to reduce the vertical scrolling that is predominant in the Salesforce Classic UI. The elements of the old UI still exist; they've just moved around.

Here are some common changes that occur on a new Lightning Experience record page, as shown in Figure 3-14:

>> **Standard fields are summarized at the top of the page.** The top part of a record displays standard field information. When scrolling down, the record name is anchored so you never forget which record you're seeing details about.

>> **The Edit and New Record buttons are shifted to the right.** Edit and Delete buttons still exist. They're just offset a bit to the right. If you can't see one of your buttons listed, click the little triangle to the right of existing buttons, to see a list of additional ones.

>> **Related lists appear as cards.** For some objects, this appears in the middle part of the record, below the record header. For other objects, related lists appear on the right-hand side. They all take the form of cards, where a few fields are exposed to give people some context around that record.

>> **Activity buttons have been changed to subtabs in the Activity subsection.** For some objects, the Activity subsection appears in the middle part of the record, below the header. For other objects, the Activity area is in the right-hand column. The Salesforce Classic buttons are gone, replaced by subtabs that still allow you to log a call, or create a new task, event, or email.

>> **Record details have been moved to the new Details subsection.** This is meant to both reduce the amount of vertical scrolling, while also allowing you to quickly get to additional fields on your record. Custom links also appear here.

>> **The Chatter feed is nested in the new Collaborate subsection.** You'll see all the posts from your Chatter feed here, related to whatever record you're on. You'll be able to post a comment, share a link, or create a poll just as you did before, under respective subtabs. Again, this helps reduce the vertical scrolling on a record.

FIGURE 3-14: Dissecting the Account record.

Chapter 4

Personalizing Salesforce

Salesforce was built by salespeople for salespeople. The tool had to be simple to use, relevant to the business of selling, and customizable so that you could use it to do your job more effectively.

The My Profile page captures information that you want your colleagues to see about yourself, to improve collaboration across your company. Think of it as a directory listing for everyone who works in Salesforce.

From the My Settings page (formerly known as the Personal Setup page), you can personalize details of your application to better suit the way you look at and manage your daily tasks. And if you capitalize on the tools available in Salesforce, you can give yourself an edge against the competition and your peers.

In this chapter, we describe how to update your personal information in My Profile, modify your settings by using My Settings, change your display, and access Salesforce anytime, anywhere.

Completing the My Profile Page

The My Profile page acts like a cross between a corporate intranet page about yourself and a news feed about your collaborations within the company. Later, we talk more about Chatter and how the concept of feeds appears in many places in Salesforce. For now, think of feeds as proactive status updates across your company so that people interested in the same things (like an account, contact, or opportunity) can follow each other and stay up to date on the latest news.

To locate and update your My Profile page, follow these steps:

1. **After logging in to Salesforce, click your name in the upper-right corner of the Salesforce page and select the My Profile list option.**

   Your profile page appears. In the left column is room for a photo, some contact details, and some statistics based on various interactions on the feed. The feed is the middle column that shows your most recent activities (similar to a feed on a social network). An overview about yourself, and what Chatter groups you belong to, is accessible from the Overview tab to the right of the Feed tab (see Figure 4-1).

FIGURE 4-1:
Reviewing the My Profile page.

2. **To upload a photo, click the outline of the head in the left column, and then click Upload.**

   The Upload Profile Photo box appears.

3. **Click the Browse button to upload a small square photo of yourself.**

   A file selection window opens so that you can browse to and select your photo from your computer.

REMEMBER

Though you may prefer to submit a photo of your pet (as we did) or the back of your head, don't forget that this is for work collaboration. Help your fellow employees out (especially the newer ones) by posting a clear photo of yourself.

4. **After you've clicked your photo file, click Open.**

5. **Click Save on the Upload Profile Photo screen.**

Voilà! Your photo appears. A smaller version of your photo will now appear to the left of your name within any Chatter feeds so that you can be quickly identified.

Now, to update your contact information so that people know a little more about you, follow these steps:

1. **To the right of the Contact heading, click the pencil icon.**

The Edit Profile page appears. The email associated with your Salesforce account appears, along with other contact information. Complete what you feel is necessary for co-workers who need to reach you.

2. **Click the About tab on the Edit Profile page.**

Update information here to give your co-workers some more background about yourself.

3. **Click Save All when done.**

The updates are now reflected on the My Profile page.

This profile page is especially helpful for companies with users who aren't all in the same location.

Using the My Settings Menu

My Settings, which you access by clicking your name after you've logged in to Salesforce, is the enhanced user interface for what used be called the Personal Setup page. In fact, if you don't see My Settings after clicking your name, your organization probably signed up for Salesforce prior to this feature's existence and the administrator hasn't opted to enable it yet (more on that later). You can still follow along and update your settings, because this is largely a visual update to what was the old Personal Setup page.

My Settings is a set of tools and options that you can use to customize Salesforce according to your individual preferences. You can decide to show only certain tabs, synchronize your Salesforce data with your email program, set how often you want to get Chatter updates, and work with Salesforce while you're not connected to the Internet.

Salesforce makes it easy for you to better personalize your system by providing all your setup tools in one area.

To locate and navigate your My Settings area, follow these steps:

1. **Click your name in the upper-right corner of any page, and select the My Settings option from the drop-down list.**

   The My Settings page appears, and you see a Quick Links and Desktop Add-Ons section (depending on your permissions), as shown in Figure 4-2.

FIGURE 4-2:
Looking over the My Settings page.

TIP

If you didn't find a My Settings link below your name, don't worry. This just means that you're on the old user interface. You can still follow along by clicking your name, then selecting the Setup option in the drop-down list, and then clicking the Personal Setup link in the left sidebar.

The My Settings page lists each of its main headings in an expandable sidebar. The Quick Links in the body of the page and the sidebar work hand in hand, but we like to use the sidebar so that we don't get lost.

2. **Click each of the section headings to expand them and see the full range of options (see Figure 4-3).**

   Subsections appear. The body of the page doesn't change if you simply expand the section within the sidebar.

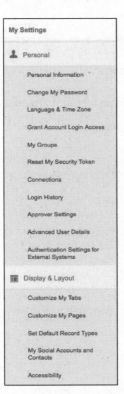

FIGURE 4-3:
Expanding the
sections.

3. **Click any subsection.**

   The details for that subsection appear.

4. **Click the Back button in your browser to return to the previous page, or click another section heading to open that heading's page.**

   You've mastered basic navigation on the My Settings menu.

Modifying Your Personal Information

By expanding the Personal heading, you can keep your user record current, set preferences, and customize your display to suit your tastes.

Updating your user information

In Salesforce, you have a user record that corresponds to you. You can use that record to keep other users up to date on your contact information.

To find out how to navigate to the My Settings area, see the preceding section.

To modify your user record, follow these steps:

1. **Click the Personal heading on the sidebar (refer to Figure 4-2).**

   A series of options appears below the heading.

2. **Click the Personal Information link.**

   Details of your user record appears in Edit mode. Review the accuracy of your personal information and update it.

   Especially if you travel frequently, make sure that you update your time zone both in Salesforce and on your laptop, reflecting your current location. This is particularly important if you're managing your schedule and synchronizing with offline tools, such as Outlook.

3. **When you're done, click Save.**

   Your user record appears again with the updated information.

Changing your display

If you log in and feel as if you really need only a fraction of the tabs or a select number of related lists, you can customize your display. Your administrator can still override your personal setup, if necessary — for example, after installing an AppExchange application that comes with additional tabs.

Salesforce already provides many standard tabs and groups some of them into apps that you choose from the Force.com app menu. Companies can also create their own tabs. Most users just don't need to see all those tabs at the same time.

To customize your tabs, follow these steps:

1. **Click the Display & Layout heading on the My Settings sidebar (refer to Figure 4-3).**

   The Display & Layout heading expands.

2. **Click the Customize My Tabs link if you want to add, remove, or change the order of your tabs within an app.**

   The Customize My Tabs page appears.

3. **Select which app's tab set you want to customize from the Custom App drop-down list.**

   The default Selected Tabs list changes when you change the Custom App selection. Salesforce pregroups its tabs into several standard apps for various common business functions. Depending on your business, having these tabs visible may be perfect, or you may want to see more or fewer tabs.

4. **Use the Add or Remove arrow buttons to highlight a tab and then add it to or remove it from your display, respectively, as shown in Figure 4-4.**

   For example, if you're in marketing and spend most of your time with leads, you may decide to add the Campaigns tab and remove the Customizable Forecasts tab from your Sales custom app.

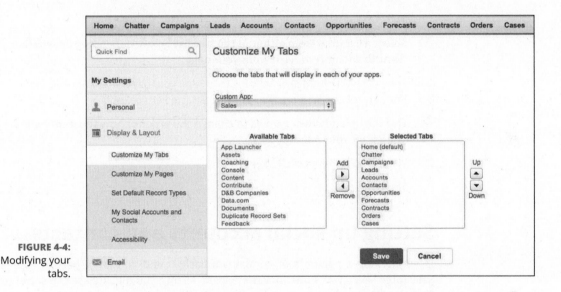

FIGURE 4-4:
Modifying your tabs.

5. **Use the up and down arrows to change the order of the tabs.**

   The only exception is that you can't move or remove the Home tab.

6. **When you're done, click Save.**

   The My Settings page reappears, and your tabs reflect your changes.

Customizing pages

You can also personalize your display by changing the layout on a record page. Doing so enables you to see the most relevant sections first. For example, if you work in a call center, you may want to see cases at the top of your related lists on an account page.

To customize the display of a page, follow these steps:

1. **Click the Display & Layout heading on the My Settings sidebar (refer to Figure 4-3).**

   The Display & Layout section expands on the sidebar.

2. **Go to the Customize My Pages subsection and select a specific tab that you want to modify (the Accounts tab, for example). Then click the Customize Page button.**

   The Customize My Page page appears for the tab you selected.

3. **Select a list item from either of the two list boxes, depending on whether you want to add or remove it from your page.**

   For example, if you sell directly to customers, you may want to remove the Partners related list from the Account's Selected List column.

4. **Use the up and down arrows to change the order of how the items will appear on your page layout.**

5. **When you're done, click Save.**

   The Customize My Pages page reappears.

Setting up social accounts and contacts

If researching a person's or company's background is a large part of your job, Salesforce saves you some mouse clicks by letting you quickly see the social profiles associated with accounts, contacts, leads, and person accounts right from that particular record.

To activate viewing of social accounts and contacts, follow these steps:

1. **From the My Settings page, click the Display & Layout heading.**

   The Display & Layout section expands to show its subsections.

2. **Click the My Social Accounts and Contacts subsection.**

   The My Social Accounts and Contacts detail page appears.

3. **Make sure that the Use Social Accounts and Contacts check box is selected.**

   A list of social networks appears. If you have a LinkedIn, Twitter, or Facebook account, this will allow you to later sign in to those social networks from within Salesforce, to see profiles for the people and companies that you're researching.

4. **Select any check boxes next to the social networks that you'd like to have enabled (see Figure 4-5).**

    Don't worry, the ability to see an account's or contact's social network information is available only to the individual Salesforce user who enables this for himself. Your colleagues will need to enable this for themselves, and have accounts to those social networks, if they want to take advantage of this feature.

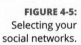

My Social Accounts and Contacts

See social profiles for your accounts, contacts, leads, and person accounts—directly in Salesforce.

Social Accounts and Contacts

☑ Use Social Accounts and Contacts ⓘ

Social Networks

☑ See Twitter information ⓘ
☑ See Facebook information ⓘ
☑ See Klout information ⓘ
☑ See YouTube Videos ⓘ

FIGURE 4-5:
Selecting your social networks.

After Social Accounts and Contacts is enabled, you'll only be able to see as much as your account on that social network allows you to see, and what the person or company that you're looking at wants you to see.

Granting login access

When you need help from your administrator, Salesforce.com customer support, or customer support from a third-party AppExchange package that was installed in your organization, you can grant any of these folks temporary login access to your account. By gaining access to your account, the person helping you can provide better assistance from your perspective, because she can view your pages as you do.

To grant login access, follow these steps:

1. **Click the Grant Account Login Access subheading from the Personal section of the My Settings page (refer to Figure 4-3).**

    The Grant Account Login Access page appears.

2. **Grant support and/or administrator access for a duration of up to one year by selecting the appropriate time frame from the Access Duration picklist.**

   Your administrator, Salesforce.com support, or the AppExchange vendor's support contact will be able to log in as you through the expiration date.

3. **When you're done, click the Save button.**

   The My Settings page appears.

TIP

If you're an administrator and a user has granted you access, you can log in to the user's account as follows: Below the Manage Users heading on the Setup sidebar, click the Users link and then select the Active Users picklist view. From the list of users displayed, click the Login link to the left of the user's name.

Setting Up Salesforce1 for Your Mobile Device

It feels like a given that any application you frequently use will also be accessible from your mobile device. Whether you're flying to Hong Kong for an important meeting and need to update critical information on your tablet, or you're in a cab looking up a contact's address on your phone, Salesforce1 was built with the user in mind to accomplish these tasks.

Downloading and installing Salesforce1

In today's world of tablets and mobile devices, you can be anywhere and access Salesforce. To best experience Salesforce from your mobile device, find the Salesforce1 app in the iTunes App Store (if you're an iPhone user) or the Google Play marketplace (if you're on the Android operating system). They're free to download and you get instant access to your most-viewed accounts, contacts, opportunities, cases, leads, and any other custom tabs specific to your company.

WARNING

The downloadable Salesforce1 app is not supported on the BlackBerry; however, some BlackBerry users (Z10 and Z30 phones) can still access the mobile browser app.

To download and install Salesforce1 on iOS via the App Store, follow these steps:

1. **From the home screen of your iPhone or iPad, select the App Store icon.**

   The App Store home page appears.

2. **In the Search field, type Salesforce1.**

   A list of search results appears.

3. **Select the Salesforce1 app in the list of search results.**

   The Salesforce1 app page appears.

4. **Tap Free and then tap Install to install the app.**

   You may have to enter your iTunes account and password for the download to begin.

   The download begins and finishes, and the app appears on your home screen.

5. **Select the Salesforce1 icon on your home screen and click I Agree.**

   You're prompted to enter your Salesforce account's username and password.

6. **Select Login once you're done to enter Salesforce1 and get started.**

Now that you've installed Salesforce1 on your device, let's talk about the configuration options you have to make it your own.

Configuring Salesforce1 for your needs

Much of Salesforce1 at this point is just enabling it for your users and organization. However, there are a few things you can customize and tweak to make it easy and efficient to work in the field. You can define the users who can access Salesforce1, customize how data appears in it, create actions to add new records, and tweak it to make it match the look and feel of your company's branding. Let's look at how to find and accomplish some of these configurations.

Salesforce makes this customization simple by giving administrators the Salesforce1 Wizard, which guides users with step-by-step customization options to make sure admins don't overlook any features.

To start configuring Salesforce1, navigate to the Setup menu, and follow these steps:

1. **Click Salesforce1 Quick Start from the menu's left-hand sidebar (see Figure 4-6).**

   The Salesforce1 Setup page appears.

2. **Click the Launch Quick Start Wizard button.**

   The Quick Start Wizard page appears.

FIGURE 4-6:
Using the
Salesforce1 Quick
Start menu.

3. **Click Let's Get Started.**

In the first step, you can set up the left-hand navigation menu for your users in the Salesforce1 mobile app. You can reorder or remove items using a drag-and-drop interface.

4. **Click Save and Next to move onto arranging your Global Actions.**

Global Actions allow users to create new records quickly and easily, but these records aren't tied to any other records in Salesforce. For example, an opportunity record won't be automatically tied to an account record. For more information above global actions and how to create them, see Chapter 17.

5. **Click Save and Next and then Create Compact Layout to move onto creating a compact layout.**

The compact layout used by Salesforce1 determines which key fields will be displayed at the top of the record detail display on the app. For example, you can choose to display a contact's name, email, and phone number at the top of your contact records in Salesforce1 for quick viewing.

6. **When you're finished, click Save and Next to preview your basic configuration thus far.**

Here you can look at different aspects of your configuration and see a simulation of the mobile app.

7. **After previewing what Salesforce1 will look like, click Next to invite some pilot users to take a test drive and give you feedback.**

   This page allows you to email those users directly. Start typing their names in the To field and, if they exist in Salesforce, they'll be suggested as you type (see Figure 4-7).

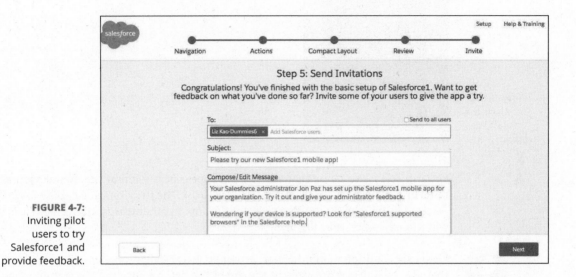

FIGURE 4-7: Inviting pilot users to try Salesforce1 and provide feedback.

8. **Click Send and then Finish when you're done.**

   Congratulations! The basic setup of Salesforce1 is complete and you're taken back to the setup menu. Now you can configure some other aspects of the app, such as in-app or push notifications, the appearance and branding of the app, or user access to it.

Navigating in Salesforce1

The Salesforce1 application is very easy to navigate and was designed in a way that is similar to many other apps you probably use. Let's look at a few navigation tips and tools to get you well on your way to using the app like a pro.

The Salesforce1 Navigation menu is where you should begin. You can toggle the navigation menu by selecting the menu icon on the top left of the app (see Figure 4-8).

REMEMBER

The Navigation menu is customizable, so if the default configuration doesn't meet your organization's needs, you can change the items that appear and the order in which they do.

FIGURE 4-8:
Using the
Salesforce1
Navigation menu.

You can select the items that will always appear at the top of the menu, such as tasks or dashboards. This is called the *selected list.* The first item you choose for the Selected list will be the landing page for the app. In other words, that's what users will first see when they log in.

TIP

Keep user adoption in mind when setting up your Navigation menu. Put the items that users will use most often at the top of the list, because the Navigation menu is not user-specific and the entire organization will see the same Selected list.

Under the Selected list, you see a Recent list, which shows you the most recent objects you've accessed, either on the browser or mobile version of Salesforce.

Finally, the last section is the Apps menu.

REMEMBER

Anything that is represented as a tab in Salesforce can be visible to a user in the Navigation menu. Users can only see the tabs and items in the Navigation menu that they have permission to access via their Salesforce profiles.

To customize Salesforce1 navigation, go to the full site, and follow these steps:

1. **Choose Setup ⇨ Mobile Administration ⇨ Salesforce Navigation.**

   The Chatter Settings page appears.

2. **Use the Add and Remove arrows to move the items you want into or out of the Selected column. Use the Up and Down arrows to rearrange the order of the items in the list.**

   The item named Smart Search Items becomes your Recent list (discussed earlier) and expands into multiple items that you've recently accessed.

Anything above the Smart Search Items element becomes part of the Selected list in the menu, and anything below it falls under the Apps list in the menu.

3. **When you're done, click Save to save your work.**

   Your navigation setup is complete! Now you can log in via your mobile device to see the changes you've made.

TIP

There is a great tool that you can download via the Google Chrome Web Store, called Salesforce1 Simulator. It displays a large mobile interface on your desktop where you can toggle and preview the changes and customizations you've made to Salesforce1.

Importing Your Contacts

One of the keys to making Salesforce productive for you from day 1 is to get your contacts into the system. If your contacts exist primarily in Microsoft Outlook, you may be better off synchronizing your data. Otherwise, Salesforce provides easy-to-use wizards that help you import contacts and accounts. See Chapter 9 for the details on importing, and see your administrator if your data goes beyond the limits of the Import Wizard. (For example, if you have historical activity linked to contacts, you can't import those records by using standard wizards.)

Working with Salesforce Remotely

For many companies, Microsoft Outlook is a critical piece of the workday: It's how people communicate with customers and schedule meetings. Salesforce lets you synchronize with Outlook so that key conversations or meetings in Outlook can be reflected and saved in Salesforce. And if you're a road warrior as well, Salesforce provides various ways to log in from your mobile device and close that deal, without having to squint too much looking at that smaller screen.

Salesforce for Outlook is an updated version of what was previously known as Connect for Outlook. The new version (and, hence, the name evolution) allows you to automatically (or manually — it's your choice) record Microsoft Outlook emails, meetings, and tasks into Salesforce. In the following sections, we show you how to install and configure Salesforce for Outlook for your specific synchronization needs.

If you're the administrator responsible for maintaining accurate data in Salesforce, encourage your company to adopt Salesforce as the system of record or "the single source of truth" for customer interactions. For example, tell users to make updates to accounts and contacts in Salesforce rather than in Outlook. Then have them configure Salesforce for Outlook to allow Salesforce to win if a data conflict occurs between Salesforce and Outlook. By doing this, you can reduce common synchronization issues and influence greater Salesforce adoption.

In most cases, installing Salesforce for Outlook is a simple process. If you connect to the Internet via a proxy server or if your company has a firewall, you may want to consult with your IT department.

To install Salesforce for Outlook, follow these steps:

1. **From the My Settings page, choose Desktop Add-Ons ⇨ Salesforce for Outlook on the sidebar.**

   The Salesforce for Outlook page appears.

2. **Click the View My Configuration button.**

   The Salesforce for Outlook configuration that is specific to you appears. It shows predetermined settings and objects that will be synchronized. This lets you know what is and isn't going to be syncing with Outlook. And depending on your administrator's configuration, you may be able to modify these settings. In case you disagree with the settings, you get to talk with your administrator first before you actually sync anything.

3. **Click the back arrow on your browser and click the Download button on the Salesforce for Outlook page.**

   Salesforce for Outlook is only available for Microsoft Windows operating system users.

   An executable (.exe) file downloads. Before continuing to Step 4, make sure that you've closed Outlook on your computer by choosing File ⇨ Exit from the Outlook toolbar.

4. **Double-click the executable file to install Salesforce for Outlook.**

   Select your language, and complete the Installation Wizard.

5. **Open Microsoft Outlook to complete your Salesforce for Outlook settings.**

   The Setup Wizard appears.

6. **After reading the brief welcome message, click Next through the series of setup windows.**

7. At the final window, click the Install button.

When setup is successful, you arrive at the Congratulations screen.

8. Click the Finish button.

In the lower-right corner of the screen, you should see a small gray logo of Salesforce for Outlook. This means that it's installed and waiting for Microsoft Outlook to be opened.

9. Open Outlook.

A Salesforce for Outlook login window appears. Enter your Salesforce username and password in the appropriate boxes. Then advance to the next screen.

10. Review your synchronization settings.

11. Click an email to open it.

If the email already exists within your Salesforce organization, the contact or lead associated with it will appear in the Salesforce side panel in your Outlook window.

12. If you want to save that email to Salesforce, associated with that contact or lead, click the small envelope icon to the right of the person's name in the Salesforce side panel.

The email is now recorded in Salesforce as an activity.

13. Click Finish.

REMEMBER

If you discover that you accidentally deleted records in Salesforce while synchronizing, you can go to your Recycle Bin and restore those records within 15 days from the date you deleted the records.

Chapter 5

Working in Salesforce

I n Salesforce, there are common ways that records behave, and there are common things you can do when you're on a specific record. Even if different companies use Salesforce for very different business processes, there's still a fundamental commonality of creating a new record, and tracking something someone did, in order to get the benefit of collaboration and using Salesforce as a source of truth.

By managing activities in Salesforce, for example, you can better coordinate with your team, quickly assess what's going on in your accounts, and focus on the next steps to close deals or solve issues.

In this chapter, you find out how to create records, manage your activities, and send emails from within Salesforce. Finally, we cover where you can go for help.

Managing Records

By using the Create New drop-down list on the sidebar of any page in Salesforce, you can easily add new records into Salesforce. You may find yourself in the position of having deleted important files. Don't worry — Salesforce gives you a way to put them back in their rightful spots before anyone notices that they're missing.

Creating records

To create a record (by using Contacts as the example), follow these steps (which can be applied to all Create New *Items* on the picklist):

1. **On the home page, select the Contact option on the Create New picklist, as shown in Figure 5-1.**

   A New Contact page appears in Edit mode.

2. **Complete the fields, as necessary.**

   Even while you're in Edit mode, the Create New picklist is available.

3. **When you're done, click Save.**

   The Contact detail page appears. Here, you can begin tracking information.

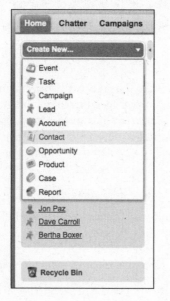

FIGURE 5-1:
Creating records
by using the
Create New
drop-down list.

Resurrecting records from the Recycle Bin

Occasionally, you delete a record and regret it. Don't panic — the Salesforce Recycle Bin gives you 15 days to restore recently deleted records, including any associated records (such as activities deleted in the process) and your credibility.

To restore a deleted record, follow these steps:

1. **On your sidebar, click the Recycle Bin link.**

    The Recycle Bin page appears. If you're an administrator, use the View picklist to view and restore records deleted within the last 15 days by other users.

2. **Navigate the list as you would a normal list page until you find the desired record or records.**

3. **Select the check box(es) in the Action column corresponding to the record(s) that you want to restore.**

    You can click the Select All link to select all the records on the page.

4. **When you're done, click the Undelete button.**

    The Recycle Bin page reappears, and a link to your restored record appears in the sidebar below Recent Items.

There is a maximum amount of space that the Recycle Bin can contain, before it starts automatically deleting the oldest files first, as long as they're at least two hours old. The space is 25 times your organization's total megabytes (MB) of storage, which you can find by choosing Setup ⇨ Administer ⇨ Data Management ⇨ Storage Usage.

Detailing the Record

After you create and save a record, the record appears on its own detail page (see Figure 5-2 for an example using the Contact object). You can use the detail page to update the record fields or manage and track activities and common operations on the related lists displayed below the record. In this section, we show you how to navigate the detail page.

Some of the features that we describe in the following sections may not be enabled by default in your organization. If you can't locate what we're talking about, have your administrator choose Setup ⇨ Build ⇨ Customize ⇨ User Interface to turn on any of these capabilities.

Saving time with hover links

At the top of any record's detail page is a row of several links. Each link corresponds to a list of other records related to the current one. The label for each link consists of the name of that type of record, as well as the number that are related. So, when you're looking at an Account detail page, instead of scrolling down the page to see whether any contacts exist, you can see how many exist right at the top. But wait, it gets better: You can click the link and immediately jump down to the bottom of the detail page to where that related list is normally found. And if you want to be even more efficient, instead of clicking the link, just hover your mouse over it. Salesforce will show you a preview of the related list that even includes buttons to create new records and clickable links to existing ones.

FIGURE 5-2: Looking over the detail page of a new Contact record.

Using links and buttons on the detail page

At the top of any record's detail page, you can use several links and buttons to perform different actions. Go to any detail page and try these out:

>> **Toggle between list and details.** If you've arrived at a record from a list view, you'll see in the upper left of the page a Back to List link. Click that to return quickly to your list view. Then click the Back button on your browser to return to the detail page.

>> **Edit a record.** Click the Edit button to edit the record (if you have permission to do so). The record appears in Edit mode. Click the Cancel button to return to the detail page, or click Save to save the record.

>> **Delete the current record.** Click the Delete button to delete the current record that you're viewing (if you have permission to do so). Click the Cancel button in the pop-up window if you change your mind about the deletion.

>> **Share the record with other users.** Click the Sharing button. (This button doesn't appear on all records.) Click the Back button within your browser to return to the detail page.

>> **Quickly jump to the corresponding related list farther down the page.** Click the related list "hover links" at the top of each detail page, if enabled by your administrator. Alternatively, hover your mouse over the link to open a snapshot of the records displayed in that related list.

>> **View a printable version of the page in a new window.** Click the Printable View link in the upper right, and then click the Print This Page link in the upper-right corner of the window to print a copy of the entire page. Believe it or not, some users still like to print good old-fashioned hard copies that they can review while traveling (hey, we can't always have access to the Internet or a cellular connection).

Modifying records with inline editing

To cut down on the number of steps you have to take when you update records in Salesforce, you can edit fields directly in detail pages.

TECHNICAL STUFF

Make sure that your administrator has enabled this feature.

Follow these steps to edit a field directly in that detail page, without having to go to another page. Salesforce calls this *inline editing*.

1. **Hover your mouse over any field on a record that you own (or have permission to edit).**

Figure 5-3 shows the email address of a contact within a company being updated.

An icon appears to the right of a field, telling you whether you can edit that field. Here's what the various icons mean:

- *Pencil:* This icon appears to the right of editable fields, which become highlighted.

- *Padlock:* This icon appears to the right of fields that you can't edit.

- *None:* You can edit a field that doesn't have an icon, but not with the inline editing feature. You have to edit the record the old-fashioned way, using the Edit button.

FIGURE 5-3:
Editing a field inline.

Email   bond_john@acmegrandh

2. **Double-click an editable field and update the information in that field.**

3. **Press Enter to complete editing that field.**

4. **After you finish editing all the fields you want for that record, click the Save button for the record.**

TECHNICAL STUFF

If you happen to delete information in a field that requires something in it, don't worry. Salesforce has a couple stop-gap measures to prevent you from messing things up. An Undo arrow icon appears before you save the record, and Salesforce is smart enough to remind you about required fields before letting you save your changes.

Capitalizing on related lists

Related lists. Say it three times so you don't forget the term. By designing the page with related lists, Salesforce enables you to gain 360-degree customer visibility and ensure that more detailed information is only a click away. For example, if you open an Account detail page for one of your major customers and scroll down below the record fields, you can see multiple contacts, activities, opportunities, cases, attachments, and so on listed as links from organized related lists. And if you don't see these links, you have work to do.

Looking things up with lookup hovers

On any detail page, you can hover your mouse over a lookup field to get a pop-up preview of that other record's contents. Figure 5-4 shows a preview of the account record by hovering over a contact's company name.

FIGURE 5-4: Hovering over a lookup field provides a preview of that record.

Contact Detail		Edit	Delete	Clone	Request Update
Contact Owner	Liz Kao-Dummies6 [Change]
Name	Mr. John Bond
Account Name	Grand Hotels & Resorts Ltd
Title	VP, Facilities
Department	Facilities
Birthdate	8/21/1951
Reports To	[View Org Chart]
Lead Source	External Referral
Mailing Address	1234 N. Michigan Avenue, Suite 4321 Chicago, IL 60601, USA
Languages	English
Created By	Liz Kao-Dummies6, 11/1/2015 12:44 PM
Description	

Account   View   Edit

Account Name   Grand Hotels & Resorts Ltd [View Hierarchy]

Parent Account

A *lookup field* is any field that actually links to another record. A lookup field's content is underlined to show that it acts as a link to another record. (Just don't confuse lookup fields with the set of related lists that appears below the main body of a record's detail page.)

Reviewing Activities

Activities in Salesforce are scheduled calendar events and tasks. In many ways, the events and tasks in Salesforce are just like the activities you use in Microsoft Outlook, Google Calendar, or any other productivity application. You can schedule events on your calendar, invite people to meetings, book a conference room, and add tasks to your to-do lists so that you don't forget to get things done.

However, Salesforce takes activities further: You can easily link events and tasks to other related records, such as accounts, contacts, and so on. You can view activities both in the context of a relevant item (for example, all activities that relate to an account) and as a stand-alone from your calendar and task lists in the comfort and convenience of your home page. And, if you're a manager, Salesforce allows you to stay up to speed on your direct reports and how they're spending their time.

You can use activities in Salesforce to track all the significant tasks and events involved in acquiring, selling, and servicing customers. Think about all the actions that you and your teams perform to accomplish your job — meetings, calls, emails, even the occasional physical letter — and imagine the value of having all that information in one place at your fingertips. You can have such a place in Salesforce, and you can easily link your activities together in an organized fashion.

Salesforce features several types of activities that you can access from the Open Activities and Activity History related lists displayed on many of the major records, including accounts, contacts, leads, opportunities, and cases. In this chapter, we focus on events and tasks, but in the following list, we briefly explain all the various activity records you can track in Salesforce:

>> **Task:** Essentially a to-do. Use this activity record as your online yellow sticky note. It's an activity that needs to be completed, but it doesn't need a specific time or duration associated with it. For example, if you know that you're supposed to follow up with a contact by sending a written letter, you can create a task such as Send Letter.

>> **Event:** A calendared activity. An event has a scheduled time, date, and duration associated with it. It can also have invitees associated with it, as well as be a recurring thing that happens on a regular basis. Examples of common events are meetings, conference calls, and tradeshows.

>> **Log a Call:** A task record of a completed call. Use Log a Call during or after a call to make sure that you capture important details. For example, use it when a contact calls you and you want to record comments or outcomes from the discussion.

>> **Send an Email:** Logs an activity for an email that you send to a contact or a lead. You can send emails from Salesforce or a third-party email product, and capture that information directly inside Salesforce.

Creating Activities

Before you can begin managing your time or activities in Salesforce, you need to know the easiest and most reliable way to add events and tasks.

Creating an event

When you want to schedule activities that have a particular place, time, and duration, use event records. By using event records, you and your sales teams can keep better track of your calendars.

You can create an event from your home page, its calendar views, or the Open Activity related list of a record. The best method to choose often depends on what you're doing. If you're carving out meetings on a specific day, add events from your Home tab calendar's Day View. If you're working on a customer deal, you might create the event from an opportunity record. The end result is the same.

TIP

If you're just getting accustomed to filling out records in Salesforce, create events from the record that's most directly associated with the event. By using this method, many of the lookup fields are prefilled for you. So, when you save, you ensure that you can find the activity quickly because it's linked to all the right records.

To create an event from a relevant record (such as a contact or account record), follow these steps:

1. **Enter a name in the search field in the upper left, next to the Salesforce logo. Search for the record to which you want to link the event.**

    For example, if you want to schedule a meeting about an account, you search for the account name.

    When you click Search, a Search Results page appears.

2. **Click the name of the particular record you want.**

    The record's detail page appears.

3. **Scroll down to the Open Activities related list on the page and click the New Event button, as shown in Figure 5-5.**

A New Event page appears. If you created this event from a relevant record, the name of the person or the related record is prefilled for you.

FIGURE 5-5:
Creating an
event.

Open Activities	New Task	New Event	New Meeting Request
No records to display			

4. **Fill in the relevant fields.**

Pay close attention to the required fields highlighted with a vertical red bar. Depending on your company's customization, your event record may differ from the standard, but here are tips on some of the standard fields:

- *Assigned To:* Defaults to you. Use the Lookup icon (the little magnifying glass) to assign the event to another user.

- *Subject:* The event's subject, which appears on the calendar. Click the combo box icon. A pop-up window appears, displaying a list of your company's event types. When you click a selection, the window closes and your selection appears in the Subject field. To the immediate right of your selection's text, customize the subject by adding a brief description. For example, you might click the Meeting link and then type **Define Requirements** to explain the event's purpose.

- *Related To:* The standard event record shows two drop-down lists that you can use to link the event with relevant records, as shown in Figure 5-6. One relates to certain types of records — an account, opportunity, or case. The other relates to a person — a contact or lead. First, select the type of record and then use the associated Lookup icon to select the desired record. For example, if you select Opportunity from the first drop-down list, you can use the Opportunity icon to find a specific account.

TIP

If you use the Related To fields on activities, you'll rarely have problems finding an activity later. For example, if you sell through channel partners, you might associate a meeting with a partner contact, but you might relate the meeting to an end-customer account. When you save the event, it appears on the related lists of both records.

- *Time:* Allows you to specify the start time and end time. You can use basic shorthand and avoid unnecessary keystrokes. For example, type **9a** for 9:00 a.m. or **2p** for 2:00 p.m.

FIGURE 5-6:
Linking the event to related records.

- *Recurrence:* Allows you to create a series of events that repeat over a duration of time. This saves you from manually re-creating an event for each occurrence. You can set the frequency of the event, and optionally, when the last occurrence of the recurrence (got that?) happens.

5. **Click Save.**

   The page you started from reappears, and the event appears under the Open Activities related list for the associated records. The event also appears on the home page of the user assigned to the event.

   Alternatively, click the Save & New Event or Save & New Task button if you want to immediately create another activity. A new activity record appears in Edit mode.

Using pop-up reminders

Similar to many calendaring applications, Salesforce triggers pop-up reminders about events at a set time before the event is scheduled to start. If you live your life daily in Salesforce and have the application constantly logged in on your machine, this feature will gently remind you via a pop-up window, to make sure that you don't forget an important meeting with a customer.

TECHNICAL STUFF

Make sure that your browser's pop-up blocker protection is set to allow pop-ups that come from the Salesforce domain. Otherwise, if your browser has the pop-up blocker feature turned on, when you create an event, a little warning box appears every time your browser tries to display a reminder box.

If, on the other hand, you're the type that lets pop-up reminders pile up on your computer screen, or if you log in to Salesforce infrequently (what sacrilege!), you can disable this feature. From your name in the upper-right corner of the Sales-force app, choose My Settings⇨Calendar & Reminders⇨Reminders & Alerts and deselect the Trigger Alert When Reminder Comes Due check box, along with any of the other boxes that are selected by default. Remember to click Save after you finish.

Creating a task

Some sales reps refer to tasks as action items; others call them reminders or to-dos. Whatever your favorite term, use task records when you want to remind yourself or someone else of an activity that needs to get done.

You can create a task from the My Tasks section of your home page or from the Create New drop-down list on any page within Salesforce. We use both methods, depending on whether we're planning out our weeks or strategizing about a particular account, contact, or other record.

To create a task from the relevant record, follow these steps:

1. **Enter a name in the search bar for the record to which you want to link the task and click the Search button.**

   For example, if you want to set a task to review a proposal that relates to an opportunity, search for the opportunity name. After you click Search, a Search Results page appears.

2. **Click the name of the record you want.**

   The record's detail page appears.

3. **Select Create New Task from the sidebar or click the New Task button on the Open Activities related list of a record, as shown in Figure 5-7.**

Open Activities			New Task	New Event	
Action	Subject	Name		Task	Due Date
Edit | Del	Meeting	John Bond		☐	12/12/2015 6:00 PM

FIGURE 5-7:
Creating a
new task.

Either way, the result is the same. A New Task page appears.

TIP

When creating tasks, go to the record that the task is most directly related to before adding the task. By taking this path, you ensure that your task is easy to find because it's automatically associated with the correct record and its account. For example, if you're creating a task to follow up on an email to a contact, you most likely add the task from the contact record.

4. **Fill in the relevant fields.**

   Like the event record, your fields may vary, but here are some tips on adding a task:

   - *Assigned To:* Defaults to you. Use the Lookup icon to assign the task to another user.

   - *Subject:* The task's subject, which appears on the My Tasks section of the Assigned To's home page. Click the combo box icon. A pop-up window appears, displaying a list of your company's activity types. When you click a selection, the window closes and your selection appears in the Subject field. To the immediate right of your selection, add a brief description. For example, you might click the Send Letter link and then type **Introduction** to explain the task's purpose.

   - *Related To:* Shows two drop-down lists that you can use to link the task with relevant records similar to the event fields. First, select the type of record, and then use the associated Lookup icon to select the desired record.

   - *Priority:* Denotes the task's importance. High-priority tasks display an exclamation point (!) to the left of the activity on the assigned user's home page.

   - *Status:* Defines the status of the task.

   - *Due Date:* The date by which you expect the task to be completed. This is typically optional. Clicking your cursor in this field makes a calendar window pop up; you can select a date from this calendar.

5. **Click Save.**

   The page that you started from reappears, and the task displays under the Open Activities related list for the associated records. The task also appears in the My Tasks section of the home page of the user who's assigned to the task.

Make sure that you set your My Tasks view on the home page so that your tasks are included in the filter. The view defaults to Overdue, which can confuse some people when they don't see a recently created task in that area.

Always link your tasks with the relevant records in Salesforce. Otherwise, you run the risk of losing valuable customer information that might have been captured in that task.

Logging a call

Sometimes, you perform a task and just want to log the activity after the fact. For example, a contact calls you on the phone, or you get stopped in the coffee room by your boss to talk about a customer issue. In these situations, instead of creating a task, saving it, and then completing it, use the Log a Call feature.

When you click the Log a Call button, you're simply creating a task record that has a Completed Activity Status. To log a call, go to the record that the call relates to (an account or lead record, for example) and follow these steps:

1. **Scroll down to the Activity History related list and click the Log a Call button.**

   The Log a Call page appears, displaying fields for a completed task at the top of the page and fields for a follow-up activity at the bottom of the page.

2. **Fill out or modify any of the fields to log the call.**

   The Status field is preset to Completed, as shown in Figure 5-8.

FIGURE 5-8:
Logging a call.

3. **If applicable, add another related task by filling out the fields below the Schedule Follow Up Task header.**

   Although certain fields are labeled as required, the follow-up task is optional.

4. **Click Save when you're finished.**

   The detail page that you started from reappears. The call record appears under the Activity History related list. If you set up a new follow-up task, that record appears under the Open Activities related list.

Instead of using the Notes feature in Salesforce to track details of your interactions with customers and prospects, we recommend using Log a Call to record this type of information. Tasks allow for easier reporting, timestamping, editing, and viewing capabilities. You can even track interactions with multiple people at once using the Shared Activities feature. If you don't see this feature when creating a Task, ask your Salesforce Administrator to turn it on.

WARNING

If you're an administrator and someone asks you to allow Shared Activity tracking, you could enable that by choosing Settings ⇨ Customize ⇨ Activities ⇨ Activity Settings ⇨ Allow Users to Relate Multiple Contacts to Tasks and Events. However, this is an irreversible request, and you should reflect on the majority use case for this. For example, in some financial services businesses, tasks often involve contacts in addition to your prospect. However, no one's going to use this (maybe not even the person who asked for it) unless it's properly announced, along with benefits derived from its use.

Organizing and Viewing Activities

You can view your activities from the home page and from a specific record's Open Activities or Activity History related list. If you're planning your calendar, use the home page. If you're working from a particular account, contact, or other item, you can get better context on pertinent activities from the related lists on the record.

After you create (or are assigned to) activities, you probably want to view them so that you can prioritize and complete them.

TIP

On the home page, change the default view in the My Tasks section to All Open or to Today, depending on how efficient you are, so that you can see all tasks that you still need to complete. The current default view, Overdue, only shows you tasks after the due date has passed, which we have found to not be many users' first choice.

If you're planning around a specific record, such as a contact or opportunity, you can view linked activities from the Open Activities and Activity History related lists located on a detail page.

The two related lists work hand in hand. An event record automatically moves from the Open Activities related list to the Activity History related list when the scheduled date and time pass. A task record remains on the Open Activities related list until its Status is changed to Completed; then the record appears on the Activity History related list.

To view activities from a detail page, follow these steps:

1. **Open a saved record.**

   The detail page of the record appears. The saved record appears at the top, and related lists are at the bottom of the page.

2. **Scroll down until you see the Open Activities and Activity History related lists.**

   If you already created related activities, activity links appear in the lists.

3. **Click an item listed under the Subject column.**

   The activity record appears.

Updating Activities

Things happen: Meetings get canceled, and small tasks suddenly become big priorities. With Salesforce, you can perform many of the actions that a normal time-management tool would allow you to do, including delegating activities to other users, rescheduling, editing information, deleting records, and so on.

You can do the following basic functions by clicking buttons at the top of an activity record:

>> **Edit:** Update any of the fields in the record whose fields now appear, and make sure that you save.

>> **Delete:** Delete the record. A pop-up window appears in which you can confirm the deletion.

>> **Create a Follow Up Task:** Generate a related task. A New Task page opens, prefilled with information from the prior record.

>> **Create a Follow Up Event:** Schedule a related meeting. A New Event page appears, prefilled with information from the prior record.

Assigning activities

Sometimes, you may create activities and assign them to others (intentionally, not because you're trying to shirk your duties). Sales development reps often do this as they set up meetings for their account executives. Salesforce lets you easily reassign tasks and events.

To assign an activity, open the activity record and follow these steps:

1. **Click the Edit button.**

2. **Click the Lookup icon to the right of the Assigned To field.**

   A pop-up window appears, displaying a list of your Salesforce users.

3. **Use the Search field to search for the user or select the user from the list.**

   After you make a selection, the pop-up window disappears, and your selection appears in the Assigned To field.

4. **Click Save.**

   The activity record reappears, and the Assigned To field has been modified.

Completing a task

When you're done with a task, you want to gladly get it off the list of things to do. You can mark a task as complete from your home page or from the Open Activities related list in which the task link is displayed.

To complete a task, follow these steps:

1. **If you're viewing the task from an Open Activities related list, click the Cls link (Salesforce shorthand for "Close") to the left of the task. If you're looking at the task on the home page, click the X link in the Completed column.**

   Both links have the same result when clicked: The task appears in Edit mode, and the Status field changes to Completed. (Your company might have its own terminology for the Completed status.)

2. **Type any changes and click Save.**

   Some reps update the Comments field if they have relevant new information. The detail page reappears, and the completed task now appears under the Activity History related list.

Understanding Email Fields in Salesforce

Email is a fundamental method for communicating with customers, prospects, and friends. By using email correctly, you can better manage your sales territory and be more responsive to customers. However, by not using email appropriately, you can leave a bad impression or lose a client.

If email is an indispensable part of your business, you and other users can send email from Salesforce and track the communication history from relevant records, such as accounts, contacts, opportunities, and cases. This capability is helpful if you inherit a major customer account, because you can potentially view all the email interactions from a single account record.

In this section, we show you best practices for sending a basic email, mass emailing, and using templates.

An email in Salesforce is an activity record comprising fields for the message and for the people you want to keep in the loop on the message.

The email record comes with standard fields that people commonly use when sending email. Most fields are self-explanatory, but the following list summarizes some additional fields:

>> **Related To:** Use this field to relate the email to an account, opportunity, campaign, case, or other standard or custom object record in Salesforce, depending on your edition. By completing this field, the email is stored under the Activity History related list of that record. See the "Creating and sending email" section, later in this chapter.

>> **Additional To:** Use this field to type in additional primary recipients. They don't have to be contacts or leads in Salesforce.

>> **Attachment:** Of course, you know what an email attachment is, but we want to let you know that the size limit is 10MB per email message within Salesforce.

Setting Up Your Email

Before you begin emailing people from Salesforce, check out a couple of setup options that can save you time and headaches. In the following sections, we show you how to personalize your outbound email, as well as how to build personal email templates for common messages that you send to people.

Personalizing your email settings

When you send an email via Salesforce, the recipient can receive the message just as if you sent the email from your standard email program. The email message appears as if it came from your business email address, and you can use a standard signature to go with your message. And if the recipient replies to your email, that reply email comes right to your standard email inbox. To pull this off, though, you need to personalize your email settings in Salesforce.

To set up your email, follow these steps:

1. **Choose** *Your Name* ⇨ **My Settings** ⇨ **Email** ⇨ **My Email Settings.**

   The My Email Settings page appears in Edit mode.

2. **Modify the first two required fields, as necessary, to specify the outgoing name and the return email address.**

3. **Select the Yes radio button if you want to send a blind carbon copy (BCC) to your standard email inbox.**

   That way, you can still keep emails in customer folders in your email application.

4. **Modify the Email Signature field.**

   If you're personalizing your email settings for the first time, you might notice a default signature from Salesforce. This message appears at the bottom of your email in lieu of your signature. Unless you're using Personal Edition, go ahead and change it.

5. **Click Save.**

   The Email page under Personal Setup appears, and your settings are modified.

Building personal email templates

If you ask your top sales reps about sending email, they'll probably tell you that they don't re-invent the wheel every time they send certain messages to customers. It's a waste of their time, and time is money. Instead, they use templates and form letters to send the same message with less work.

In your standard sales process, you probably send a variety of emails to customers, including

>> Letters of introduction

>> Thank-you notes

>> Responses to common objections

>> Answers on competition

Although you do need to personalize a message to fit the specific details of a customer, you probably use certain effective phrases and sentences over and over again. Instead of searching for a prior message and cutting and pasting, you can create personal email templates and improve your productivity.

To create a personal template, follow these steps:

1. **Choose *Your Name* ⇨ My Settings ⇨ Email ⇨ Email Templates.**

   An Email Templates page appears.

2. **Select the My Personal Email Templates folder in the drop-down list, if it's not already set to that.**

3. **Click the New Template button.**

   Step 1 of the New Template Wizard appears.

4. **Select the radio button for Text, HTML, Custom, or Visualforce to set the type of email that you want to create, and click Next.**

   - *Text:* Uses a basic text-only template without any formatting

   - *HTML:* Uses a previously created letterhead and supports HTML formatting

   - *Visualforce:* Lets you create an email template within a Visualforce page

   - *Custom:* Lets you paste previously created HTML code as your template

   The next page of the wizard appears, and the content of the page depends on the choice you made. Using HTML is most common and has certain advantages, both from appearance and tracking standpoints, but older email programs cannot receive HTML email.

5. **If you select Text in the previous step, complete the template fields provided (see Figure 5-9) and then click Save.**

   You can use the template only after you select the Available for Use check box.

   After clicking Save, a Text Email Template page for your new template appears in Saved mode with an Attachments related list.

6. **(Optional) Attach a document.**

7. **If you select either HTML option (HTML or Custom) in Step 4, enter the properties for the email template and click the Save & Next button.**

   If you choose to build your email template with a letterhead, you have to select a previously created letterhead and then a layout by using the drop-down lists provided. After you click the Next button, the Step 3 page of the wizard appears.

FIGURE 5-9:
Create a text
template.

REMEMBER

You can create HTML or Custom email templates only if you have the Edit HTML Templates permission. See an admin if you don't have the right permissions.

8. **Create the HTML version by typing and formatting the content and copying and pasting merge fields.**

9. **Click Preview to review your work and, when you're done, click the Save & Next button.**

   The Step 4 page of the wizard appears.

10. **Enter the text version of the email template.**

    Customers who can't or don't want to receive HTML emails can receive the text version. If the message is similar or identical to the HTML version, click the Copy Text from HTML Version button and modify the content as needed.

11. **Click the Save button.**

    An HTML or Custom Email Template page for your new template appears in Saved mode with an Attachments related list, which you can use for attaching standard documents.

We show you how to use your email template in the later section "Using email templates."

Creating letterheads

If you're a system administrator, you can create and save custom-branded letterheads to ensure that all your templates have a similar look and feel.

To create a letterhead, follow these steps:

1. Choose Setup ⇨ Administer ⇨ Communication Templates ⇨ Letterheads.

If this is your first time visiting, an Understanding Letterheads page appears. You can bypass it by clicking the Next button.

2. Click the New Letterhead button.

The Letterhead Properties section of the New Letterhead Wizard appears.

3. Select the Available For Use check box. Then fill in the required fields marked in red and optionally enter a description.

If you don't want to let anyone use the letterhead just yet, you can leave the Available For Use check box deselected for now.

4. Click the Save button.

The Letterhead Details section of the New Letterhead Wizard appears (see Figure 5-10). This is where you can graphically design your letterhead.

FIGURE 5-10:
Create a
letterhead.

5. **Click the Edit Background Color button.**

The Background Color window opens with the default color as gray. You can set it to any HTML color code or use the Paint Can button to select from a color chart. When you're done, click the OK button to close the window.

6. **Click the Select Logo button.**

The Attach File window opens to let you select from any image that has already been uploaded to the Documents tab in Salesforce. When you find the file you want, click its name to select it and close the window.

TIP

Make sure the document is marked as an externally available image.

7. **Click the Edit Header Properties button.**

The Header Properties window opens. You can specify the background color, the horizontal and vertical alignment, and the height of the Header section to ensure that your logo looks great. When you're done, click the OK button to close the window.

8. **Click the Edit Top Line button.**

The Top Color and Height window opens. If you don't want a top line, you can set the line color to the same as your background and set the height to 0. When you're done, click OK to close the window.

9. **Click the remaining buttons to make additional edits to your letterhead.**

You can configure the middle and bottom lines, the footer properties and logo, and the body background color, just as you did in the previous steps.

10. **Click the Save button.**

A preview of your new letterhead is shown. You can always make additional changes by clicking the Edit Letterhead button.

Sending Email from Salesforce

You can send an email to any lead or contact stored in Salesforce with a valid email address. By sending from Salesforce, you can ensure that you and your team members can keep track of critical outbound communications to customers and prospects.

Creating and sending email

You can initiate your outbound email from many different records in Salesforce, including opportunity, account, case, campaign, lead, and contact records. To create and send an email, go to the relevant record and follow these steps:

1. Click the Send an Email button on the Activity History related list.

A Send an Email page appears, as shown in Figure 5-11. The Email format is in Text, with a Switch to *Format* link appearing to the right of it. Alternatively, click the Send an Email button in the HTML Email Status related list to default to HTML format. Either way, if you change your mind, you can always switch formats on the Send an Email edit page.

FIGURE 5-11:
Composing an email.

If you have organization-wide email addresses set up in Salesforce, you can select one as your From address. If not, your email address will default as the From address.

2. Decide in what format you want to send your email:

- *Switch to Text Only:* You want to send the message using only text — no HTML. A dialog box appears to warn you that any HTML formatting will be removed. When you click OK, the box disappears, and the format is switched.

- *Switch to HTML:* Send your message in HTML format. If you decide to send your email with HTML, you get an added bonus of being able to track your email (see the later section "Tracking HTML emails").

3. **Type the recipient's name in the To field and then click the Lookup icon at the right of the field to search for the contact or lead.**

   A pop-up window appears, containing a search tool and a list of search results.

   TIP

   If you send an email from the relevant lead or contact record, you can eliminate this step because the To field is prefilled. But remember to use the Related To field to associate the email to other records, such as an opportunity.

4. **Select the correct person by clicking the name, or refine your search by modifying the name or using wildcards; then click Go.**

   When you select the recipient, the pop-up window disappears, and the To field is populated with your selection.

5. **Use the Related To drop-down list to associate the email with the correct type of record, and then click the Lookup icon to the right of the adjacent field to find the exact record — similar to the process in Steps 3 and 4.**

   Depending on which record you started from, the Related To drop-down list might already be filled.

6. **In the Additional To field, type additional primary recipient emails.**

   These folks get their email on the To list. They don't have to be contacts or leads.

7. **Clicking the CC link or the BCC link lets you copy other contacts or users to the email.**

   A pop-up window appears, containing a drop-down list for co-workers at your company and for contacts of the account. Select names in the Contacts list box, use the double arrows to include them as recipients, and then click Save. The pop-up window disappears, and the CC and BCC fields reflect your selections.

8. **Click in the CC or BCC fields and add additional email addresses, as needed.**

   Salesforce allows you to send emails to people who aren't contacts, leads, or users. Just type the email address directly in this field.

   If you want to use an email template, stop here and go to the next section.

9. **Complete the Subject and Body fields of the message and then click Send.**

   If your contact or lead in the To field doesn't yet have an email address, this absence is flagged before you send the email. A Click Here to Edit the Email Address link appears that you can click to associate an email address with the record without having to leave your Send an Email page.

The record that you started from reappears, and a link to a copy of your email appears in the Activity History related lists of the records that you linked.

Using email templates

In the section "Building personal email templates," earlier in this chapter, we show you how to create a personalized template. In this section, you find out how to send an email that uses a template you created. First, create an email (as described in the preceding section), and then follow these additional steps before you send it:

1. **Before you modify the Subject and Body fields, click the Select Template button at the top of the page.**

   A pop-up window appears, displaying a list of available templates.

2. **Click the Folder drop-down list and select the folder where you saved your template.**

   The pop-up window refreshes, displaying a list of available templates based on your folder selection, as shown in Figure 5-12.

Folder	My Personal Email Templates ⬦		
Name		**Type**	**Description**
Dummies Edition 6		Text	

FIGURE 5-12: Available email templates.

3. **Select the desired template by clicking the relevant link in the Name column.**

   The pop-up window disappears, and the page reappears with content based on the template that you selected.

4. **Modify the message to further personalize the email and then click Send.**

   The record you started from reappears, and a link to a copy of your email appears under the Activity History related lists of the linked records.

TIP

Due to Saleforce's presence in so many sales organizations, a whole ecosystem of third-party vendor applications have sprouted that sync externally sent emails with Salesforce. Go to www.appexchange.com and search in the Email and Calendar Sync category to learn about the options available with your email system.

Sending Mass Email

If you struggle to stay in touch with prospects or customers on a regular basis, you can use Salesforce to send mass emails and lighten your workload. Mass email is particularly helpful for sales reps who send common messages that don't require a lot of personalization. For example, if you're an institutional sales rep selling shares of a hedge fund, you might want to send a monthly email newsletter to sophisticated investors specifically interested in your fund.

REMEMBER

When sending mass email, Professional Edition users can send a maximum of 250 emails at a time. Enterprise Edition users can send as many as 500 emails, and Unlimited Edition users can send as many as 1,000 emails. A company is limited to 1,000 emails per day.

You can send a mass email to contacts or leads — the method is similar.

To send out a mass email, go to the Contacts home page or Leads home page, and follow these simple steps:

1. **Click the Mass Email Contacts link or the Mass Email Leads link (depending on which home page you're on) under the Tools section.**

    The Recipient Selection page appears.

2. **Specify the recipients that you want to include in the email from the View drop-down list and click the Go button.**

    If you find the recipients you want, skip to Step 5.

3. **If you can't find the view that you want from the View drop-down list, click the Create New View link.**

    The Create New View page appears. In most circumstances, you need to create a custom view.

4. **To create the new view, fill in the information that you want to use to filter the recipients for your mass email and then click Save.**

    For example, if you want to send an email to all customer contacts located in New York, you can build a view. (See Chapter 17 for general details on how to create custom views.) When you click Save, the Recipient Selection page reappears, displaying a list of contacts that meet your criteria.

REMEMBER

Any of your leads or contacts that have the Email Opt Out check box selected are automatically omitted from these lists.

5. **Review the list and select the check boxes to designate the contacts to whom you want to send the mass email.**

Contacts or leads that don't have email addresses lack an available check box in the Action column.

6. **When you're satisfied with your selections, click Next.**

A Template Selection page appears, where you can select an email template from the email template folders and associated lists.

7. **Use the Folder drop-down list to locate the right folder and template.**

You can skip this step if you already see the desired email template on the list results.

8. **Select the desired email template by selecting the appropriate radio button in the Name column, and then click Next.**

9. **Review the content for the mass email and then click Next.**

A Confirmation page appears, summarizing the number of contacts that will receive the mass email.

10. **Select the appropriate check boxes if you want to receive a blind copy, store an activity, and/or use your signature.**

11. **Give this mass email a name in the Mass Email Name field.**

12. **Use the radio buttons to select whether you want to send the email now or schedule it for delivery (set the time and date in the Schedule for Delivery On and Time Zone fields).**

13. **When you're done, click Send.**

A Complete page appears, confirming the delivery of your mass email.

Getting Help and Setting Up

In the upper-right corner of any Salesforce page, to the left of the Force.com app menu, you find a set of links that can help you get more out of Salesforce:

» **Your Name:** This picklist menu is labeled with your full name. Click the down arrow next to your name to select links to edit your personal profile information or your personal settings.

» **Setup:** Click this link to open a page containing the Force.com home page for all things under the hood. If you're an administrator, you'll be able to administer and customize Salesforce for your company from Setup.

>> **Help:** Click this link to open a window that contains the Salesforce Help community with a search bar and additional tabs for accessing documentation, getting technical support, getting billing assistance, and signing up for training and certification.

TECHNICAL STUFF

If the Developer Console link appears in the *Your Name* menu, ignore it for now. This link is for technical administrators who use it to analyze or troubleshoot automated processes and the use of Apex code.

Chapter 6

Collaborating in the Cloud

Every one of us has been the new guy or gal at a company at some point in our lives. Even if you received a formal orientation and a review of the organizational chart (a luxury that you shouldn't take for granted), do you remember still having to meander around, finding that person who has the answers? Or maybe you're an old-timer who is extremely busy but always willing to answer a newcomer's questions because you remember how overwhelming it was when you first started.

Organizations have huge amounts of varying types of knowledge: formal and informal, documented and verbal, current and outdated. Very rarely is knowledge shared in one centralized location. Even when a company is pretty diligent about communicating, the sheer volume of information and the speed at which current information gets outdated can be overwhelming. Chatter bridges the gap between sharing useful information and information overload by allowing you to communicate quickly with colleagues, as well as keep track of progress and updates on topics as they happen.

In this chapter, we discuss how Chatter, when used correctly, works to eliminate all that information chaos by providing a central place where Salesforce users can update statuses, post and respond to questions, and see recent activity on records to easily collaborate in a private and secure environment. We walk you through setting up your profile, updating your status, and using groups and feeds so that your sales, marketing, and customer service organizations can work together even more effectively.

TIP

At the time of this writing, Chatter has three license types. A Salesforce license already comes with full Chatter features, but there are also three different Chatter-specific licenses for colleagues who don't need to be in Salesforce, but could still benefit from collaborating with people who work in Salesforce often. The free license just lets users see status updates from others, but they can't click into any customer relationship management (CRM) tabs, like Accounts or Contacts. The external license is like the free license, but it's intended for customers and other external users. You can add them to specific Chatter groups for collaborative projects, but they can't see your Salesforce data. Chatter Only (or Chatter Plus) is an additional charge for users who may only need to see Accounts and Contacts, and some custom apps, but not Opportunities. All these options are for colleagues who don't need to be in Salesforce but could still benefit from collaborating with people who work in Salesforce often. If you're a daily user of Salesforce, your license comes with Chatter.

REMEMBER

Each profile, group, and status update you make is a record in Salesforce, which adds to your data and storage usage numbers. Salesforce has also set some limits on the number of posts and comments that are stored in Salesforce (and for how long). It's usually not an issue, but if your organization has a bunch of die-hard super-users (and what organization doesn't?), always check with your account executive for more details.

Preparing to Use Chatter

When you get a new car, it's tempting to just drive away as soon as you're handed the keys, but taking a few minutes to read the owner's manual may serve you better. The same holds true for Salesforce Chatter. By spending a little extra time preparing, you can ensure a successful implementation of this powerful feature and ensure your standing as a Salesforce hero in your company.

TIP

Here are some key actions that we recommend for every Chatter implementation:

>> **Get key executives of your organization to use Chatter.** Engage executives early, help them update their profiles (more on that later), and show them how easy it is to follow other employees. They'll love the

communication-improvement aspect of Salesforce Chatter and will encourage their employees to post regular updates.

» **Allow the most informational objects to be followed.** If you have a popular product or brand, you may get hundreds of leads a day in Salesforce. Being able to track Chatter on leads is important, especially if you can selectively choose which records to monitor. Other types of records (such as Products) probably won't change that often and, thus, don't warrant tracking via Chatter. As part of your preparation, you have to determine which objects make sense to track for your business.

» **Prepare for the change.** Your organization may not have processes in place to provide routine updates to management. People naturally resist change, especially change that embraces sharing what they're doing. When you put together your communications plan introducing Salesforce Chatter, be sure to focus on the timesaving aspect and reassure people that it's not a surveillance tool used by Big Brother. It's meant to encourage collaboration.

» **Lead by example.** Show users how to find and follow your profile. Then be sure to post status updates about the work you're doing so that they can get a feel for how it works. You can even create polls via Chatter to encourage participation.

» **Establish basic posting guidelines.** Your colleagues may already be used to an informal posting functionality of social-networking sites, but before they post personal information in Chatter, set some basic guidelines. Here are some ideas to get you started:

- Keep Chatter updates related to business matters.

- Don't post anything you wouldn't want to be seen by your CEO, HR department, or peers.

- Never post confidential information that isn't widely available elsewhere in your organization.

- Keep statements constructive and professional. Leave the flame wars and boorishness to anonymous forums.

» **Provide training sessions and FAQs.** Education is the key to success for any Salesforce implementation. Training and documentation not only improve adoption but also ensure that users make fewer mistakes. The same holds true for implementing Chatter. It might seem easy to "just turn it on," but if people aren't all on the same page on when and how to use the tool, information that's posted won't be helpful, which will affect adoption rates.

An FAQ list is a basic question-and-answer document that your users can reference. In addition to the previous guidelines, you can include sample status updates (good and bad ones) and instructions on common tasks. See Chapter 8 to find out how you can create a reusable email template that includes your FAQs and guidelines.

>> **Continue adoption.** When new employees join your company, be sure to bring them onboard them with training, and review your FAQs and Chatter guidelines with them. This will ensure that they continue the success of your Chatter implementation and prevent any embarrassing mistakes.

Understanding Key Chatter Terms

Here are some Chatter-related terms to familiarize yourself with:

>> **Profile:** A page about a specific person in your company who is using Salesforce. A profile can include the person's name, a short bio, contact information, and a photo, for example. The one for yourself is accessed from the top menu, via your name. That page is called My Settings, and we discuss how to update that in Chapter 3.

>> **Feed:** A Chatter feed shows a chronological list of activities performed by people or records within your company's Salesforce instance.

>> **People:** A collection of people within your company who have Chatter profiles.

>> **@:** Pronounced *at,* type this symbol and then immediately the name of a co-worker whom you want to include in your post, in the hopes of giving him a specific heads-up or asking him to join in the conversation. If you have emails allowed and the user you are mentioning has opted to receive email notifications from Chatter activity, the user will get an email notifying him of that specific post.

>> **Following/Unfollowing:** The act of following (or unfollowing) a person or record to see (or no longer see) her feed updates. These can include comments, posts, and updates to certain fields within a record. Other people in your Salesforce organization can also choose to follow you.

>> **Post:** A type of update that you make about yourself that's added to your feed for others to see. Because it's called a *post,* you're usually posting an update to some work most likely associated with a record.

>> **Comment:** A response that you write based on another person's feed activity. For example, if an opportunity that people are following is finally won, your CEO could comment on the feed and say, "Congratulations, team!"

- » **Like:** A very quick way to cast your vote saying that you also approve of a particular post or comment.

- » **Share:** A quick way to share a post with your followers or a specific group.

- » **File:** A document (up to 2GB in size) that can be attached to a post or comment. It can come from your computer or from within files you own in Salesforce.

- » **Group:** A way to collaborate with specific people. People can join these freely, or you can make them private so that people have to request entry or be invited, and its contents are not seen by nonmembers.

Turning On Chatter

Chatter is automatically enabled for all new customers. However, if you subscribed a long time ago or turned it off, then before your company can begin using Chatter, your system administrator has to make some minor changes to your Salesforce configuration.

The first step in using Chatter is activating it in Salesforce Setup. Follow these steps:

1. **Choose Setup ⇨ Customize ⇨ Chatter ⇨ Chatter Settings.**

The Chatter Settings page appears.

2. **Select the Enable check box.**

Several more sections appear.

3. **Review the fields that have defaulted to having the check box selected.**

- • *Allow Group Archiving:* This allows groups without any activity over a 90-day period to be archived so that group clutter is minimized. Sometimes people create groups for one-time events; this option allows the organization to archive a group, which keeps this group information in the system without letting new users join or add to the conversation. You can search for them if needed.

- • *Allow Records in Groups:* This allows the addition of account, contact, lead, opportunity, contract, campaign, case, and custom object records to groups. You still need to include the Add Record action in the group publisher layout if you want users to be able to add records to the groups.

- *Allow Rich Link Previews:* When people post a URL, a preview of a photo or video from that URL is shown.

- *Allow Customer Invitations:* This allows Chatter users to invite people outside of your company's email domain into your organization via a private group. They won't have access to anything outside of that group.

- *Enable Actions in the Publisher:* Allows you to add actions to the publisher layout, as well as the order in which they appear. You can add these actions on the home page, Chatter tab, and records themselves.

- *Allow Today Recommendations:* This enables Chatter feed recommendations within the Salesforce1 mobile app. The Chatter feed includes recommendations for users, such as suggesting groups to join.

- *Allow Users to Edit Posts and Comments:* This allows certain users to modify posts and comments. The users are authors of the post or comment, record owners, or Chatter moderators.

- *Allow Users to Compose Rich Text Posts:* Allows users to use rich text in their posts so that they can use formatting or bullets.

TIP

If some of your users want external people to be invited into a private Chatter group, pause for a moment and think about that external user's user experience. Is this a great way to collaborate on a project? Will they mind having to log in to a different system on a regular basis to share information? What if they have their own instance of Salesforce — will they get mixed up logging into two organizations' Chatter conversations every day? Every situation is different, and you can't control 100 percent of it. But make sure that your employees know that adoption by the external person is highly dependent on the context and expectations set.

Locating Chatter on Your Home Page

After your administrator turns on Chatter, you'll notice it at the top of your home page when you log in to Salesforce.

As shown in Figure 6-1, after you set up your profile, Chatter shows a photo of you, today's date, and a feed of status updates from yourself and others whom you're following. All this occurs in the middle section of your home page.

The rest of your home page is still there. Your tasks, dashboard, and calendar have just moved down the screen. You can always click the Hide Feed link right below your top photo to, well, hide the Chatter feed.

FIGURE 6-1:
Viewing your
Chatter feed.

Profiling Yourself

The first thing you should do when starting Chatter is to update your profile. When you click your name anywhere in the Chatter feed or click My Profile below your name in the upper-right menu area, you're taken to your My Profile page. Your profile page is your work profile, displaying your profile picture, more information about yourself (your background, contact information, past roles, hobbies, and so on), a history of your status updates, the co-workers who follow you, and the co-workers and Salesforce records that you follow.

REMEMBER

Your profile is also what others see when they click your name, which means that profiles work like a company directory. Be sure that you don't include any information in your profile that you don't want *everyone* in your company to see.

To update your My Profile page, refer to Chapter 4.

Keeping Everyone Informed with Posts

Part of what makes Chatter work is letting your co-workers — even maybe your boss — know what you're up to. In return, you can find out what they're doing. In this section, we show you how to post as well as how to comment on others' posts.

Posting a status

Posts are what your followers see. You can update posts to let others know what you're working on, to ask questions, or to share files or website links. The inspiration comes from status updates on websites, such as Facebook and Twitter, that play an increasing role in people's personal lives. If you have a Facebook or Twitter account, you'll pick up Chatter in no time.

To make a post, follow these steps:

1. **Click the Chatter tab or the Home tab.**

   Either option takes you to a page with a Chatter feed in it.

   If you're at the home page, your Chatter feed must be showing. If it's not, click the Show Feed link below your photo at the top of the page.

REMEMBER

2. **Make a post in the open field near the top of the page where it says, "Share an update, @mention someone."**

3. **(Optional) Attach a file or a website link, or append a poll to your update by clicking the File, Link, or Poll icon, respectively, directly above the Status box. These may appear under the More drop-down list on the right.**

   You may want to link to an interesting article that you read online or upload a file with a presentation you're working on.

4. **Click the Share button to publish your update.**

   Your post is published.

5. **(Optional) From the small drop-down list to the right of your post, select the Delete option to remove it.**

   If you ever make a typo or post something embarrassing, you can always delete that entry and make it disappear from the feed.

Commenting on posts

When you're following people, you start seeing their posts in your Chatter feed on the home page. Chatter allows you to add comments to posts, thus creating and managing multiple conversations in an organized fashion.

To add a comment to someone's post, follow these steps:

1. **Locate the post in the Chatter feed.**

2. **Click the Comment link below the post.**

3. **Type your comment in the indented field that appears below the post.**

4. **Click the Comment button when you're done writing.**

Your comment appears indented below the original update, as shown in Figure 6-2.

FIGURE 6-2: Commenting on a post.

Choosing What to Follow

Before you can follow anything, your administrator needs to enable Chatter on certain objects. *Objects* are types of records. They're the words (for example, Accounts) that appear at the top of your Salesforce page; you can click these words, and then they look like highlighted tabs. (For a review of how to navigate the default objects in Salesforce, turn to Chapter 3.)

Your administrator and executive stakeholders should decide which objects to first turn on for following: typically, the one or two objects that your Salesforce users collaborate on the most, such as Opportunities.

Configuring your Chatter feeds

After you determine which objects need to be followed, you can enable Chatter for those objects:

1. **Choose Setup ⇨ Customize ⇨ Chatter ⇨ Feed Tracking.**

The Feed Tracking page appears, as shown in Figure 6-3.

2. **Click the name of an object in the Object list on the left side.**

The Fields In page for that object appears.

Feed Tracking

Enable feed tracking for objects so users can follow records of that object type. Select fields to track so users can see feed updates when those fields are changed on records they follow.

Object	Tracked
Account	2 Fields
Asset	
Campaign	
Case	2 Fields
Coaching	0 Fields
Contact	3 Fields
Content Document	0 Fields
Contract	
Dashboard	
Event	
Feedback Request	0 Fields
Goal	0 Fields
Group	7 Fields
Lead	3 Fields
Metric	0 Fields
Opportunity	5 Fields
Order	
Order Product	
Performance Cycle	0 Fields

Fields in accounts

[Save] [Cancel]   ☑ Enable Feed Tracking   Restore Defaults

You can select up to **20** fields.

Account Name	☑	Account Number	☐
Account Owner	☑	Account Site	☐
Account Source	☐	Active	☐
Annual Revenue	☐	Billing Address	☐
Clean Status	☐	Customer Priority	☐
D&B Company	☐	D-U-N-S Number	☐
Data.com Key	☐	Description	☐
Employees	☐	Fax	☐
Industry	☐	NAICS Code	☐
NAICS Description	☐	Number of Locations	☐
Ownership	☐	Parent Account	☐
Phone	☐	Rating	☐
SIC Code	☐	SIC Description	☐
SLA	☐	SLA Expiration Date	☐

Help for this Page

FIGURE 6-3:
Selecting fields on objects to follow.

3. **Select the Enable Feed Tracking check box.**

4. **Select each check box for the fields that you want to track with Chatter.**

   Select fields that others will want to be notified about when a change occurs to that field, for example, Areas of Interest, Next Step, Status, or Stage.

TIP

   You get a maximum of 20 fields on any given object that you can track with Chatter. You may be able to expand this number for an additional cost.

5. **Repeat for other objects. When you're done, click Save.**

Following people

When you first start Chatter, the feed will be empty because you're not following anyone. In this section, we show you how to follow people in your organization.

TIP

Follow the people in your organization who are working on things that interest you or that affect what you're doing so that you can join the conversation. All the people you can follow are listed on the All People subsection of the People heading on the left sidebar of the Chatter app.

To follow people, follow these steps:

1. **Click the Chatter tab from the home page.**

   The Main Chatter feed appears.

2. **From the left sidebar, click the People heading.**

   The People heading expands to show the All People subsection.

3. **Click the All People subheading.**

The All People list appears.

4. **Find people to follow using one of these methods:**

- *Find someone specific.* Type that name (such as that of your CEO) into the Quick Find search bar. The list of people automatically updates while you're typing. Look for key executives, peers, and other movers and shakers within your company.

- *Browse for names.* Scroll down the first page and click Next to see the next page of names.

Be picky about whom you follow first so that you don't get overwhelmed with all the updates you'll be getting in your feed.

Figure 6-4 shows a list of people and whether you're following them.

When you click a person's name, you go to his or her Profile page.

REMEMBER

All People

🔍 Type a Name...	
Name ↑	Following
Kao-Dummies6, Liz Chief Executive Author	✓ Following
Paz, Jon Executive Vice Author	
User, Integration	✓ Following
User, Security	Follow

FIGURE 6-4:
Finding people to
follow.

5. **After you locate someone you want to follow, click the Follow link that appears in his row.**

You're now following that person, and the link toggles to Unfollow in case you want to unfollow him in the future. By default, the followed person receives an email notifying him that you're following him so that he can likewise choose to follow you back — or not. His posts now show up in your Chatter feed as long as you have your feed unhidden.

Your secret is safe

Only internal users of your company's Salesforce instance can see your Chatter posts and comments, depending on where you enter that update. (Read through the earlier section for more information on how to update your status.)

As far as having outsiders or Google see your updates, you're safe because Chatter uses the built-in privacy and security functionality of Salesforce. Internal users can see whatever you post, if they have access to the record you're posting on or about. So if you post from your home page that you're looking for a notary, everyone can see that (what's the point if they can't?). But if you're on the Opportunity record for "Big Secret Government Deal" and make a post there asking about a notary, only people who can see that opportunity will be able to see your post.

Following feeds

One of the key differentiators of Chatter, as compared with other social networking sites — or other services that attempt to bring social networking into the workplace — is that you can also follow nonhuman things in your Salesforce database. Sounds crazy, right? This feature means that you can follow specific opportunities, accounts, contacts, leads, price lists, cases, and any changes that are made to those records. You can even create or follow groups, focused on a single competitor, region, or vertical. Being able to choose what things you want to stay in the loop about makes Chatter highly relevant to what you need to be successful at work.

To follow a record feed, click the Follow link under the record's name on the record's detail page. Below that link you'll see who else is following that record.

Whenever someone changes a tracked field in an opportunity, for example, you know about it. If you're a sales manager, you can choose to follow a strategic opportunity that one of your reps has been toiling over. The moment she updates that Opportunity Stage field to a Closed-Win, it appears in your feed. If you have key executives following that opportunity, too, they can provide comments that amount to a virtual high-five for all to see.

When you follow a specific record (see Figure 6-5), your profile photo appears as a follower of this object on the record's page so that others will know you're interested in this record.

You can also add comments to specific records, just as you can with people you follow (see the earlier section, "Commenting on posts"). They appear in your feed on your home page and on the feed on the record's page.

REMEMBER

Only users with read access to a record will be able to see any posts that you make on that record. To read more about profiles and permissions, visit Chapter 21.

Opportunity
United Oil Installations

Customize Page | Edit Layout | Printable View |

Hide Feed   Click to add topics

Post   File   New Task   More ▾   ✓ Following

Write something...   Share   **Followers**   Show All (1)

🔍 | Show All Updates ▾

Liz Kao-Dummies6 changed Close Date from 10/11/2013 to 12/11/2015.
Comment · Like · November 8, 2015 at 9:56 AM

« Back to List: Opportunities

Products [0] | Open Activities [0] | Activity History [0] | Notes & Attachments [0] | Contact Roles [0] | Partners [0] | Competitors [0] | Stage History [2]

Opportunity Detail   Edit   Delete   Clone

Opportunity Owner	Liz Kao-Dummies6 [Change]	Amount	$270,000.00
Private	☐	Expected Revenue	$243,000.00
Opportunity Name	United Oil Installations	Close Date	12/11/2015
Account Name	United Oil & Gas Corp.	Next Step	
Type	Existing Customer - Upgrade	Stage	Negotiation/Review
Lead Source		Probability (%)	90%
		Primary Campaign Source	
Order Number		Main Competitor(s)	
Current Generator(s)		Delivery/Installation Status	Yet to begin

FIGURE 6-5:
Following a record.

Being Part of a Group

Similar to finding people to follow, you search for groups to join. By following a group's feed, you can collaborate with a specific subset of people within your company on a regular basis.

REMEMBER

Posts made to a private Chatter group can be seen only by members of the group, system administrators, and those with the View All Data permission.

Understanding Salesforce Chatter groups

Chatter groups in Salesforce are subsets of people who collaborate on a project, event, or idea. You can create a Chatter group for all sorts of different projects. For example, that company retreat may warrant a Chatter group to broadcast updates and answer questions. A specific branch or office could have its own Chatter group. Similarly, you can create Chatter groups for a wide variety of use cases — product lines, organization-wide competitions, and so on. Just make sure that these groups are kept professional and don't become a channel to talk about personal lives or your weekend plans.

Joining a group

To find a group to join, follow these steps:

1. **Click the Chatter tab.**

The Chatter feed appears.

2. **Click the Groups heading in the left sidebar.**

The Groups heading expands to show several subsections.

3. **Select the Active Groups subheading.**

A list of active groups appears. You can see which groups you're a member of by looking at the Membership column to the right of the group's name.

4. **Use the search bar to look for specific group names.**

While you type, the list automatically changes to show the results of your search.

TIP

If you don't find a group that you want to join, create a new one yourself. See the next section, "Creating a new group," on how to create a group from scratch.

5. **Click a group's name to view the Group detail page.**

This provides more details about the group.

6. **Click either of these two links:**

- *Join:* Join a public group.

- *Ask Owner:* Ask the owner for permission to join a private group.

Creating a new group

Communication is key when working in teams. With groups, you can set up private feeds where team members can discuss their work outside their normal feed. This feature is extremely useful for sensitive projects to ensure that online conversations remain secure. You can set up public groups as well for less-confidential discussion.

To set up a new group, follow these steps:

1. **Click the Groups heading on the left sidebar of the Chatter tab.**

The heading expands. The Recently Viewed Groups home page appears, listing existing groups.

2. **Click the New Group button.**

The New Group page appears.

3. **Type the name of your group.**

4. **Enter a description to further distinguish it from other groups.**

5. **Select whether you want to have this group automatically archived after 90 days of inactivity.**

6. **Set the Group Access as Public or Private:**

   - *Public:* Anyone can join the group or see its feed.

   - *Private:* Only members, system administrators, and people with the View All Data permission can see and add posts to the feed.

7. **Click Save.**

   Your new group's page appears. You can add members by clicking the Add/Remove link on the right side.

Managing Chatter Notifications

If Chatter Emails was enabled by your system administrator when Salesforce Chatter was activated, you have the option to be notified via email whenever someone (or something) you're following has made a post.

You can set your preferences as follows:

1. **Choose** *Your Name* ⇨ **My Settings** ⇨ **Chatter** ⇨ **Email Notifications.**

2. **Select the Receive Emails check box to ensure that you receive emails about updates.**

3. **Select the appropriate check boxes corresponding to the events for which you want to be notified, and how often.**

4. **Click Save.**

Using Chatter Effectively

Here are a few ideas on how your company can benefit from Chatter if some people are reluctant to get onboard:

>> **Help Sales sell smarter.** Follow key accounts and strategic opportunities. Ask others for references to help you close a specific deal. Create a group to team up to win against a competitor.

- **»** **Market more effectively.** Get feedback on updated presentations and other marketing materials by attaching them to status updates. Share noteworthy press mentions. Follow leads to find out more about which types of prospects are converting.

- **»** **Improve customer service.** Receive and provide help on cases. Discuss potential work-arounds and technical solutions in a private group. Collaborate on creating the most succinct answer to common customer issues.

- **»** **Define a Chatter code of conduct.** If you have different generations of employees at your company, they're going to react very differently to this tool. Establish basic norms to ensure that this doesn't turn into yet another medium to post cat photos.

- **»** **Install Chatter Desktop or Chatter Mobile.** Get proactive alerts on your computer screen whenever someone or a record you're following makes an update so that you're never out of the loop.

- **»** **Skim posts from your mobile device.**

3 Closing More Deals with Sales Cloud

Chapter 7

Tracking Leads

O ften, we hear frustrated salespeople say, "We could hit our numbers if we just had enough leads to fill our pipeline." Leads are the building blocks by which many companies drive their sales.

Loosely defined, a *lead* is a person or a company that may be interested in your services. Some organizations refer to them as *visitors* because they haven't shared any information about themselves yet. Others call them *prospects* because a lead has to be someone who has expressed interest in your service. Whatever your favorite terminology is, you can use leads to efficiently follow up on sales inquiries, aggressively attack new markets, and vastly improve your sales pipeline.

In this chapter, you can discover all the basic tricks you need to convert leads into revenue. You need to get your existing leads into Salesforce, and update them when you follow up with them. Also, we discuss how to convert a lead into an actual opportunity that you can link to an account and a contact. For online marketing or email managers or administrators, we devote an entire section to how you can manage and maintain your lead database. Finally, we review how to expand your leads with Data.com.

Introducing the Lead Record

A *lead record* consists of a number of fields that you use to capture information about a potential lead. A lead record has two primary modes:

>> **Edit:** In Edit mode, you can modify the fields.

>> **Saved:** In Saved mode, you can view the fields and related lists.

The standard record comes predefined with several fields. Most of the terms are immediately clear, but if you want specific definitions, click Help in the upper-right corner of Salesforce. Here are the most important standard fields:

>> **Lead Owner:** The person who owns the lead. If no one owns the lead, Salesforce can automatically place the lead in a queue or assign it to a specific individual (though we don't recommend that, because users take vacations, get sick, or leave the company, and should always have a backup). You can then assign the lead to a group of users (for example, "Corporate Sales — West Region"), who can take leads in the order in which they arrive in the queue.

>> **Lead Status:** One of three required fields on a lead record. Lead Status is a drop-down list of values, and this field is critical if you want to follow a standard lead process. We talk more about lead status in the nearby sidebar, "Building an effective lead process."

>> **Lead Source:** A standard, but not required, field on a lead record. If you use it, you can define and track the sources of your leads by using this field.

REMEMBER

Lead sources are the originators of leads that come knocking at your door. These can be related to broad communication channels (a toll-free number, cold call, or web form, for example), more specific types of marketing venues (trade show, print ad, partner referral, and so on), or a blend of both. It's up to you. Always remember to balance your desire to get really granular data with the tolerance of the users who often have but a few seconds to customize this field (alongside other fields). And if you really want to track granular details of where leads are coming from, seriously consider using campaigns or a third-party marketing automation tool, described further in Chapter 15.

TIP

When you first get a lead, you'll likely want to qualify that lead to make sure that a sales opportunity really exists for you. For example, maybe you want to be certain that the lead has the budget and a real interest and isn't just kicking tires. A marketing-qualified lead is a lead that meets your sales and marketing's teams qualification requirements to hand over the discussion to a salesperson. Teams in the Marketing or Sales department can own this responsibility.

BUILDING AN EFFECTIVE LEAD PROCESS

The key to a successful lead program that contributes to sales is a well-constructed lead process built into your Lead Status drop-down list. Salesforce provides a default list of four statuses: Open, Contacted, Qualified, and Unqualified. These statuses may appear straightforward, but they require definition because those four choices may not mirror your process or your terminology. The good news is that after you define the statuses that relate to your business, your administrator can quickly modify the values. The process starts with the Lead Status field, but it doesn't end there.

Here are some additional suggestions for how you might construct your lean, mean, lead-generating machine:

- Create fields to capture qualification criteria.

- Make it clear at what point in the process a lead should be converted to an opportunity.

- Decide who'll manage the lead program and what that entails. Usually that's the same person who sends out email campaigns. Make sure that he or she has sufficient permissions to administer the lead database.

- Figure out at what point in the process a lead should be deleted or archived.

- Set up queues, if it makes sense, to manage the workload and drive the competitive spirit.

- When you figure out your process, train your users so that everyone knows what's expected of him or her.

You'll have your own definition of what qualifies as a lead, so jot it down, and then seek out someone to customize your lead record. (See Chapter 17 for the how-to details on building fields, rearranging your layouts, and other design tricks.) You'll have greater success with leads if you collect the right information.

REMEMBER

Writing useful Help text and descriptions for each field you create is vital to a healthy customer relationship management (CRM) system. It may seem laborious at first, and you may write terribly unhelpful descriptions. But fast-forward 6 to 18 months when new team members are scratching their heads wondering why certain fields were created and you can't remember why. Do yourself and your teammates a favor: Write down who requested a field and for what purpose.

Setting Up Your Leads

Before you can begin working your leads, you need to add the lead records into Salesforce. In the following sections, we show you three quick approaches for lead creation, and if needed, how to share your leads with the right people. If you want to capture leads from your website, see Chapter 15 for details on generating Web-to-Lead forms.

Adding new leads

The best way to manually create a lead is to use the Create New drop-down list on the sidebar. To create a lead using this method, follow these steps:

1. Select the Create Lead item from the Create New drop-down list.

A New Lead page appears in Edit mode, as shown in Figure 7-1. The only prefilled field is the Lead Status field.

FIGURE 7-1:
Filling out a lead record.

2. Fill in the fields as much as you can.

At a minimum, you must complete the Last Name and Company fields.

TIP

You can add a list of target companies as leads, even if you don't yet know the names of the right people. In certain cases, you may have only the name of a company because you know you want to target it, but you don't yet know whom to call. You can work with incomplete information. In these cases, we recommend that you type **?** or **unknown** in the Last Name field so that you know this information is missing.

3. **When you're done, click the Save button or the Save & New button.**

   Here's the difference between those two buttons:

   - *Save:* When you click Save, the lead record appears in Saved mode, and your changes are displayed in the fields.

   - *Save & New:* Salesforce knows that salespeople commonly add multiple leads before working them. When you click Save & New, the lead is saved, and a New Lead page appears in Edit mode.

WARNING

When entering or editing records, click the Save button or the Save & New button when you're done. Otherwise, you don't save the information that you just typed for that record. If you make this mistake and haven't yet logged out of Salesforce, try clicking the Back button on your browser (as opposed to hitting your head in frustration), which should get you back to the record in Edit mode. Then click Save and breathe a sigh of relief.

Cloning an existing lead

If you're developing relationships within a particular company and you want to enter multiple leads for that company, you can save time by cloning leads. For example, say that you already created a lead record for Sergey Brin at Google. When you talk to his assistant, he courteously refers you to Larry Page. In this case, cloning can save you many extra steps.

To clone a lead record from an existing lead, follow these steps:

1. **Click the Clone button at the top of the lead record.**

   A new lead record appears in Edit mode. All the information is identical to the previous lead record.

2. **Edit the information on the new lead, where appropriate.**

   Pay attention to what's prefilled because you want to avoid inaccurate information on the new lead record.

REMEMBER

3. **Click Save when you're done.**

   The newly created lead reappears in Saved mode. To verify this, click the link to the older lead, which you can find in the Recent Items section on the sidebar.

Importing your leads

If you already have a file of leads, you probably want a faster way to get them into Salesforce than entering them manually. You need special permissions to import leads (as well as other types of records), so if you're able to do this, find your administrator, tell her what you're trying to do, and have her provide you with the "import leads" permission.

TIP

Although you can import up to 50,000 leads at once, test an import with 5 or so leads first, just to make sure that you know what you're doing. After the test data is imported, review your new lead records to make sure that they contain all the information that you want to have brought in. Delete the test records, refine your import file, and then run through the final import.

WARNING

If you're a new salesperson who just came from a competitor and you happened to bring all your leads with you to upload into your new company's CRM system, hold up. Dumping tens of thousands of pieces of unreviewed data into your nice CRM system is terrible practice. You're just moving potentially dirty data from an old home into a new one. Think that's someone else's problem? Just wait until people start going through it and finding quadruplicates, old job titles, and other pollution. Instead, take a more measured approach. Can you name the top 50 companies that you should be targeting? See how many leads are from any of those companies, and start with that as an upload. Broaden your range slowly.

To import lead files, follow these steps:

1. **On the Leads home page, click the Import Leads link at the bottom of the page, below the Tools heading.**

   The Data Import Wizard appears, providing you with a process to import your records, plus helpful hints.

2. **In your existing lead file or system, compare your fields against the lead fields in Salesforce. Map all your fields between your current system and Salesforce.**

   If you can map all the necessary fields, move to the next step. If not, add fields to the lead record by customizing Salesforce. (See Chapter 17 for simple instructions on adding fields.)

TIP

While someone is mapping the fields from your current system to Salesforce, you should also be talking with your company about cleaning up that data. Now's a good time to discuss which of your current system's fields are still needed in the new world. Some fields may have been used several years ago, but no one's been filling them in since you can remember, and no one's bothered to remove or hide them from the current system. Even worse, no one can recall what those fields were for, or maybe you have multiple fields with very similar names! Also, you could have lots of duplicate or partial records. Talk with your company and your Salesforce consultant about best approaches to cleaning up this information.

TECHNICAL STUFF

Mapping is a technical term for matching one field to another field, typically in different databases, to properly move data. For example, in Microsoft Outlook, you type a corporation's name into the Company field. In Salesforce, you typically use the Account Name field. These two different labels have the same meaning. Mapping is the process by which you decide that data from the Company field in Outlook should correspond to the Account Name field in Salesforce.

3. **Export your file.**

   You may have leads in an existing database or spreadsheet, such as Microsoft Excel, Oracle CRM On Demand, or Microsoft Dynamics. Most systems like these have simple tools for exporting data into various formats. Select the records and the fields that you want. Then, export the file and save it in a .csv format. If your leads are already in spreadsheet format (such as Excel), just resave the file in .csv format.

4. **Review your lead data.**

   You've probably heard the old adage "garbage in, garbage out." Regardless of whether your company spent some time with initial housecleaning before this step, it's important to review the data again at this point. Clean up your information before you bring it into Salesforce so that you can save yourself the effort later.

5. **When you're done with the preparation, click Launch Wizard on the Data Import Wizard.**

   The first page of the Data Import Wizard appears, as shown in Figure 7-2. In the first step, the wizard wants to confirm what type of data you'll be importing. In this example, we select Leads. The progress bar moves along to the second step.

FIGURE 7-2:
Uploading the lead file.

6. **Complete the fields in Step 2 of the wizard.**

The wizard next asks what you want to do in your import. You choose whether you're adding new records, updating existing ones, or a combination of both.

Assuming that you already prepared your file, follow these steps:

a. *Select the matching type.*

If you want Salesforce to avoid importing duplicate records, choose whether you want to identify a duplicate lead by matching Salesforce ID, name, or email. If a lead record with the matching criteria already exists in Salesforce, that record is updated with the information in your file.

b. *Select a default lead source, if relevant.*

c. *Apply an assignment rule if you want leads to route directly to assigned reps.*

If you don't use an assignment rule, all the leads that you import are assigned to you unless you otherwise specify a lead owner in the file. (See the section "Creating assignment rules for automatic routing," later in this chapter.)

d. *Select the check box if you want to use assignment rule settings to send email notifications to the record owners.*

e. *Select the check box if you want assign all the leads to campaigns.*

f. *Select the check box if you want to trigger workflow rules and processes to new and updated records.*

See Chapter 17 for tips on improving workflow.

g. *When asked where your data is located, either drag your file from your computer's desktop to the "Drag CSV file here to upload" section, or select one of the file options depending on the file's original source (like CSV, Outlook CSV, Gmail, and so on).*

7. **When you're done with this part of the wizard, click Next.**

The Edit Field Mapping page appears for this object.

8. **Map the fields between your file and Salesforce and then click Next.**

The Edit Field Mapping page displays all the Salesforce lead fields in a column that correspond to the fields in your file. Simply go through the list of fields and select the field from the corresponding file that you're importing that maps to the Salesforce field, as shown in Figure 7-3. Any column headings in your source file that don't have an obvious Salesforce equivalent will be identified with the word *Unmapped* in red letters.

After you click Next, the Review and Start Import page appears if you have no possible errors. Otherwise, this step may bring up warnings about problems with the data or let you know about fields that you haven't mapped. If you discover an error, you can click the Back button and refine your mapping, or even close the wizard so that you can improve your import file. You may have to start over, but at least you avoid importing bad or incomplete data.

A summary of information about the import is displayed, confirming what fields will and won't be imported, and what type of import you'll be doing.

9. **When you're satisfied with the summary, click the Start Import button.**

A pop-up window appears to let you know that the import is in progress. Click OK to close that window and get sent to the Bulk Data Load Job page, which identifies the progress of the import.

FIGURE 7-3:
Mapping the lead fields.

10. **Check the lead records that you imported.**

Salesforce sends you an email after your file has been successfully imported. To check your handiwork, click the Leads tab to go to your Leads home page. In the View drop-down list, select Today's Leads to see a list of the leads that were created today. Click the link for a lead that you just imported and review the information for accuracy.

Importing leads is one of the fastest ways for you to set up your leads in Salesforce so that you can begin working them.

Accepting Leads from a Queue

If you're a rep assigned to a queue, you can access the queue in the View drop-down list on the Leads home page. The queue list page looks just like a regular list page, but you can use it to grab and claim leads. (See the section "Making use of lead queues," later in this chapter, for details on setting up queues.)

To pull leads from a queue and make them your own, go to the Leads home page and follow these steps:

1. **Select the queue name from the View drop-down list.**

   The queue list page appears.

2. **Select check boxes in the Action column to the left of leads that you want to claim.**

   Your manager may have specific guidelines. This is your chance to click into some records and try to pick the hottest leads.

3. **Click the Accept button.**

   The queue list page reappears, minus the lead(s) that you selected.

TIP

Another way to keep your leads organized is to make sure that multiple versions of the same person don't show up in Salesforce. This can wreak havoc as people update activity information on different records for the same person. Salesforce detects whether duplicate records already exist and merges them for you. Read the next section to see how to deduplicate lead records.

Following Up on Leads

After you receive a new lead, you want a quick way to follow up and determine what you caught: a big one, a warm one, or just another person kicking tires. Your company may already have a standard lead qualification process, but the following sections talk about some of the ways that you can use Salesforce to pursue leads.

Tracking leads with related lists

How can you remember all the interactions that took place with a lead? Some of us have a hard enough time remembering what we did yesterday, let alone three weeks ago with 200 leads. Related lists on a lead record can help you capture all that information so that it's at your fingertips the next time you talk to a lead.

If you're looking for typical ways that salespeople use lead-related lists on a lead record, read the following list for an example:

>> **Log a Call:** The next time you respond to a lead and want to record what you said, click the Log a Call button and enter the details.

>> **New Task:** You plan to call the lead back next Friday when you know that the gatekeeper is on vacation. Click New Task and set a tickler for yourself for Friday. (See Chapter 5 for details on how to fill out a new task record.)

>> **Send an Email:** You get through to the lead, and he asks you to send him an introductory email about your company. Click the Send an Email button to send and track the email directly from Salesforce. We talk more about sending email through Salesforce in Chapter 5.

>> **New Event:** The lead agrees to a demo. Click New Event and schedule a meeting so that you don't forget.

TIP

At some point, you may decide that a lead can't become a qualified opportunity at this time. In that case, you can archive the lead by changing its status. Archiving inactive leads allows you to get a sense of how many leads are still being worked.

Converting qualified leads

When you decide that a lead is actually a qualified opportunity, you can start using Salesforce's full opportunity tracking system. To do so, you must convert the lead to an opportunity. This conversion gives you two benefits:

>> **It allows you to track multiple contacts within an account, which you can do more easily than tracking a single individual lead.** In other words,

if you have ten leads from Microsoft, they aren't linked with each other in Salesforce. But, by converting a lead, you create an account called Microsoft and you link all the Microsoft co-workers as contacts for the same account.

>> **Your goal is to ABC (always be closing), so the sooner you can start managing opportunities and not just leads, the healthier your pipeline and wallet.** For a qualified lead, your sales process begins where your lead process ends.

REMEMBER

When deciding whether to add names of companies or businesspeople as leads or as accounts with contacts, remember that the leads module of Salesforce is non-relational from lead to lead. If you're serious about going after a particular company, and the interrelationships of business contacts will be important, we recommend that you add the target as an account, rather than as a lead.

To convert a lead to an opportunity, follow these steps:

1. **Click the Convert button on a lead record that you want to convert.**

   The Convert button is located at the top and bottom of the lead record. A Convert Lead page appears (see Figure 7-4).

Convert Lead
Dave Carroll   Help for this Page

Leads can be converted to accounts, contacts, opportunities, and followup tasks.
You should only convert a lead once you have identified it as qualified.
After this lead has been converted, it can no longer be viewed or edited as a lead, but can be viewed in lead reports.

[Convert] [Cancel]

Convert Lead | = Required Information

Record Owner	Liz Kao-Dummies6
Send Email to the Owner	☐
Account Name	Create New Account: Oracle ▾ View
Opportunity Name	Oracle- ☐ Do not create a new opportunity upon conversion.
Converted Status	Closed - Converted ▾

Task Information

Subject		Status	Not Started ▾
Due Date	[11/8/2015]
Priority	Normal ▾

FIGURE 7-4:
Converting a lead.

2. **Complete the required fields.**

   Required fields are highlighted in red. Here's a summary:

   • *Record Owner:* If the lead owner remains the record owner, don't change the selection. If the owner changes, click the Lookup icon and choose from the list of users. Select the Send Email to the Owner check box, if needed.

- *Account Name:* If Salesforce doesn't find an account that closely matches the Company field from your lead, it creates a new account record. In the event that it does find a match, select an option from the drop-down list, depending on whether you want to create a new account or associate the lead to the existing account.

- *Opportunity Name:* If you want to create an opportunity, complete this field by giving the opportunity a name. (We typically recommend that the name of an opportunity be the account name followed by a hyphen and then a summary of the product interest — for example: Amazon – New Hardware.) You don't have to always create an opportunity record when you convert a lead. Sometimes, the lead that you're converting is associated with an existing opportunity. In these situations, select the Do Not Create a New Opportunity upon Conversion check box to avoid creating a new opportunity.

- *Converted Status:* Salesforce prefills this field with the default value that your company has chosen for a qualified lead. Don't change this field unless your company has multiple selections for a qualified lead.

- *Task Information:* You can create a follow-up task right in these fields, but you don't have to. Complete these fields only if it saves you a step.

3. **When you're done, click the Convert button.**

   If Salesforce finds a contact record that matches your lead, you can decide to associate it with the existing contact record. Otherwise, a contact record appears for your former lead. That contact is linked to an account corresponding to the lead's Company field, and all associated records from related lists are carried over. If you chose to create an opportunity in Step 2, you can see the opportunity on both the account and contact record's Opportunity related lists.

Maintaining Your Lead Database

If you're a system administrator or a lead manager who has the right permissions (we specify those permissions in the following sections), one of your greatest challenges is managing what hopefully will become a large pool of leads.

Lead databases can become unwieldy over time, so you need to keep them clean. For example, say that you work for a company that regularly collects leads from industry conferences. Someone who hadn't read this book ended up importing a lot of leads into Salesforce without any review beforehand. After a year, your leads database may have many duplicates and plenty of garbage. Salesforce provides a number of simple tools to make short work of cleaning up your leads and other tasks.

The biggest problems we see with leads involve creating a regular cadence around assigning, identifying duplicate records, merging them together (also known as *deduping*), transferring, archiving, and deleting. We know: You hate to get rid of anything. However, sometimes it's necessary and relatively painless.

Making use of lead queues

If you have a sales team made up of multiple people (often called sales development reps [SDRs]) responsible for harvesting leads collectively, you may want to set up lead queues. For example, some companies hire SDRs to handle leads on a first-come, first-served basis. You may just find that your reps work harder if they all have an equal chance to go after a fresh pool of leads.

If you're an administrator or user who has permission to customize Salesforce, you can set up lead queues. Follow these steps:

1. **Choose Setup ⇨ Administer ⇨ Manage Users ⇨ Queues.**

   A Queues page appears.

2. **Click New to create a new queue.**

   The New Queue page appears in Edit mode, as shown in Figure 7-5.

FIGURE 7-5: Creating a new lead queue.

3. **Name the queue and specify the Lead object to associate with this queue.**

4. **Add members to the queue.**

   Members can be users, groups, or roles in your company who'll be part of the queue. For example, you may label the queue Western Field Sales and then choose users who make up the Western Sales team.

5. **When you're done, click Save.**

   You can now use this queue when you organize and reassign lead records.

REMEMBER

Lead queues can be viewed in the same place on your Leads home page where you view your lead views. The name of the lead queue is automatically added to the drop-down list for the lead views. Pretty neat, huh?

Finding and merging duplicate lead records

Before following up on a new lead, click the Find Duplicates button on the specific lead record to see whether a record already exists. You probably know that duplicates frequently occur with leads. For example, if you capture leads from your website, the same visitor may fill in your web form multiple times, even with the best of intentions. Instead of wasting your time or upsetting the existing lead, check first for duplicates.

By checking for duplicates, you may increase your chances of a qualified lead. When you merge duplicate records, the remaining record inherits not only the information you select but also linked records on related lists.

REMEMBER

To merge lead records, you must be the lead owner of the records, the lead owner's manager (that is, the lead owner must be subordinate to you in the role hierarchy), or a system administrator.

To find and merge duplicate leads, follow these steps:

1. **Go to a lead record that you suspect or know has duplicates.**

2. **Click the Find Duplicates button at the top of the lead record.**

   A Search for Duplicates page appears, in five sections. The first section determines how you want to search Salesforce for duplicates. By default, Salesforce looks for a duplicate with a matching name, company, email address, or phone number. The remaining four sections show any matching lead, contact, account, or opportunity records, based on the default matching criteria.

3. **Select or deselect search criteria boxes to narrow or expand your search. Click the Search button to return updated results.**

Records matching any of the selected search criteria appear in their appropriate sections.

4. **Review the duplicate lead records and select a maximum of three records to merge.**

In Salesforce, you can merge only three records at a time.

5. **Click the Merge Leads button in the Matching Leads related list.**

A Merge Leads page appears, displaying, side by side, the selected records and their fields.

6. **Compare the information and select the radio buttons to choose the values that you want to retain.**

TIP

At the top of each column, you can also choose to keep all the values from one record by clicking the Select All link.

7. **When you finish reviewing, click the Merge button.**

A pop-up window appears, prompting you to validate that you want to perform the merge. After you click OK, the merged lead reappears. Any records from related lists are kept.

REMEMBER

Minimize the subjective decision making that needs to happen when an end-user is reviewing conflicting criteria within matching leads. Do this by establishing some clear rules to your teams so they don't get frustrated spending time trying to re-research everything. For example, if there is contradictory employee size information in duplicate records, establish that the tiebreaking field is the one whose data most closely matches the employee size as reported in Data.com, or some other master source of truth.

Creating assignment rules for automatic routing

If your company generates a lot of leads, assignment rules can help distribute the workload and get leads to the right users. Assignment rules give you a better chance to keep leads from becoming stagnant. A lead *assignment rule* is a feature that lets the administrator define who should receive a lead and under what conditions. For example, if your reps have sales territories defined by zip codes or countries, you can use those zip codes or countries to dictate who gets what leads.

To create a lead assignment rule, follow these steps:

1. **Choose Setup ⇨ Build ⇨ Customize ⇨ Leads ⇨ Lead Assignment Rules.**

If you haven't yet set the default lead owner, the Lead Settings page appears, asking you to select the default lead owner. The buck stops with this person or queue, as far as lead routing goes. After you make this selection, Salesforce returns you to the Lead Assignment Rules page.

2. **Click New to create a new assignment rule.**

The New Lead Assignment Rule page appears in Edit mode.

3. **Enter a title in the Rule Name field, select the check box if you want to make it the active assignment rule, and click the Save button.**

The Lead Assignment Rule page reappears. You can have only one active rule at a time, but the rule can have multiple entries. Click the rule name to go to the detail page for that rule.

4. **Click New in the Rule Entries related list.**

A Rule Entry Edit page appears.

5. **Complete the steps as follows:**

a. *Enter a number in the Order field to set the order in which the rules will be evaluated.*

b. *Select criteria to define the rule.*

See Chapter 17 for details on selecting criteria. In this case, you might enter **ZIP Code Equals 02474.**

c. *Use the drop-down list and Lookup icon to select the user or queue.*

d. *Use the Lookup icon to choose an Email Notification Template.*

You can set the assignment rules to send email alerts to recipients of new leads.

6. **When done, click the Save button or the Save & New button.**

Here's what happens when you click each button:

- *Save:* When you click Save, the New Lead Assignment Rule page reappears.
- *Save & New:* When you click Save & New, a new Rule Entry Edit page appears, and you can repeat Steps 5 and 6 until you finish.

Transferring leads

You may need to transfer leads for a variety of reasons. For instance, after you set up your lead records in Salesforce, you need to give them to the right people on a different team. Or maybe some reps just weren't following up, so you took their leads away after swatting their noses with a rolled-up newspaper.

To transfer leads, you must be an administrator or a user with Manage Leads and Transfer Leads permissions. If you want to reassign many leads at the same time, take these steps:

1. **From the Leads home page, select a view from which you can see some leads that you want to reassign.**

   The list page appears.

2. **In the Action column of the lead list, select the check boxes to the left of the lead records that you want to assign to someone else.**

3. **Click the Change Owner button at the top of the page.**

   The Change Lead Owner page appears.

4. **Select the user or queue that you intend to reassign leads to, and then click Save.**

   The lead list reappears, and the lead owners have been changed. The new lead owner can be optionally notified via email of this ownership change. Just select the Send Notification Email check box before clicking the Save button.

TIP

If you're an administrator, you can use the Mass Transfer Leads tool in Setup to accomplish the same goals of reassigning en masse. See Chapter 22 for details on mass-transferring leads.

If you're reassigning one lead at a time, you can transfer ownership directly from a lead record. Follow these steps:

1. **On the lead record, to the right of the Lead Owner field, click the Change link.**

   The link is in square brackets. The Change Lead Owner page appears.

2. **Select the user or queue that you're assigning the lead to.**

   You use this same page when you're assigning multiple leads.

3. **(Optional) Select the Send Notification check box to notify the new owner of the reassignment.**

4. **When you're done, click Save.**

   The lead record reappears, displaying your ownership change.

Changing the status of multiple records

An administrator or a user who has Manage Leads permissions can change the status of multiple records at the same time. This feature comes in handy if, during a process, a lead manager reviews leads prior to assigning them to reps.

To change the status of multiple leads at the same time, follow these steps:

1. **From the Leads home page, select a view.**

   The list page appears.

2. **In the Action column of the lead list, select the check boxes to the left of the lead records that require a status change.**

   To select all the leads in this view, select the check box to the left of the Action column header, which selects all the leads on this page.

   For example, if you're eyeballing a list of leads from a trade show, you might select obviously bogus leads.

3. **Click the Change Status button at the top of the page.**

   The Change Status page appears.

4. **Select a status from the New Status drop-down list and click Save.**

   The lead list reappears.

If you require industrial-strength deduplication tools, a number of proven technology partners handle deduplication within Salesforce, plus a variety of other data management tasks. You can check out these offerings on the AppExchange directory by searching for "data cleansing" in the search bar.

Mass-deleting lead records

Periodically, be sure to delete records that are unqualified or of no value to your company. You must be an administrator to mass-delete records.

Some companies add a To Be Deleted value to their Lead Status field to denote garbage. Then, periodically, the administrator deletes those records.

If you want to delete multiple records at a time, follow these steps:

1. **On the Leads home page, click the Mass Delete Leads link below the Tools heading.**

   A Mass Delete Leads page appears, including a three-step deletion wizard.

2. **Review the steps and then type the search criteria for the leads that you want to delete.**

   For example, if you want to delete unqualified leads, enter a filter in which Lead Status Equals Unqualified.

3. **Click the Search button.**

   The page reappears, displaying your results at the bottom of the page.

4. **Select all records or just the records that you want to delete by selecting the appropriate check boxes.**

   To select all the search results for deletion, click the Select All link at the top of the list.

5. **Click the Delete button after you complete selecting the records for deletion.**

   The search results are updated to omit the record(s) you deleted.

TIP

When deleting records, always be cautious, but don't overly stress out. When you delete records, that information is placed in your Recycle Bin, and you can access records for 15 days. To undelete a record, click the Recycle Bin link on your sidebar, find the record, and undelete it. Then, count your blessings and breathe into a paper bag until the panic attack subsides.

Building Your Lead Database with Data.com

Data.com (www.data.com) is an online source of millions of business professionals and Dun & Bradstreet (D&B) information about companies. It's used to compare, update, and clean lead information in your Salesforce org, against information that exists with D&B. Data.com's partnership with D&B provides industrial-strength, third-party validation of lead information, because many people who sign up for things online can often use as little real information as possible when they're in the early stages of researching a product. Data.com has several product lines that meet different needs and varying budgets.

Here's a high-level overview on how it works:

1. **From within Salesforce, Data.com flags any of your lead data when a discrepancy exists between the information you have and what's in Data.com.**

You get to choose which lead fields Data.com reviews to determine this and which flagged records you want to be updated. Don't worry: You can also lock certain records so they're not reviewed.

2. **You can mine Data.com for new leads based on certain criteria (like Industry = Manufacturing, State = California, Company Revenue = $500 million–$1 billion) that you choose, to build your own custom prospecting list.**

    Data.com searches its database for matches and adds them to your Salesforce database on a regular basis.

3. **Companies using Data.com, especially its data sourced from D&B, use this information as an objective source of truth when it comes to deciding on what data in a field is more trustworthy.**

    So, if one sales rep swears that a company has enough employees to categorize that account as his, but Data.com's employee size is different, you can go with what's in Data.com and assign that account to its rightful owner.

Data.com has a few different products to help with each aspect of deduping or list building. To get more information, visit its website at www.data.com.

IN THIS CHAPTER

Understanding the account record

Using the account related lists

Keeping your accounts up to date

Chapter 8

Using Accounts

W ho are your customers? What do you know about them? What are their top compelling business problems? If you have trouble answering any of these questions, pay close attention to this chapter. Here, we discuss how to use Salesforce to manage your accounts.

In Salesforce, an *account* is a company that you do business with or have done business with in the past. Accounts can include all types of companies — customers, prospects, partners, and even competitors. Among the top reasons why companies implement any customer relationship management (CRM) tool is that they need a centralized place where they can store account data, to prevent themselves from searching all over the place for critical customer information. With Salesforce, you can keep all your important account information in one place so that you and your team can apply that knowledge to sell more and keep customers happy. For example, if you work for a pharmaceutical company, you can use the accounts area to manage your territory of hospitals, clinics, and top offices and capture everything from call reports to business plans.

In this chapter, we describe all the ways you can use accounts to manage and track companies. First, you need to get your important company lists into Salesforce and organize them according to the way that you work. Then, you can find out how to make the best use of the account record to profile your companies. Finally, you can discover how to capitalize on the account-related lists to gain a 360-degree view of your customers and ensure that no one drops any balls.

Getting Familiar with the Account Record

You use an *account record* to collect all the critical information about the companies with which you interact. That account record is supported by other records (contacts, opportunities, cases, activities, and so on) that collectively give you a complete view of your customer. From this vantage point, you can quickly take in the view from the top, but you can also easily drill down into the details.

Here's a short list of valuable things you can do with accounts:

>> Import and consolidate your lists of target accounts in one place.

>> Enter new accounts quickly and maintain naming consistency.

>> Create parent/child relationships that describe how companies' divisions or subsidiaries relate to each other.

>> Realign sales territories.

>> Segment your markets with ease.

>> Eliminate paper-based business planning.

>> Assign account teams to better serve your customers.

>> Track your top customers and deemphasize nonstrategic ones.

>> Define the movers and shakers within an account.

>> Monitor information from your account's social network.

>> Manage your channel partners.

Understanding standard account fields

An account record comprises fields that make up the information on a company that you're tracking. A record has two modes:

>> **Edit:** You can modify fields.

>> **Saved:** You can view the fields and the account's related lists, which are located below the record fields.

An account record also comes preconfigured with a set of fields commonly used for account management. Most of the standard fields are self-explanatory, but in the following list, we highlight certain terms that warrant greater definition:

>> **Account Owner:** This required field identifies the person in your organization who owns the account. An account record has only one owner, but many users can still collaborate on an account.

>> **Account Name:** This required field represents the name of the company you want to track.

>> **Account Site:** The Account Site field goes hand in hand with the Account Name field when you're distinguishing different physical locations or divisions of a company. This field, although not required, is very important if your company sells to different locations of a customer with decentralized buying patterns. For example, if you sell mattresses to HappyDaze Hotels but each HappyDaze hotel buys independently, this field is useful for classifying different sites.

>> **Type:** This is one of the fields on an account record that classifies the relationship of an account to your company. The Type field consists of a drop-down list of values, which can prove critical if you want to differentiate types of companies. For example, if you work for a software company that uses value-added resellers (VARs) to sell and service your products, you may want to select Reseller as one of your drop-down list values.

>> **Rating:** Use this drop-down list to define your internal rating system for companies that you're tracking. Salesforce provides default values of Hot, Warm, and Cold, but you can replace these with numbers, letters, or other terms based on how you want to segment companies.

TIP

See Chapter 17 for instructions on customizing account fields, such as the Type and Rating picklists.

Building parent/child relationships

If you sell into different locations or divisions of a company and you're currently challenged by how to keep this information organized, use account hierarchies to solve your problem. In Salesforce, you can link multiple offices of a company together by using the Parent Account field on an account record. And you can create multiple tiers to the hierarchy if your customer is organized that way.

To establish parent/child relationships, follow these steps:

1. **Create accounts for the parent and subsidiary companies.**

If you need help with this step, turn to Chapter 5 for information on how to create new records.

TIP

You can skip this step if the accounts are already created. However, you may want to type a term such as **Headquarters** or **HQ** in the Account Site field to signify which account is the parent.

2. **Click the link in your Recent Items list in the left sidebar for the subsidiary account (a *child account*) that you want to link and then click Edit.**

   If it's not in the Recent Items list, search and find the child account you want to link and click Edit.

   The record appears in Edit mode.

3. **To the right of the Parent Account field, click the Lookup icon.**

   A pop-up window appears, containing a Search field and a list of recently viewed accounts.

TIP

If you see the parent account in the most-recently viewed results list, skip to Step 5.

4. **Search for the parent account by typing the name of the account in the Search field and then clicking Go.**

5. **From the list of results, click the name of the company to select the parent account (as shown in Figure 8-1).**

FIGURE 8-1:
Select a sample parent account.

🔍 **Lookup**

| United Oil & Gas | Go! | New |

You can use "*" as a wildcard next to other characters to improve your search results.

< Clear Search Results
Search Results

Account Name	Account Site	Account Owner Alias	Type
United Oil & Gas Corp.	HQ	LKao	Customer - Direct
United Oil & Gas, Singapore	Singapore	LKao	Customer - Direct
United Oil & Gas, UK		LKao	Customer - Direct

The pop-up window closes, and your selection appears in the Parent Account field.

6. **(Optional) To further denote the child account, use the Account Site field.**

   Some companies use city, state, country, division, and so on, depending on how they organize their accounts. For example, if Big Box Office Supplies, Inc., has locations in Dallas and Atlanta, you could type the city into the Account Site field for each child account so that you can tell which is which.

7. **Click Save.**

   The child Account detail page appears.

8. **To view the account hierarchy, click the View Hierarchy link to the right of the Account Name field on the child account record.**

   An Account Hierarchy list page appears, and like other lists, you can click an item to go to a specific account.

Performing Actions with Account Related Lists

Fields on an account record are useful for storing important data specific to a company. But where do you go to capture all the critical interactions and relationships when you're working an account? To keep track of these details, use the related lists located on the Account detail page.

Many of the actions on account related lists are common to other modules. For example, major modules, such as Accounts, Contacts, Opportunities, and Cases, all have related lists for Open Activities, Activity History, and Notes & Attachments. Instead of being redundant, we point you to Chapter 5 for details on using related lists to track tasks and calendar events. In the following sections, we describe certain related lists that are unique to the account record.

Defining contact roles

Many sales reps do a great job of collecting business cards for contacts within an account, but this action alone doesn't get them closer to a sale. Contacts and their titles often don't tell the whole story about decision makers and the chain of command within an account. To use contact roles in Salesforce, your administrator must proactively reveal this related list on the account record — you can find details on how to do this in Chapter 17.

To better define the buying influences on an account, go to an account record and follow these steps:

1. **Review your records in the Contact related list.**

   If important contacts are missing, add them first, which we describe in Chapter 9.

2. **Click the New button on the Contact Roles related list.**

   The Account Contact Role Edit page appears.

3. **Type the name of a contact in the Contact field and then click the Lookup icon.**

   A pop-up window with your search results appears.

4. **Find the correct contact:**

   - *The contact is part of the search results.* Click the link for that contact's name.

   - *Your search doesn't find the contact.* Refine your search, or click the New button to create the contact record and then select the contact you find or create.

     TIP

     This is only true if "Quick Create" is enabled for your organization.

     After you select the contact, the pop-up window disappears, and the Contact field is filled in.

5. **Select the Correct Role from the Role drop-down list.**

   The default roles are strategic, rather than mere job titles. If the right role for your contact doesn't appear, advise your system administrator to edit the roles. Many companies match these roles with their particular sales methodology identifiers.

6. **Select the Primary Contact check box if the contact is your primary contact; then click the Save button or the Save & New button:**

   - *Save:* The Account detail page reappears, and your contact appears on the Contact Roles related list for that account's record.

   - *Save & New:* A new Account Contact Role Edit page appears, and you can associate another contact to a role immediately.

Displaying an account's opportunities

Over the course of managing an account, you'll hopefully uncover specific opportunities to sell that company your products or services. You can use the Opportunity related list to quickly perform the following tasks:

>> Stay aware of all open opportunities that you and your team are pursuing on an account.

>> Add new opportunities and link them automatically to the account.

>> Edit and delete opportunity records with a single click.

>> Gauge the progress of an account by quickly seeing all open and closed opportunities at their various sales stages and amounts.

See Chapter 10 for the scoop on managing opportunities.

Viewing cases

Account health is much more than measuring the growth of sales for a customer. After selling, sales reps want to stay informed of customer service issues so that they can continue to keep their customers satisfied, resolve issues early, receive warnings about potential landmines, and track potential upsell opportunities. Use the Cases related list to view all the open and closed customer service cases that relate to an account.

TIP

If your company relies on a channel sales team to manage partners, distribute leads, and bring in revenue, consider using Salesforce Communities, which is available in Enterprise and Performance editions for an extra charge. This partner relationship management (PRM) application gets your partners on board with using Salesforce to manage all the details of their activities with your company and your joint deals. Go to Chapter 12 for a more in-depth discussion.

Tracking your account teams

If you're fortunate enough to work with large companies, you probably know that it takes a team of people to win complex deals and maintain large accounts. The Account Owner field may identify the primary person in charge, but often you need to know who to go to for a specific purpose, or maybe the account owner is just out sick. Account teams lets you list all the individuals at your company who work with an account and detail their specific roles.

1. **Choose Setup ➪ Customize ➪ Accounts ➪ Account Teams.**

The Account Team Setup page appears.

2. **Click Enable Account Teams, select the Account Teams Enabled check box (as shown in Figure 8-2), and then click Save.**

The Page Layout Selection page appears, allowing you to select all the Account page layouts to which you want to add the Account Teams related list. If you have account types (and layouts) that never require team collaboration, don't add the related list to these.

3. **Select the account page layouts to which you want to add the Account Teams related list and click Save.**

The Account Team Setup page appears, where you can choose to define team roles for your organization. This step is optional.

Account Team Setup

Enable or disable the ability to define account teams and use teams for accounts.

☑ Account Teams Enabled

[Save] [Cancel]

FIGURE 8-2:
Enabling Account
Teams.

Now that Account Teams are enabled for your organization, to give credit to your team and make sure that others know whom to call, go to an account record and follow these steps:

1. **Scroll down to the Account Team related list or click the Account Team hover link at the top of the page.**

   If you don't see the Account Team related list, have your administrator activate the feature in Setup.

2. **Click the Add button to add up to five team members.**

   The New Account Team Members page appears, as shown in Figure 8-3.

FIGURE 8-3:
Add account
team members.

3. **Use the Team Member lookups to select fellow users of Salesforce who work on this account.**

   You can always go back and add more later.

4. **(Optional) Specify the sharing access you want to give for this account, its opportunities, and its cases.**

5. **Select the appropriate role in the Team Role drop-down list.**

6. **Click Save.**

   You're returned to the account record's detail page with your account team listed.

Maintaining Your Account Database

The more you use Salesforce for account management, the more important it is to maintain it over time.

In the following sections, we show you simple tools for keeping your account database up to date.

Increasing account accuracy with Data.com

Everyone has his or her own way of entering a company name, but when each sales rep uses his own method, it leads to duplicate account records. Instead of arguing over whose method is best, you can use Data.com to provide you with the correct name.

Data.com provides top-quality data from Dun & Bradstreet and is available in Salesforce for an added charge. You can use it to automatically clean your account records, providing you with up-to-date information for 83 account fields. Sales reps can also use Data.com to instantly import new accounts and contacts into Salesforce. Whether you're augmenting your existing data or starting from scratch, Data.com can provide the data you need without ever having to leave Salesforce.

Deleting account records

If you (or a subordinate) own accounts that need to be deleted, you can delete them one at a time by using the Delete button on the account records. The one caveat here is that some companies remove your permission to delete accounts altogether. If this is the case or if you want to delete many accounts at one time, consult with your system administrator. System administrators are the only users in your company who have the ability to mass-delete records. (Kind of startling to realize that geeks have all the power, isn't it?)

WARNING

When deleting account records, remember that you're also deleting associated records. So, if you're deleting an account, you can potentially be removing contacts, activities, opportunities, and other records linked to the account. You can rectify a mistakenly deleted record within 15 days of your deletion by retrieving it from your Recycle Bin, but be careful before deleting records.

Chapter 9

Developing Contacts

I f you've been selling for more than a few years, you probably have a big golden list overflowing with business contacts. And if you're just starting out, you probably wish you had one. But how much do you know about those contacts? Where do you keep track of the personal and business information that you've collected throughout the years?

Salesforce enables you to plan, manage, and capture all the important interactions that you normally have with your prospects and customers. Just imagine the value that keeping this shared information in one place can have for you and your teams.

By using the Contacts section in Salesforce, you can effectively keep all your most important contacts together in one place, easily link them with the accounts they work for, gain insight into the relationships between contacts, and capture the critical personal drivers of each contact that are so key to your selling success.

In this chapter, we discuss how to use Salesforce for your contact management needs. You can also find out how to build your contact database by adding information directly or by importing your existing files. Later in the chapter, we describe how to organize your contacts lists so that you can quickly find the people you want to talk to. We also show you how to maintain the integrity of your contact data by editing contact records, merging duplicate records, and deleting old records. These tasks allow you to start putting your contacts to work for you.

Understanding the Contact Record

A *contact record* is the collection of fields that consists of the information about a person you do business with. Unlike a business card or a lead record in Salesforce, however, a contact is linked to an account. Like other records, the contact record has two modes: an *Edit* mode, in which you can modify fields, and a *Saved* mode, in which you can view the fields and the contact's related lists (which are located below the fields).

A contact record comes preconfigured with a standard set of fields commonly used for contact management. The exact number isn't important because your company might add or subtract fields based on the way you want to track your contacts. Most of the standard fields are self-explanatory, but in the following list, we highlight a few fields that are less obvious:

>> **Contact Owner:** This is the person in your organization who owns the contact. A contact has only one owner, although many users can still collaborate on a contact.

>> **Reports To:** This lookup field on the contact record allows you to organize your contacts hierarchically.

>> **Lead Source:** This drop-down list defines where you originated the contact.

>> **Email Opt Out:** This check box reminds you whether a contact should be emailed.

>> **Do Not Call:** This check box reminds you whether a contact can be called.

REMEMBER

Privacy is a big issue with companies and the selling tactics they employ. Nothing damages a customer relationship more than a contact who's contacted when he or she has asked not to be. To protect your contacts' privacy, be diligent about the Email Opt Out and Do Not Call fields. Users in your company should always check the contact record before calling or marketing to a contact.

Customizing Contact Information

After you complete the standard fields, you never have trouble knowing where to reach your contacts. Whether they take your call is another question, though.

Think about all the personal or professional information that you commonly collect on your best contacts. For example, if Michael Jordan is your client, you may like to know that he loves golf and fine cigars and has five kids. And he's always driven to be number one.

PRECISION TARGET MARKETING

A leading telecommunications provider wanted to improve the coordination between sales efforts and marketing programs. Over the course of a year, the provider's marketing department planned numerous campaigns that included direct marketing, trade shows, customer case studies, client outings, and so on. In the past, marketing managers wasted substantial time trying to extract contact information from the sales teams. By customizing the contact record to collect important personal and business information, and then training sales reps to update custom fields on contacts in Salesforce, the company has realized substantial savings in time and better productivity in targeted marketing programs.

TIP

Ask yourself these questions while you customize your contact record:

>> What professional information is important in your business (for example, prior employers or associations)?

>> What personal information can help you build a better relationship?

>> How do you evaluate the strength of your relationship with the contact?

>> What probing questions do you commonly ask all contacts? (For example, what are their current initiatives and business challenges?)

We always advise keeping it simple, but if any specific fields are missing, write them down and seek out your system administrator. (See Chapter 17 for the details on how to build fields and other design tricks.) Salesforce can help you remember important details about your contacts, and you can use that information to build better relationships.

Entering and Updating Your Contacts

Your contact database is only as good as the information it contains, so Salesforce has multiple ways for you to get your contacts into the system. You can either start from scratch and manually create new contact records, or if you already have contacts on a spreadsheet or in another tool, you can use Salesforce's simple wizard to import your contacts within minutes. In the following sections, we discuss quick and simple ways to get started and how to update records.

Entering new contacts

Because contacts belong to accounts, the best, most reliable way to create contact records is by starting from the relevant Account detail page. From the Account detail page, you can then add a contact by using either the Create New drop-down list on the sidebar or the New button on the Contacts related list. The result is the same in both situations, and Salesforce automatically prefills the Account lookup field. By doing this, you can always find your contact, and your contact's activities also appear in a list on its Account detail page.

To create contacts by using this best practice, follow these steps:

1. **Search for the account, and then click the appropriate Account Name link on the Search Results page.**

   The Account detail page appears.

2. **Click the New button on the Contacts related list.**

   The Edit mode of a new contact appears, as shown in Figure 9-1.

FIGURE 9-1: Completing fields on a contact record.

3. **Fill in the fields as much as you can or as required.**

   The Account field is prefilled with the account you were working from.

4. **When you're done, click one of the following buttons:**

   - *Save:* After you click the Save button, the Contact detail page appears. On this page, you can click the Edit button whenever you need to modify information on the record.

- *Save & New:* Clicking this button saves the current contact record and automatically opens a new, blank contact record in Edit mode.

A link to the first contact appears in your Recent Items list in the left sidebar.

Importing your contacts and accounts

If you already have contact lists from another database (such as Excel), you can use the Data Import Wizard to create multiple contact records in Salesforce and be done in no time. The Data Import Wizard is located in the Tools sections of either the Accounts or Contacts home page.

TIP

When you import accounts, you can import just companies and their associated information, or you can import companies and their related contacts in one action. Which route you take really depends on your existing data and what you want in Salesforce.

To import your contacts and accounts automatically, follow these steps:

1. **Click the Contacts tab to go to the Contacts home page, and then click Import My Business Accounts & Business Contacts under the Tools section.**

The Import Business Accounts & Business Contacts Wizard appears, which includes four steps for importing records, plus helpful hints.

TECHNICAL STUFF

If you're a system administrator for Salesforce, you can click the Import My Organization's Accounts & Contacts link, which allows you to import substantially more records at one time with different owners. If you're an administrator, that link also appears under the Tools sections of the Accounts or Contacts home pages. What's the big deal? Most users can import 500 records at a time, but if you're a system administrator, you can import 50,000 at a time and leap over tall buildings in a single bound.

2. **In your existing contact tool or file, compare your current fields with the fields in Salesforce. Add fields to the account or contact records by customizing Salesforce.**

If you can map all the information you currently have to fields in Salesforce, move on to Step 3. If you have to add fields to Salesforce to match fields, see Chapter 17.

3. **Export your file.**

You may have contacts and accounts in an existing database, such as Zoho CRM, Microsoft Dynamics, Microsoft Access, or Microsoft Outlook. Most systems like these have simple tools for exporting data into various formats. Select the records and the fields that you want to export. Then export the file and save it in a comma-separated values (CSV) format. If your accounts are already in spreadsheet format, such as Microsoft Excel, just resave the file in the CSV format.

4. **Review and prepare your data in Excel.**

Refine your accounts and contacts before bringing them into Salesforce or clean them up after the import — it's up to you. Some sales reps prefer to make changes on a spreadsheet first because they're more accustomed to spreadsheets.

When preparing your import file, keep these points in mind:

- Enter your column headers in the first row. We recommend renaming column headers to be consistent with the field names in Salesforce. For example, you could rename the Company field from Outlook as Account Name.

- To import data for your entire company (available as an option only to system administrators), add a column for Record Owner to signify who should own the record in Salesforce. Otherwise, as the person importing, you own all the records from the file.

- To differentiate locations of a company (for example, Sony in Tokyo versus Sony in New York), add a column for Account Site and update the rows in your file to reflect the different sites.

- Link accounts in the import file by adding columns for Parent Account and Parent Site and by filling in fields as necessary to reflect the hierarchy.

- Make sure that a Type column exists and that fields are filled to correspond to the types of companies you track (customers, partners, prospects, competitors, and so on).

- For files with more than 500 rows, divide the master file into smaller files to fit the Import Wizard's size limitation. You have to repeat the Import Wizard for each of the smaller files.

- To import contacts and accounts at the same time, add a column for the billing address fields if those addresses are different from the contacts' mailing addresses.

For more hints on importing, click the Help and Training link and check out the Training and Support information in Salesforce by searching for the keyword *Importing*.

TIP

When you're figuring out how to import data into Salesforce, we recommend testing an import with five or so records first, just to make sure that you know what you're doing. After importing the test data, review your new records to make sure that they contain all the information you want to have brought in. Delete the test records, refine your import file, if necessary, and then run through the final import.

5. **After preparing the file, and clicking the Import My Organization's Accounts & Contacts link, click Launch Wizard.**

The Data Import appears in a new window.

6. **Choose Accounts and Contacts under the Standard objects tab in the left window and choose what you want to do with them.**

You can add new records, update existing Salesforce records, or update and add new ones at the same time.

7. **Click Add New Records and choose the unique identifier for the records.**

If you want Salesforce to avoid importing duplicate records, choose whether you want a duplicate contact to be identified by matching name or email. If a contact record with the matching criteria already exists in Salesforce, Salesforce updates that record with the information in your file.

8. **Drag and drop your CSV file into the right window, as shown in Figure 9-2, and click Next when you're done.**

The Edit Field Mapping page appears, where you can edit your data mapping.

FIGURE 9-2:
Using the Launch Wizard to prepare for your contact import.

9. **Map the contact fields between your file and Salesforce, and when you're done, click Next.**

If you're importing only accounts, skip this step. Otherwise, just go through the field mapping, click the Change link to modify the auto-mapped fields, and click the Map link to map your unmapped fields to Salesforce, as shown in Figure 9-3.

FIGURE 9-3:
Mapping contact fields.

TECHNICAL STUFF

Mapping fields is simply the process by which you associate a field from one database with a field in another database so that your data appears in the right fields. For example, if you're importing your contacts from Outlook, you want data from the field called Company in Outlook to map to the field called Account Name in Salesforce. Take your time when making the mappings. Pay attention to which screens are for account-specific fields and which screens are for contact-specific fields.

10. **Review your selections and import to make sure you didn't forget anything, and when you're ready click Start Import.**

This step basically warns you about problems with the data or lets you know about fields that haven't been mapped. If you discover an error, you can click the Previous button and refine your mapping, or even close the wizard so that you can improve your import file. You might have to start over, but at least you avoid importing bad or incomplete data.

When you click Start Import, an Importing page appears to confirm that your import is in progress.

11. **Click OK and later check the records that you imported.**

Salesforce sends you an email after it successfully imports your file. To check your import, click the Contacts tab to go to your Contacts home page. Use the Recent Contacts section drop-down list to select the Recently Created option, and a list of the contacts that were recently created appears. Click the link for a contact that you just imported to double-check that the information is accurate.

If you're importing both accounts and contacts, scroll down on an applicable account to verify that all the right contacts are linked from your import file. Click into a specific account and contact record and check to see that the information matches your import file.

Researching contacts on social networks

Visiting a company's website may tell you about its location and phone number, but it won't help you figure out which sports team to mention when calling a customer. For detailed insight on a person's likes and dislikes, you have to turn to social networks. We all do it. Before dialing that prospect's phone number, we look up the person online to see a picture and find out more about him or her. Sure, it's a little creepy, but it definitely helps you avoid saying the wrong thing.

With Social Contacts, Salesforce lets you link to your existing social network accounts and then search and select the right profiles for your contacts from right inside Salesforce. The best part is, from then on, every time you visit that contact, his picture will appear in the upper-left corner of the page with links to his social network profiles.

Updating contact fields

While you work with your contacts, you may need to modify contact information. To update a contact, follow these steps:

1. **Type the name of your contact in the Global Search field at the top of any Salesforce page and click Search.**

   A Search Results page appears.

2. **Click the desired Contact Name link.**

   The Contact detail page appears.

3. **As with any record, double-click any field that has a pencil icon to its right to edit that field.**

   If a field doesn't have an icon at the right of the field, click the Edit button at the top of the record to make changes. A padlock icon means that you can't edit that field.

4. **Update the fields as necessary and then click Save.**

   The Contact detail page reappears.

Cloning an existing contact

If you want to add a contact that's similar to an existing record, cloning can save you keystrokes and time. To clone a contact, go to the existing contact and follow these steps:

1. **Click the Clone button at the top or bottom of the contact record.**

A new contact record in Edit mode appears. All the information is identical to the previous record.

2. **Edit the information on the new contact record, where appropriate.**

Pay attention to what's prefilled because you want to avoid inaccurate information on the new contact record.

3. **When you're done, click Save.**

You created a new contact without altering your existing contact.

Organizing Your Contacts

When you have all or a portion of your contacts entered in Salesforce, you can begin to organize them to suit the way you sell.

In the following sections, we show you how you can use list views and other tools from the Contacts home page to provide greater focus for you and your sales teams. We also show you an important feature of the contact record that lets you build powerful organizational charts (also called *org charts*) for contacts of an account. (See Chapter 17 to find out how to use standard and custom contact reports.)

Using contact list views

A *contact list view* is a list of contacts that match certain criteria. When you select a list view, you're specifying criteria to limit the results that you get back. The advantage of using a list view versus searching is that you can use the list view over and over again. For example, if you like to send a card on a contact's birthday, you can benefit from a preset list view for this month's birthdays.

The Contacts home page comes with several predefined list views, including

>> **All Contacts:** Provides a list of all the contact records entered into Salesforce. Depending on the way your company has set up your security model, you may not see this view or its results.

» **Birthdays This Month:** Generates a list of contacts whose birthdays land in the current month (assuming that you collect that information).

» **New This Week:** Generates a list of contacts that have been created since the beginning of the week.

» **Recently Viewed Contacts:** Allows you to look at a list of contacts that you've recently viewed.

You use a predefined contact list view in exactly the same way that you use any list view (detailed in Chapter 17) or the predefined list view for any other record.

Creating custom contact views

If you want special lists for the way that you track your contacts, we recommend building custom list views, just as you do for any other record. (For an example of how to create a custom view, see Chapter 17.) For example, if you sell medical equipment, and once per month you like to call your contacts who are dentists, you can create a list view to simplify your work.

Developing Organizational Charts

Having 20 contacts associated with an account is great, but you may not be any further along in understanding the pecking order. In practice, sales reps have been building org charts to strategize on accounts ever since someone thought up org charts, but often, the charts resided on whiteboards and PowerPoint presentations. (And whiteboards are tough to lug around.) By using the org chart feature in Salesforce, you can quickly define the reporting structure for your contacts and use that structure to more easily identify your relationships with your customers.

To build an org chart in Salesforce, follow these steps:

1. **Add all the contacts for an account.**

See the section "Entering and Updating Your Contacts," earlier in this chapter, for details about adding records.

2. **Go to the contact record for a person who's low on the totem pole and then click the Edit button.**

The record appears in Edit mode.

3. Type the name of the contact's boss in the Reports To field and then click the Lookup icon to the right of the field (it looks like a little magnifying glass).

A pop-up window that contains search results appears.

4. Select the correct contact or refine your search until you can select the right contact.

The pop-up window disappears, and the Reports To field is prefilled with the selected contact, as shown in Figure 9-4.

Contact Information	
Contact Owner	Jon Paz
First Name	Mr. — Jerry
Last Name	Forbes
Account Name	Edge Communications
Title	VP, Technology
Department	Technology
Birthdate	12/2/1965
Reports To	Sean Thomas
Lead Source	--None--

FIGURE 9-4: Selecting the boss.

5. Click Save.

The Contact detail page appears.

6. Click the View Org Chart link that appears to the right of the Reports To field on the contact record to display the hierarchy.

An Org Chart list page appears, and like other lists, you can click a link to go to a specific contact.

TIP

Some sales reps run into certain challenges based on the way they create the org charts in Salesforce. One such challenge is gaps; you just may not know or even care about the entire reporting structure. By getting creative and building place-holder contacts, you can avoid pitfalls. For example, if you sell to both the business side and the technology side of a customer, create a contact record called "IT Organization" and another called "Business Organization" and then align your contacts accordingly. This technique also works well for *orphans*, where you know one contact in a department and don't want to leave the contact out of the org chart for the entire account.

IN THIS CHAPTER

Demystifying opportunities

Creating new opportunities

Changing opportunity records

Organizing opportunity lists and contact roles

Using Chatter to follow opportunities

Chapter 10

Tracking Opportunities

Your sales pipeline is the lifeblood of your business. It's the list of deals that can help you achieve your sales targets. But try as you might, you can probably never close every deal in your pipeline. Things happen: Budgets get slashed, projects get tabled, you lose to a competitor, decision makers change. So, you need enough deals to give yourself the chance to hit and exceed your revenue goals in a given time frame.

An *opportunity* in Salesforce is a sales deal that you want to track to an ultimate conclusion (ideally, a win). The opportunity record has tools to help you efficiently track and close a sale. By using Salesforce, you can manage more opportunities at the same time and pursue each opportunity with greater precision. For example, if you're a Salesforce sales rep, you can use opportunities to follow a standard process, link distribution partners, associate products, strategize against competition, record your actions and other notes, and more. And you don't have to waste precious time updating a pipeline spreadsheet. Instead, you or your manager can generate the current pipeline with the click of a button.

In this chapter, we show you the techniques and best practices for using opportunities to track sales. First, you find out the most reliable way to create opportunities. Then we discuss how to view them in the manner that makes sense to you. You can also discover how to update your records so that your information is current and how to use Chatter to follow opportunities.

Getting Familiar with the Opportunity Record

An *opportunity record* is the collection of fields that make up the information on a deal you're tracking. The record has only two modes: In Edit mode, you modify fields; in View mode, you view the fields and the opportunity's related lists.

An opportunity record comes preconfigured with several standard fields. Most of these fields are self–explanatory, but be sure to pay attention to these critical ones:

» **Amount:** This field displays the intended, best-guess amount of the sale. Depending on the way your company calculates the pipeline report, you might use numbers that include total contract value, the bookings amount, and so on.

» **Close Date:** Use this required field for your best guess as to when you'll close this deal. Depending on your company's sales process, the close date has different definitions, but this field is commonly used to track the date that you signed all the paperwork required to book the sale.

» **Expected Revenue:** This read-only field is automatically generated by multiplying the Amount field by the Probability field.

» **Forecast Category:** This field is typically hidden, but every opportunity automatically includes a value. Each sales stage within the Stage drop-down list corresponds to a default forecast category so that higher-probability opportunities contribute to your overall forecast after they reach certain stages.

» **Opportunity Owner:** This person in your organization owns the opportunity. Although an opportunity record has only one owner, many users can still collaborate on an opportunity.

» **Opportunity Name:** This required text field represents the name of the specific deal as you want it to appear on your list of opportunities or on a pipeline report.

TIP

When naming opportunities, you and your company should define a standard naming convention for the Opportunity Name field so that you can easily search for and distinguish opportunities from a list. We recommend that the opportunity name start with the account name, then a hyphen, and then the name of the customer's project or the product of primary interest. This naming convention makes for readable reports later on.

» **Private:** If you want to keep an opportunity private, select this check box to render the record accessible to only you, your bosses, and the system administrator.

» **Probability:** The *probability* is the confidence factor associated with the likelihood that you'll win the opportunity. Each sales stage that your company defines is associated with a default probability to close. Typically, you don't need to edit this field; it gets assigned automatically by the Stage option that you pick. In fact, your administrator might remove write access from this field altogether.

» **Stage:** This required field allows you to track your opportunities, following your company's established sales process. Salesforce provides a set of standard drop-down list values common to solution selling, but your system administrator can modify these values.

» **Type:** Use this drop-down list to differentiate the types of opportunities that you want to track. Most customers use the Type drop-down list to measure new versus existing business and products versus services, but your system administrator can modify it to measure other important or more specific deal types, such as add-ons, upsells, work orders, and so on.

REMEMBER

When customizing your opportunity fields, take into consideration the patience and attention spans of your end-users. Keep the record as simple as possible to ensure that all your important fields actually get filled in. If you add many fields, you might make the opportunity record harder to use, which then puts user adoption of Salesforce at risk. At the same time, you'll have greater success with opportunities when you can easily capture what you want to track.

Entering Opportunities

Before you can begin using Salesforce to close opportunities, first you must get the records into Salesforce. The best method for creating a new opportunity is to start from the relevant account or contact record, which guarantees that the opportunity associates to the correct record, making the opportunity easily trackable. And if you add the opportunity from a contact, you link both the account and the contact at the same time.

To create an opportunity, go to the relevant Account or Contact detail page and follow these steps:

1. **Select the Create Opportunity option from the Create New drop-down list on the sidebar.**

   Alternatively, scroll down the detail page to the Opportunities related list and click the New button. The result is the same. The Edit mode of a new opportunity appears (see Figure 10-1). The Account Name field is conveniently filled in for you.

FIGURE 10-1:
Completing opportunity fields.

2. Fill in the fields as much as you can or as required.

At a minimum, you must complete the required fields. Depending on how you set up your opportunity record, you might have to fill in additional required fields, all of which are highlighted in red. See the section "Getting Familiar with the Opportunity Record," earlier in this chapter, for more details on common required fields.

3. Click Save when you're done.

The Opportunity detail page appears. You can click the Edit button on this page at any time if you need to modify the record.

TIP

If you have the good fortune to need to enter multiple opportunities, one after another, instead of clicking the Save button, click the Save & New button. A new opportunity record appears in Edit mode. You have to fill in the Account Name field, but this technique can save you time.

TECHNICAL STUFF

If your company has legacy databases that contain deal information and you want this data to be in Salesforce as opportunities, you can't use an import wizard to migrate your records like you can with leads, accounts, and contacts. If this is a current challenge, seek out your technical staff, system administrator, Salesforce rep, or a Salesforce consultant. With business guidance, a person with the technical know-how can use the Apex Data Loader to import opportunities and other records into Salesforce, which can help you avoid wasting time manually re-inputting opportunities. See Chapter 22 for additional tips and tricks on migrating data.

Modifying Opportunity Records

After you add opportunities to Salesforce, you can make changes to your records when deals progress, stall, or fade away. In the following sections, we cover three common practices: editing, sharing, and reassigning.

Updating opportunity fields

In the course of working with your opportunities, you inevitably collect information that you want to save directly in the opportunity record. Every time you capture important data on your opportunity, remember to update your record by following these steps:

1. **Click the Edit button on the opportunity.**

You can also hover your mouse over the specific field that you want to edit. If a pencil icon appears to the right of the field, double-click the field to edit it. (If you see a padlock icon instead, that means the field is not editable, on purpose. Move along and pick another field to update.)

Alternatively, if you're already in an account or contact record that's linked to the opportunity, scroll down to the Opportunities related list and click the Edit link to the left of the desired opportunity. The result is the same. The Opportunity Edit page appears.

2. **Update the fields, as necessary, paying particular attention to keeping fields such as Amount, Close Date, and Stage up to date.**

Nine out of ten times, those fields play key roles in your company's sales pipeline reports. By keeping your information up to date, you and other users can get a true measure of the opportunity's progress.

3. **When you're done, click Save.**

The opportunity reappears in Saved mode. The fields that you edited are changed.

TIP

You can keep track of certain critical updates to your opportunity record by using the Stage History related list. Anytime you or one of your team members who has read-write access to your record modifies the Stage, Probability, Close Date, or Amount field, you can quickly scan this at the bottom of the opportunity record page to see who modified the record and when. See Chapter 17 for more detail on creating, updating, and cloning records, and Chapter 23 for more information about using and customizing reports.

Rolling up opportunity data onto the account record

The opportunity record carries a great deal of quantifiable information about an account, such as how many licenses were sold, the amount of a deal, and so on. By collecting and aggregating key opportunity field information onto an account record, a sales rep can quickly see how valuable a particular customer is by viewing the total number of licenses a customer currently has, how much total revenue a customer has closed with your company, and the highest deal closed with that customer, to name a few examples.

You can aggregate this summary information in two ways:

>> You can run a report that summarizes this information for you. (See Chapter 23 for more details on creating reports.)

>> Your Salesforce administrator can choose which opportunity fields you want to have summarized automatically on the account record.

To create a custom roll-up of your opportunity data onto the account record, choose Setup ➪ Build ➪ Customize ➪ Accounts ➪ Fields and then follow these steps:

1. **In the Account Custom Fields and Relationships section, click the New button.**

   The New Custom Field Wizard opens.

2. **Select the Roll-Up Summary radio button and click Next.**

3. **Enter the name of what you're summarizing in the Field Label field and click Next.**

   The Field Name field automatically populates itself based on what you enter in the Field Label. In this example, we typed **Total Deals Closed**, hit the Tab key to populate the Field Name, and then clicked the Next button.

4. **At the Define the Summary Calculation step, from the Summarized Object picklist, select Opportunities.**

   Identifying the summarized object tells Salesforce which records from which objects you want to be combined and summarized onto the account record.

5. **Select the roll-up type from the selection of radio buttons in the Select Roll-Up Type section in the middle of the page, and then click Next.**

   This selection tells Salesforce how you want the field of your choice to be summarized. You can choose a count of records, the sum, the minimum value, or the maximum value. If you choose any of the latter three options, you also have to identify which field in the opportunity you want to be summarized by using the Field to Aggregate picklist to make their choice.

You can filter out certain criteria in your result set.

If you want to summarize only records that meet certain criteria, select the Only Records Meeting Certain Criteria Should Be Included in the Calculation radio button to reveal a set of filter criteria. For example, you may want a sum of all the Amount fields for opportunities in which the Closed status equals True. (Figure 10-2 shows an example of defining the field calculation.)

FIGURE 10-2:
Defining an opportunity roll-up field calculation.

6. **Select which profiles should be able to view the new field and click Next.**

7. **Select on which page layout(s) the field should be displayed and click Save.**

Organizing Your Opportunities

When you have all or a portion of your opportunities entered in Salesforce, you can begin to organize them to suit the way that you sell.

In the following sections, you find out how you can use views and other tools from the Opportunities home page to provide greater focus for you and your sales teams. Then, for even more robust organization of your opportunity information, check out Chapter 23 for specifics on how to use standard and custom opportunity reports.

Defining contact roles

Depending on your sales process, at some early point, you need to identify the decision makers who'll influence the buying decision. Contacts and their titles often don't tell the whole story about decision makers, influencers, and the chain of command within an opportunity.

To better define the buying influences on an opportunity, go to an opportunity record and follow these steps:

1. **Click the New button on the Contact Roles related list.**

The Contact Roles page appears for that specific opportunity, displaying a list of the available contacts linked to the related account (see Figure 10-3).

FIGURE 10-3: Selecting the contact role.

Contact Roles for United Oil Installations

Save Cancel

Primary	Contact	Role
◉	No Primary Contact	
○	Lauren Boyle	✓ --None--
○	Avi Green	Business User
○	Stella Pavlova	Decision Maker
○	Arthur Song	Economic Buyer
○		Economic Decision Maker
○		Evaluator
○		Executive Sponsor
○		Influencer
		Technical Buyer
		Other

Save Cancel

2. **For each relevant contact, use the Role drop-down list to select the appropriate role.**

Salesforce comes preconfigured with a standard list of contact roles, but your company can customize this drop-down list if you need to modify the list of values. You don't have to classify a role for every contact on the list; you can just leave the Role default value of None.

REMEMBER

If the right role for your contact doesn't appear, advise your system administrator to customize the Opportunity Contract Role Picklist Values.

3. **Select a radio button to designate the primary contact.**

The primary contact typically refers to the person who's currently your point of contact. One of the benefits of selecting a primary contact is that you can list who the primary contact is on a basic opportunity report.

4. **(Optional) Click the Lookup icon to the right of empty fields in the Contact column to add other contacts who are critical to your opportunity.**

TIP

If you work with multitier selling models or if you collaborate with business partners on your deals, use contact roles to add contacts who aren't employees of an account. For example, if your customer's legal gatekeeper works for an outside law firm, you can use the Contact Roles related list to highlight the attorney's role.

5. **When you're done, click Save.**

The Opportunity detail page reappears, and your Contact Roles related list is updated to reflect contacts involved in the opportunity. If you need to add more contact roles, click the New button in the Contact Roles related list again.

Using opportunity teams

Depending on how you do business, you can identify opportunity teams so that all members working a deal can access the same record. An *opportunity team* is a set of users in your Salesforce instance that can collaborate on a single opportunity. You can also create default opportunity teams if, for example, you typically work on deals with the same account manager and presales representative from your territory.

To enable opportunity teams, choose Setup ➪ Build ➪ Customize ➪ Opportunities ➪ Opportunity Teams ➪ Opportunity Team Settings and click the Enable Team Selling check box, as shown in Figure 10-4.

Team Selling Setup

Once team selling is enabled, you can add custom fields, buttons, and links, validati be available for opportunity teams.

☑ Enable Team Selling

[Save] [Cancel]

FIGURE 10-4:
Enabling
opportunity
teams for your
organization.

Now you'll see the page layout selection page, where you can select any and all opportunity layouts to which you can add the Opportunity Team related list.

Associating an opportunity team to your opportunity

Now that you have opportunity teams enabled for your organization, you can create default opportunity teams or just create an ad hoc team and associate it with the opportunity you're working on.

To create a default opportunity team that you typically work with, click your name in the upper right of any Salesforce page and choose My Settings. Then follow these steps:

1. **In the My Settings menu on the left, select Advanced User Details.**

   The Advanced User Details page appears, with information about your profile.

2. **Scroll down to Default Opportunity Team and click Add.**

   The Add Members page appears, where you can select the users you want to add to your default team, their level of access to the opportunity, and their team role, as shown in Figure 10-5.

   You can choose to automatically add the default team to any opportunities you create or are reassigned to by selecting the corresponding check box on the Add Members page.

TIP

FIGURE 10-5:
Adding members to your default opportunity team.

3. **Click Save when you're done.**

   The Advanced User Details page reappears with your default opportunity team.

   To associate your default team to an opportunity, navigate to the opportunity record you own, scroll down to the Opportunity Team related list, and click Add Default Team.

   If you don't have a default team, or just want to associate other users to the opportunity, click the Add button on the Opportunity Team related list, and select the users, roles, and level of access there.

Following Opportunities with Chatter

If you work as part of a sales team or just have a lot of deals to keep track of, Salesforce can bring you the news on your opportunities as it happens. You are automatically set to follow updates on any opportunity you create, but sometimes, you don't want to hunt down what's happening on someone else's opportunity.

You can follow an Opportunity record by following these steps:

1. **From the Opportunity home page, click a recently viewed opportunity.**

   The Opportunity detail page appears, displaying the Chatter feed front and center, as shown in Figure 10-6.

   For more information on how to use Chatter, see Chapter 6.

FIGURE 10-6: Following an opportunity.

2. **To follow the discussion on this opportunity, click the Follow link with the green circled plus sign.**

The Opportunity page updates to show a thumbnail photo of your profile picture under the Followers section, alongside photos of other people following this record. The Follow button now appears as a Following status, with a gray "X" next to it that you click if you want to unfollow the record.

Now when there's Chatter activity on this opportunity, it appears in your Chatter feed displayed on your home page, too.

IN THIS CHAPTER

Defining products and price books

Using products and price books

Creating products

Establishing and updating product schedules

Maintaining product lists and price books

Chapter 11

Tracking Products and Price Books

A *product,* as its name implies, is a product or service that you sell to customers. Products are the individual line items that make up an *opportunity.* Depending on your goals for Salesforce, you may not need to immediately incorporate Salesforce's product-type features into your opportunities. But if you sell multiple products and services and you struggle with product-level visibility, Salesforce provides powerful and easy tools to implement solutions for users of Professional, Enterprise, or Unlimited Edition.

Using products in Salesforce benefits sales reps and people in product marketing, management, and development throughout your organization. Sales reps can quickly locate the price of a product and select products to calculate an opportunity's amount. Marketing, management, or development professionals can get vital sales information to support strategic business planning, new product development, and product life cycle management.

In this chapter, we show sales teams how to use products and price books with opportunities (if your administrator has already set that up). Before setting up products and price books, though, administrators first need to do some advanced planning. We discuss how to create a product catalog, set up schedules, and build price books. We then show you how to maintain products and price books on an ongoing basis to facilitate your sales goals. We conclude this chapter by showing you how to generate quotes that incorporate items from your product catalog so that you can email them to your contacts.

Discovering Products and Price Books

You need to know two key and interrelated terms before you can begin planning your product strategy in Salesforce:

>> **Products:** Individual items that you sell through your opportunities. All products belong to one universal product catalog. After you create a product, though, you can associate it with one or multiple price books with identical or different prices. For example, you may use multiple price books if you use one set of prices when selling to qualified nonprofit agencies and a different set of prices when selling to companies in the private sector.

A product can have an associated *schedule* based on quantity, revenue, or both. If you sell products and break out schedules to forecast revenue recognition or for planning, you can use Salesforce to reflect important schedules for products linked to opportunities.

TIP

To access the Products home page, click the Products tab. If you can't see that, confirm that the Force.com drop-down list in the upper-right corner of the screen is set to Sales (versus something like Call Center). If you still don't see it, check with your system administrator.

>> **Price book:** A collection of products and their associated prices. A product with its associated price is a *price book entry*. You can also create custom price books based on your unique sales model.

You can associate a price book, add products, and build schedules on an opportunity through the Products related list on an Opportunity detail page.

Defining standard product fields

A product record consists of a number of fields that you use to capture information about a product you sell. If you're involved in shaping products for your company, most of the standard fields are obvious. If you want specific definitions, click the Help link in the upper-right corner of Salesforce.

Here are some important pointers on understanding the standard product record fields:

>> **Product Name:** The name of your product. Make sure to use titles that are clear and familiar to your sales reps and customers.

>> **Product Code:** An internal code or product ID used to identify your product. If your existing products and product codes reside in a financial database and you want to plan for integration, make sure that the product codes are consistent.

>> **Product Description:** Text to distinguish products from each other. If you're in product management or marketing, describe your products so that they're obvious and useful for your sales teams.

>> **Product Family:** The category of the product. Use this drop-down list when building reports that reflect sales data by product category. For example, if you work for a technology value-added reseller (VAR), you may want to reflect your pipeline by families that include hardware, software, services, training, and maintenance. You can set up products in Salesforce so that each product automatically maps to a product family.

>> **Active:** This check box must be selected to make the product available to your users.

>> **Quantity Scheduling Enabled:** Select this check box to enable quantity scheduling for a product. If you don't see this check box, your administrator hasn't enabled it.

>> **Revenue Scheduling Enabled:** Select this check box to enable revenue scheduling for a product. If you don't see this check box, your administrator hasn't enabled it.

Understanding the different types of pricing

Salesforce allows you to customize your pricing based on the way you sell. If you use products in Salesforce, your company has three different options for pricing:

>> **Standard Prices:** Default prices that you establish for your products when you set up your standard price book.

>> **List Prices:** Prices that you set up for custom price books.

>> **Sales Price:** Price of a product determined by the sales rep when he adds a product to an opportunity. (See the following section for details on adding products to opportunities.)

TIP

You'll hear the terms *products* and *opportunity products* referenced when you start using Salesforce products and price books. What's the difference? Products are the base level things that your company sells. Products can be assigned to various price books and given different list prices within those price books. Opportunity products are the specific products (and prices) that are associated with a specific opportunity. Opportunity products should reflect the negotiated price and conditions for that specific opportunity.

Using Products and Price Books

Sales reps can add products with specific prices to their opportunities, and Salesforce automatically calculates the Amount field on an opportunity record. If you're a sales rep selling multiple products and managing multiple opportunities at the same time, you can take the frustration out of remembering what you offered to a customer. If you're a sales manager, you can segment your pipelines and forecasts by product lines. And if you're in product management or marketing, products in Salesforce can give you real insight into product demand from your markets.

Adding products to opportunities

To take advantage of products, your company must first set up a product catalog, as well as one or more price books. See the section "Building the Product Catalog," later in this chapter, for the how-to details on setting up your products and price books. After this is done, sales reps can add products to an opportunity by going to a specific opportunity and following these steps:

1. **Scroll down the Opportunity detail page to the Products related list and then click the Choose Price Book button.**

   A Choose Price Book page appears. If your company has made only one price book available to you, you can bypass this step and start with Step 2.

2. **Select the appropriate price book from the Price Book drop-down list and then click Save.**

   The Opportunity detail page appears again. The Products related list now shows the name of the price book in parentheses.

   REMEMBER

   On an opportunity, you can use only one price book at a time.

3. **Click the Add Product button on the Products related list.**

   A Product Selection page appears, as shown in Figure 11-1. This shows all the products in your selected price book.

FIGURE 11-1:
Finding your products.

> If the resulting list of products is too long for your tastes, you may narrow the results by entering a keyword or filter criteria, and then clicking the Search button to begin your search. The page reappears with your search results in a table at the bottom of the page.

4. Select the check boxes next to the products that you want, and then click the Select button.

An Add Products page appears with your selections and fields for you to provide line item details. The Sales Price field is prefilled with the default sales price from the price book that you selected.

5. Fill in the line item details.

You must, at a minimum, fill in the Quantity and Sales Price fields for each selected product. The Date field is typically used to reflect an expected shipping or delivery date for the product. It could also be used to determine the contracted start date of a service.

6. When you're done, click the Save button or the Save & More button.

Clicking the Save & More button takes you back to the Product Selection page. If you click the Save button, the Opportunity detail page reappears. Notice that the Amount and Quantity fields on the opportunity record have changed based on the total from the products you added.

If you need to change the details on your product selections in the course of the sales cycle, you can do this easily on the Products related list of the opportunity record.

If you find yourself unable to modify the sales price on your products, you may want to politely confirm the intent with your sales manager. Some companies lock in the sales price for sales reps so that they must adhere to a predefined discount approval policy.

Adding and updating schedules on opportunities

If you manage opportunities in which your products or services are delivered over time, you can create schedules for your products by quantity, revenue, or both. By using schedules, you and your users can benefit in multiple ways:

» **If you're on a sales team:** You get a better gauge on revenue recognition, which could be significant if that affects compensation.

» **If you're in product management:** You can better forecast and plan for the number of units that you'll have to deliver in future quarters.

» **If you're part of a services organization:** Schedules updated by reps provide a real-time gauge in planning your resources and projects.

Your system administrator must first set up your products with scheduling. (See the section "Setting Up Schedules," later in this chapter, for more specifics on schedules, and see Chapter 17 for the details on common Salesforce configuration actions.)

After scheduling is enabled for a product, set up a schedule by going to the Opportunity detail page and following these steps:

1. **Click the desired product in the Product Name column of the Products related list.**

   An Opportunity Product page appears with a Schedule related list.

2. **Click the Establish button in the Schedule related list.**

   An Establish Schedule page appears. If you see a Re-Establish button instead of an Establish button, you have an existing schedule already. Clicking Re-Establish deletes the old schedule and creates a new one by taking you to the Establish Schedule page.

3. **Complete the fields and click Save.**

   Your fields may vary, depending on whether the product is set up for quantity, revenue, or combined scheduling. When you click Save, a schedule appears based on your choices.

4. **Review and modify the schedule.**

   If the revenues or quantities aren't equal over the periods that you first established, you can type over the values in the schedule. For example, these amounts may not be equal if your customer has negotiated varying types of ramped payments, or more payments during certain times of the year to accommodate for heavier seasonal business.

5. **When you're done, click Save.**

   The Opportunity Product page reappears with the schedule you established.

Over the course of an opportunity, if terms change, you can adjust the schedule on a product by clicking the buttons on the Opportunity Product page. To access an Opportunity Product page, go to the relevant opportunity record, scroll down to the Products related list, and click the desired product link from the Product column. The Opportunity Product page for the selected product appears with a Schedule related list. You can do the following with the schedule:

>> **Modify the schedule.** Click the Edit button.

>> **Delete the schedule.** Click the Delete button.

>> **Establish the schedule all over again.** Click the Re-Establish button.

Searching for products

You can search for specific products easily by using the Find Products search tool on the Products home page.

TIP Instead of searching from the Products home page, you can search for products from your main home page. Your administrator must set this up for your company. For details on adding this home page tool, see Chapter 17 for customizing Salesforce and consult with your administrator.

To search for a product, go to the Products home page and follow these steps:

1. **Enter keywords in the Find Products search tool and then click the Find Product button.**

   A Product Search page appears with a list of possible selections, as shown in Figure 11-2.

TIP You can use the Find Products search tool to enter more keywords or filters to refine your search and again click the Find Product button. The list results change based on your criteria.

FIGURE 11-2:
Search for a
product.

2. **Click a link in the Product Name column to go directly to the product.**

   The Product detail page appears.

Building the Product Catalog

If you have a vested interest in your product strategy, be aware and take advantage of all the options that Salesforce provides for customizing products and price books. The more you plan ahead, the better you can implement products and price books for how your sales teams sell. As you make products and price books active, your sales reps can start associating products to their opportunities.

Planning products for success

For products, consider the characteristics of your products outside the standard realm that you want to analyze. In most companies, the product management or marketing teams own and maintain these records in coordination with finance. You should pull together a cross-functional team made up of sales, marketing, finance, and product management users to decide what you want to achieve from products in Salesforce. Then work with your system administrator to customize the product record to meet your specific needs. For more details on customization, see Chapter 17.

For pricing, consider whether to have set pricing on your products or whether you prefer to keep the pricing simple at the beginning. Some customers of Salesforce, for example, set the prices on their products at $0 or $1 and then depend on their sales reps to fill in the sales prices when they prepare an opportunity. Other companies invest time and effort in creating actual standard or list prices on products to provide guidance to their sales reps.

Adding products to the product catalog

Before your sales reps can begin linking products to their opportunities, you need to add the products to Salesforce.

To add a product, log in to Salesforce and follow these steps:

1. **Select the Create Product option from the Create New drop-down list on the sidebar.**

   A New Product page appears, as shown in Figure 11-3.

FIGURE 11-3:
Add a product to the product catalog.

2. **Complete the fields.**

   Your exact fields may vary, but see the section "Defining standard product fields," earlier in this chapter, for info on the standard fields.

3. **When you're done, click Save.**

   The Product detail page for your new product appears with related lists for standard prices and price books.

Changing product details in the product catalog

Over time, marketing or product managers may need to update details about a product. You can make most of your changes to a product from its detail page. Go to a specific product and take a look at this list of actions that you can perform.

(You must have "edit" permissions on products to perform these steps. See Chapter 21 for details on granting the right permissions to the right people.)

>> **Edit the product record.** Click the Edit button. For example, if the name of your product changes, you can change the product name and then save and automatically update all opportunities that include that product with the modified name.

>> **Delete the product.** Click Delete and then click OK in the dialog box that appears. In circumstances in which you're no longer offering a product but it's linked to opportunities, it's better that you deactivate or archive the product rather than delete it.

>> **Deactivate the product.** Click the Edit button, deselect the Active check box, and then click Save. Take this path if you might offer the product in the future.

>> **Delete and archive the product.** Click Delete and then click OK in the dialog box that appears. If your product is linked to opportunities, a Deletion Problems page appears with suggested options. Click the Archive link if you're still intent on deleting the product but not altering the existing opportunities.

TIP

If you want to keep your sales reps informed of any changes to your products (for example, if a product is no longer offered or if its name changed), you can use Salesforce Chatter so that any changes to a product's status or its name are reported in a Chatter feed. Interested users need to just follow the actions of the person who makes those changes (usually someone in Sales Operations), or they can follow the specific product, too. (See Chapter 6 for more information on setting up Chatter and its feeds and following users and records.)

Setting Up Schedules

If your company wants to track annuity streams, stay aware of key shipping dates, or estimate when revenue will be recognized on products, you can also set up schedules on all or some products.

Enabling schedules for your company

Your administrator first needs to enable schedules before you can add them on specific products.

TIP

If your company wants to track shipping dates with Salesforce, you need to enable *quantity scheduling.* If your company wants to measure revenue recognition or anticipate upcoming payments, be sure to enable *revenue scheduling.* If your company wants to do both, you'd enable both types of scheduling.

To set up schedules, follow these steps:

1. **Choose Setup ⇨ Build ⇨ Customize ⇨ Products ⇨ Product Schedules Settings.**

   The Schedule Setup page appears, as shown in Figure 11-4.

FIGURE 11-4:
Enable schedules for your company.

2. **Select the appropriate check boxes.**

   You can choose to enable schedules based on quantities, revenue, or both. You can also choose to enable schedules for all products.

REMEMBER

3. **When you're done, click Save.**

   The Products page reappears.

Adding and updating a default schedule

After schedules have been enabled, you can create default schedules on existing products or while you're adding new products.

By creating default schedules, you can simplify repetitive tasks for sales reps. With this setting, a default schedule is created when a sales rep adds a product to an opportunity. A sales rep can still reestablish a product schedule on an opportunity. The product date determines the start date for the installments.

TIP

If you sell a basic service with different payment plans, consider creating a unique product for each payment plan and then using default revenue schedules. By doing this, you can simplify the data entry for the rep and reduce the chance of error.

To create a default schedule, follow these steps:

1. **Select the Create New Product option on the sidebar or click the Edit button on a product record.**

   A Product page appears in Edit mode. (Make sure you didn't click Edit on an Opportunity Product record. Remember that an Opportunity Product record is different from a Product record.)

2. **Complete the fields, as appropriate.**

   Here are some tips on completing the default schedule:

   - *Schedule Type:* Select Divide if you want to divide the opportunity amount into installments. Select Repeat if you want to repeat the quantity or revenue on each installment.

   - *Installment Period:* Define the frequency.

   - *Number of Installments:* Define the duration.

3. **When you're done, click Save.**

   The Product detail page appears.

REMEMBER

If your product has both quantity and revenue default scheduling, quantity scheduling is calculated first and drives the total amount. Then revenue scheduling divides the amount.

To update a default product schedule, follow these steps:

1. **From the Products home page, search for the product whose schedule you'd like to update, using your preferred method.**

   See the "Searching for products" section, earlier in this chapter, for specifics. A Product Search page appears.

2. **Click the product name of the specific product to edit.**

   The Product page appears.

3. **Click the Edit button to update schedule information.**

4. **When you're done, click Save.**

   The Product page for your product appears with the updated information.

Managing Price Books

Some companies require just one universal price book. Many other companies, however, want custom price books based on their unique selling needs. Examples include price books that are based on the following:

>> **Geography:** For a global company, the Japanese sales team might sell a subset of the products sold by its North American counterpart (and at different prices and in different currencies).

>> **Partner tiers:** In some companies that sell via partners, strategic partners might get preferential pricing.

>> **Sales teams:** If your company is divided into sales teams that sell different products, you can use custom price books to simplify the product selection for groups.

>> **Volume discounts:** Some companies build price books based on volume purchases.

>> **Seasonality:** Some companies change their pricing based on seasonal buying patterns. You can use custom price books to communicate pricing changes to your sales reps during these periods.

If the standard price book meets your objectives, keep it simple. Otherwise, in the following sections, we show you how to set up your price books.

Adding to the standard price book

Every time you add a standard price to a product, you automatically associate it with the standard price book. You can do this while you're creating products, or you can add the standard prices after you've built the product records.

Adding standard prices while creating products

The easiest time to add a standard price is while you're creating products. To use this method, start creating a product record as you normally would (see the section "Building the Product Catalog," earlier in this chapter). Instead of clicking Save, though, follow these steps:

1. **Click the Save & Add Price button (refer to Figure 11-3).**

   An Add Standard Price page appears, as shown in Figure 11-5.

FIGURE 11-5:
Add a standard
price.

2. **Complete the Standard Price field and click Save.**

   The Product detail page appears, and a standard price displays on the Standard Price related list.

Adding or editing standard prices for existing products

You can also create the products first and add prices later. To add or edit a standard price, go to the desired Product detail page and follow these steps:

1. **Click the Add button on the Standard Price related list.**

   If standard prices already exist, you can click Edit or Edit All. The result is the same: An Add or Edit Standard Price page appears.

2. **Complete or modify the Standard Price field, as necessary, and then click Save.**

   The Product detail page reappears with any changes reflected on the Standard Price related list.

Creating a custom price book

To create a price book, you need to be an administrator or have permission to manage price books.

To create a price book from scratch, go to the Products home page and follow these steps:

1. **Click the Manage Price Books link under the Maintenance section, near the bottom of the page.**

   A Price Book page appears with a related list for recent price books.

2. **Click the New button on the Recent Price Books related list.**

   A New Price Book page appears in Edit mode.

REMEMBER

3. **Complete the fields.**

Select the Active check box if you want to make the price book available.

4. **When you're done, click Save.**

The Price Book detail page for your new price book appears with a Products related list.

Adding products to a custom price book

After the price book has been established, you can add products to it. A product listed on a price book is also referred to as a *price book entry*. To add products to an existing price book, go to a price book and follow these steps:

1. **Click the Add button on the Products related list.**

A Product Selection page appears with a search tool and a list of products.

2. **Enter keywords and filter criteria, and then click the Search button to narrow your search.**

The Product Selection page reappears with a list of products based on your search criteria.

3. **Use the check boxes on the search results to choose products and then click the Select button.**

An Add List Price page appears.

4. **Complete the fields.**

Select the check boxes in the Use Standard Price column if you want to use the standard price for the list price of a product or just enter a list price. You can select the Active check boxes to make products immediately available in the price book.

5. **When you're done, click Save (or Save & More if you want to find more products).**

After you save the product, the Price Book detail page reappears, and your selected products have been added to the Products related list.

Making global changes to price books

Maintaining accurate and up-to-date product and price lists is challenging, especially if you have an extensive product catalog and/or complex pricing. If you're responsible for such a daunting task, you can use tools that are located on the Products home page to save time.

Changing activation on price books

At times, you'll want to make a price book unavailable to sales reps. Maybe you had to raise prices on a family of products or you stopped selling a product line. You probably need to preserve the current price book because existing customers and some prospects are still being associated with those products and prices, but new customers will need to be tied to the new catalog. Rest assured that you can deactivate one or more price books almost instantly so that sales reps won't be able to tie new opportunities to old information.

To deactivate a price book, go the Products home page and follow these steps:

1. **Click the Manage Price Books link under the Maintenance section.**

The Price Book detail page appears.

2. **Create a custom price books list view to meet your needs.**

In this example, click the Create New View link to create a custom view that filters your price books by those that are active. Call it the Active Price Books view. To learn how to create a custom list view, see Chapter 17.

3. **On the Active Price Books custom list, click the Deactivate link next to a price book that you want to make unavailable.**

The custom list view reappears, and the selected price book is no longer visible in this list because it is no longer active.

To reactivate price books, you follow a similar process, the difference being that you click the Activate link adjacent to a price book listed in a custom price book list view based on Inactive Price Books.

Cloning price books

On occasion, you may want to create a price book that closely resembles an existing price book. Instead of starting from scratch, you can clone from an existing price book and then make changes, as necessary.

To clone a price book, follow these steps:

1. **Click the Manage Price Books link under the Maintenance section.**

The Price Book page appears.

2. **Click the New button on the Recent Price Books related list.**

A New Price Book page appears.

3. **Use the Existing Price Books drop-down list to select a price book to clone.**

4. **Type a unique name in the Price Book Name field, and give it a description in the Description field.**

5. **Select the Active check box when you want the new price book to be available to others for use.**

6. **When you're done, click Save.**

   The new Price Book page appears with a Products related list cloned from the existing price book.

   If necessary, click Edit or Edit All on the Products related list to change the list prices, and click Add or Delete in the Products related list to add or delete price book entries.

Deleting price books

WARNING

You can delete price books, but if the price book is associated with existing opportunities, beware. In those circumstances, we recommend the following actions:

» Deactivate (rather than delete) the price book so that the linkage between opportunities and products stays intact.

» Delete the associated opportunity records first, and then delete the price book.

» Archive the price book entries prior to deleting. Then, even if you delete the price book record, the products associated with opportunities are retained.

If you still want to delete a price book, follow these steps:

1. **On the Products home page, click the Manage Price Books link under the Maintenance section.**

   The Price Book detail page appears with related lists for active and inactive price books.

2. **Click the link for the desired price book.**

   The specific Price Book page appears.

3. **Click Delete and then click OK in the dialog box that appears.**

   If you select a price book that isn't associated with opportunities, you return to the Price Book detail page with the lists of price books. If a Deletion Problems page appears, follow the suggestions provided in the preceding bulleted list and on the Deletion Problems page.

Chapter 12

Managing Your Partners

Because Salesforce can get sales reps and managers onboard to track all their opportunities and sales-related activities, the big pipeline picture should be getting clearer for everyone. *Partners* — which might also be known in your business as third-party companies, value-added resellers (VARs), original equipment manufacturers (OEMs), wholesalers, or distributors — can also be accurately managed in Salesforce almost as if they were full-time dedicated company sales reps. It used to be difficult to create and maintain unique messages and branding for specific groups of partners. Not anymore.

Salesforce Communities extends the existing Salesforce product to partners (as well as employees and customers, optionally) and the leads and deals they bring in. Additionally, support managers and support reps within a company can more easily resolve issues for your partners.

A detailed discussion of Salesforce Communities could take up a whole book on its own. In fact, many of the details are covered in *Salesforce Service Cloud For Dummies*, by Jon Paz and TJ Kelley (Wiley), so in this chapter, we provide a high-level overview of what life is like for partners and channel reps. Then we discuss how a channel team manages its partners with Salesforce. For partners asked by their vendors to use this application, we discuss how to access and navigate Salesforce from a community. Finally, we give channel managers and administrators some pointers on how to set up a partner-focused community and begin giving partners access.

Understanding the Partner Life Cycle

Using an indirect sales force of partners to help sell your products allows you to quickly and cost-effectively expand your company's reach into markets that you might otherwise not have the resources to tackle. Some industries that are more partner intensive include high-tech, insurance, and manufacturing. In this section, we set the stage for two types of business users and describe how Communities can help.

Here are some helpful Partner terms:

>> **Vendor:** The company that's using Salesforce and for whom the channel managers work.

>> **Channel managers:** The employees within your company who manage a set of partners.

>> **Channel conflict:** What happens when your direct sales force and your indirect sales force find the same prospect to woo and start bickering about who's entitled to that lead — a clear sign that your current system is ineffective.

>> **Deal registration:** Minimizes channel conflict. These programs get your indirect sales channel registering deals with you (the vendor) to reduce the chances of other partners or the direct sales force competing for a deal.

>> **Communities:** Customizable web portals hosted by Salesforce.com that allow users to access Salesforce. Your company can set up multiple communities for partners, in addition to employees or customers.

>> **Partner accounts:** Account records that are used by channel managers to manage partner organizations, partner users, and partner activities.

>> **Partner users:** Salesforce users with limited capabilities and visibility into your instance of Salesforce. They're associated with a specific partner account and access Salesforce via a community.

Understanding a day in the life of a channel manager

Channel managers and their direct reports, channel reps, manage relationships with various types of partners and partners-in-waiting. The channel team does whatever it can to empower its indirect sales force with the right selling tools, sticks, and carrots, to make sure that the relationship is win-win.

MEASURING PARTNER PERFORMANCE

A major communication services company drove its channel sales strategy by partnering with leading wireless equipment manufacturers. Sometimes, the company was introduced to the end customer; other times, the company was involved in opportunities completely managed by the manufacturer. But in all circumstances, the company's channel managers leveraged Communities to track the partner sales performance, to improve mindshare with strategic partners, and to deepen its relationships with end customers.

With Partner Communities, channel managers now have access to Salesforce dashboards, leads, opportunities, accounts, and content records. Dashboards provide a graphical snapshot of the channel's performance so that you can see how much revenue the channel is bringing in. Leads are potential business that come either from a partner or to your company and are automatically or manually reassigned to the best partner for the job. Opportunities are the deals sourced or nurtured by your partners. Accounts can be resellers, distributors, agents — any type of partners that your business tracks. Channel managers can also use content to publish copies of sales tools, price lists, or product information for partners.

In addition to these standard tabs, you can also track partner budgets and fund claims if you run joint marketing programs, create and promote rebate programs with your partners, and more. Your administrator needs to set this up, so make sure that she reads the section "Setting Up Salesforce Communities for Your Channel Team," later in this chapter.

Understanding a day in the life of a partner

A partner's perspective is the flip side of the relationship managed by the channel manager. For example, one type of partner could be reselling your company's products. That partner works in a territory that's managed by a channel manager.

With Salesforce Communities, partner users can now access a limited view of your Salesforce information via a Partner Community. The Partner Community provides a centralized view of leads to pursue, opportunities in your pipeline, vendor documents to help with the sales cycle, and optional tabs to help with additional responsibilities, such as making fund requests. Partners get to see leads specifically assigned to them or grabbed from a general "shark tank" in which first come is first served. Additionally, partners can receive other key targeted messages on the website, update their company's information for the vendor to see, and email their channel rep, as needed. Figure 12-1 shows a sample Partner Community that you might set up for your partners.

FIGURE 12-1: Viewing a Partner Community.

Managing Your Channel with Salesforce Communities

After your administrator has set up your organization with Salesforce Communities, the channel team can easily access it from the Force.com app menu in the upper-right corner of your Salesforce window. This section provides a high-level overview of how the channel team can now use Salesforce Communities to gain better visibility into their partner relationships. We also recommend that you scan Chapters 3, 7, and 8, which talk in more detail about navigating Salesforce, as well as leads and accounts.

Enabling partner relationship management

To allow partners to take part in the benefits of communities while still providing certain privileges specific to partners (such as working leads assigned to them), you have to first turn it on.

WARNING

To enable partner relationship management, follow these steps, but note: This action is not reversible! We suggest you try out this feature in a Developer Edition instance first, or your sandbox if you own Enterprise Edition or higher.

1. Choose Setup ⇨ Build ⇨ Customize ⇨ Partners ⇨ Settings.

A page appears to enable partner relationship management (PRM).

2. Click the Edit button and select the only check box on this page to enable PRM.

You're reminded that this action is not reversible.

3. **Click the Save button.**

   The Convert External User Access Wizard appears. This wizard helps you adjust sharing settings that might allow certain records or folders to be otherwise shared with external users.

4. **Click the Continue button.**

   The three-step wizard begins.

5. **In Steps 1 through 3 of the wizard, see whether any existing sharing rules need to be updated.**

   Consider whether any records may contain information that you don't want shared with partners.

6. **Click Done when you're finished, or click Cancel if you don't have any rules to modify.**

Creating partner accounts and contacts

First, you should make sure that all your partners are represented as accounts in Salesforce, with the respective channel managers owning the partner account records. This allows channel managers to monitor and record all activities related to partners in their territory.

To create a new partner account, follow these steps:

1. **Use the Create New drop-down list on the sidebar and select the Account option.**

2. **Create the account record.**

3. **Click the Manage External Account button and select the Enable as Partner option from the resulting drop-down list.**

4. **Associate partner users to this partner account record by adding contacts.**

5. **Create a new contact, click the Manage External User button on the contact record, and select Enable Partner User for your partner user to receive his or her login and password notification via email.**

   A New User page appears, allowing you to confirm user details before saving the record and generating a password for the user.

Assigning leads to partners

By assigning leads to partners, channel managers ensure an organized way of seeing what potential business their partners are working on.

Leads may be assigned to partners by manually switching the record ownership, by assigning partner leads to a queue (also known lovingly as the "shark tank"), or by adopting a round-robin method, in which leads are routed evenly to a number of queues. Partners then have access to the queue to grab leads. (You can keep them from getting too greedy by setting a ceiling on how many leads they can accept to work on at one time.) Additionally, lead assignment rules may be set up by your administrator to automatically assign leads to partner users or partner queues based on certain rules.

To reassign a lead to a partner user, follow these steps:

1. **On the lead record, next to the Lead Owner field, click the Change link.**

   The link is in square brackets. The Change Lead Owner page appears.

2. **From the Owner drop-down list, choose the Partner User option.**

3. **Select the partner user to whom you are assigning the lead.**

   This assumes the partner's profile has been added as a member to the community you want him to join, the community has been published and can be viewable by others, and the partner user is already activated and logged in at least once to the system. If the user is not active, his name will not show up when filtering for partner users.

4. **(Optional) Select the Send Notification Email check box to notify the partner about the lead.**

5. **Click Save.**

   The lead record reappears with your ownership change. The new partner owner instantly receives a customizable email if you selected the Send Notification check box, and the lead appears in his Lead Inbox the next time he accesses the Partner Community.

You may also reassign leads in bulk (see Chapter 7).

Reducing channel conflict with deal registration

Without a well-thought-out PRM process, companies often run into channel conflict when their direct sales and indirect sales forces butt heads over who found which lead first. As the channel manager, you often have to waste time arguing with a direct sales rep and her manager over who has dibs, while the prospect waits for the internal bickering to stop. This isn't an efficient way to close a deal, and it's frustrating for the customer to often hear multiple messages (or even price quotes!) from what's supposed to be a united front. In addition, if the partner loses out on that opportunity, you've just lost some of her trust in how supportive you really are in her efforts — so why should she reveal her pipeline data early or adopt your processes?

By taking the time to design a deal registration process, concisely and consistently communicate the status of deal registrations to partners, efficiently carry out the approval for all submissions, and then be able to measure related conversion and close ratios, you can eliminate channel conflict. The deal registration capabilities of Salesforce Communities help provide clarity on what your deal registration processes are from start to finish, which can increase adoption of your partner program and help increase partner sales because the channel conflict inefficiencies disappear. However, this setup can be successful only if you invest the time to think out your deal registration process. If you have a hard time explaining it or whiteboarding it, how do you think your partners feel?

TIP

Here are some key questions to ask before establishing any deal registration program:

>> How would you describe your deal registration process, from start to finish?

>> What do partners get for registered deals? Exclusivity? A rebate? A different tier or status?

>> What do you think would increase deal registrations?

SALESFORCE TO SALESFORCE

Salesforce to Salesforce is an amazing alternative feature to Salesforce Communities that allows partners with their own instance of Salesforce to seamlessly share lead and opportunity records with vendors in real-time. Traditionally, this sharing occurred through a hairy, expensive, and drawn-out integration process. If a lot of your partners also use Salesforce, think about what partner processes you want to track.

If you have very specific custom processes that are more focused on a high volume of lead and opportunity management, you may lean toward using Salesforce to Salesforce.

If you send a lot of customized partner communications, including collateral and content distribution, and you deal with both a Salesforce-owning and non-Salesforce-owning indirect sales force, you may want to lean more toward the Partner Community.

We don't have one correct answer to give you, so make sure that you run things by your customer success manager.

>> What information do you need when a deal is registered? Balance your quest for knowledge with the partner's patience in filling out fields.

>> What's your process for approving deal registrations?

>> What criteria do you evaluate to determine who officially owns a deal?

>> Does this approval process work the same for all partners? For which categories would it be different?

>> What metrics matter to you?

Accessing Salesforce Communities as a Partner

You can strengthen your vendor relationship by accessing your vendor's instance of Salesforce from a web portal and getting first-hand access to leads, accounts, opportunities, and other tabs to manage your deals. You can get leads assigned to you in real-time — no waiting forever after a trade show ends to see which leads to pursue. You can also provide your channel managers with real-time updates on the status of deals that you're trying to bring in. That way, if you need some assistance, your channel manager can view all deal-related activity that occurred up to a certain point and provide you with the appropriate resources to close the deal. In the following sections, we give you a quick overview of accessing and navigating your Partner Community.

As a partner sales rep, you'll receive an email from your vendor's Salesforce administrator after he's ready for you to start accessing the community. The email welcomes you to the community and provides you with everything you need to log in.

In this email, click the appropriate link to log in directly to your community and change your temporary password. Remember to bookmark the URL for easy access later. After logging in and changing your password, you're brought to the home page for your Partner Community. Every time you log in to the Partner Community, you begin at your home page. You'll see that the Partner Community is organized into a series of tabs (refer to Figure 12-1). The look of your portal may resemble your vendor's branding or your own.

Viewing and updating your leads

Similar to a direct sales user's view, a partner will see a Leads tab, which contains leads that have been assigned to the partner directly or to a general queue. The queue allows channel managers to make leads available to their partners on a first-come-first-served basis while also avoiding multiple partners working on the same lead. After you claim a lead from the queue, no other partner can claim it.

REMEMBER

Play nicely. The Force.com platform is very customizable, and your vendor could set up rules for how many leads each partner can claim so that a partner with an itchy trigger finger doesn't take away all the goodies.

The leads available to you are viewable from the Lead Views list and are displayed according to columns set by your vendor. Click any column heading to re-sort your list according to that column's criteria. Click the same column header a second time to re-sort your list in reverse order.

If you see a record in your list, that's a lead in a queue that you should claim if you think you're the right partner to pursue it. You'll see that the Action column displays Accept for these types of leads.

To claim a lead from a queue, follow these steps:

1. **Click the Accept link for that record.**

   A link to the lead now appears in the Recent Items section in the sidebar. You can click it to review more information about your lead and update the lead status to begin pursuing this suspect.

2. **Click Edit to update the lead.**

   After all, you want to be able to work on all the leads that you claimed so that your channel manager sees some results.

3. **Click Save after you update the record.**

   The Lead page reappears.

Managing your opportunities

When a lead has progressed far enough in the sales process, you convert it into an opportunity. You can manage your existing opportunities and create new ones from the Opportunities tab. To update the deal information on an existing opportunity, following these steps:

1. **Click the Opportunities tab at the top of your Partner Community.**

2. **Select the My Opportunities option from the List View drop-down menu to see a list of opportunities that you own, as shown in Figure 12-2.**

FIGURE 12-2:
Viewing your
opportunities
from a
community.

3. **Click the Edit link next to the opportunity that you want to update.**

4. **Update the fields to reflect the latest developments in the sales deal.**

5. **When finished, click Save.**

   You are returned to the List View page.

Setting Up Salesforce Communities for Your Channel Team

Before setting up Salesforce Communities, your Salesforce administrator should meet with a member of the channel sales team to confirm your PRM needs. Discuss the following questions:

>> What percentage of your sales force is indirect versus direct?

>> What types of partners do you work with?

>> Do you message differently to each type of partner?

>> What are the objectives, challenges, and participation benefits for each type of partner in your program?

>> How are your channel territories broken out?

>> How are channel managers tracking partners' sales and marketing activities today?

>> How do channel managers put together their channel forecasts? How long does it take, and how accurate is the information?

Make sure that you set an appointment with your Salesforce.com customer success manager for some free advice or a blessing to go forward with using Salesforce Communities. Chances are, if answers to these questions show that your business relies heavily on an indirect sales force, yet your visibility into the channel pipeline is as clear as mud, you probably need Salesforce Communities.

Again, the information we give you is meant to prepare you to successfully implement Salesforce Communities. The details of all the cool features that you can activate are more thoroughly discussed within *Salesforce Service Cloud For Dummies*, by Jon Paz and TJ Kelley (Wiley).

4

Providing Support with Service Cloud

IN THIS CHAPTER

Understanding service and support processes

Creating cases

Using case queues

Resolving cases

Communicating the outcome

Chapter 13

Tracking the Support Life Cycle with Cases

Salesforce provides robust customer service functionality in its Service Cloud product. The module is used to track and resolve cases, using a variety of features that allow agents to respond to cases as efficiently as possible. But it's more than that as well.

With Service Cloud, you have all the tools at your fingertips to efficiently deliver excellent customer service while managing the costs of operations. In days and weeks, versus months and years, you can start and manage a fully integrated customer service strategy that supports the many channels that customers use to communicate with you. Service Cloud also provides the ability to handle web chats from customers looking for help on your website, the ability for customers to log in to a private community where they can submit new cases and check up on existing ones, and a console where agents can minimize the number of clicks and additional pages they have to open to see information about a customer.

In this chapter, we introduce you to basic customer support functionality in Salesforce, starting with its core concept: the case. We first discuss fundamental support agent processes for handling new cases; then we cover how to manage the growing caseload. For more extensive knowledge of Service Cloud and implementing its various features, check out *Salesforce Service Cloud For Dummies*, by Jon Paz and TJ Kelley (Wiley).

Walking through a Day in the Life of a Service Agent

Salesforce follows a general process when it comes to managing cases. Service agents (you may call them *support reps*) commonly perform these tasks on any given day. The specific tasks may be different in your company, but you probably see some similarities:

>> Responding to inbound emails and calls

>> Taking new cases from assigned queues

>> Validating that the inquiry is coming from an authorized contact

>> Creating a case to begin tracking efforts to resolve the issue

>> Working the case backlog, including researching solutions

>> Managing service-level agreements (SLAs)

>> Communicating the resolution to the customer

At its core, customer support is all about accepting questions and answering them in a timely and consistent manner, while providing high levels of customer satisfaction. How you handle your responses — and the scale on which you handle them — are more complicated issues.

TIP

If all your company's Salesforce users have full licenses, and you just need to capture a fairly manageable influx of basic cases, you can do that without having to purchase full-blown separate Service Cloud licenses.

Understanding the Case Record

A *case* is a record of a customer service inquiry (you may call them *tickets*), as shown in Figure 13-1. Similar to other common records, such as accounts and contacts, you capture case-related information from a single detail page. And to manage all your cases, Salesforce comes out of the box with all the tools that you need for routing, queuing, and escalating cases, plus complying with SLAs, if that applies to your company.

FIGURE 13-1:
Introducing the
case record.

A case record comes preconfigured with standard fields and two icons commonly used for case management. Most of the standard fields are self-explanatory, but in the following list, we highlight key fields that are less obvious:

>> **Status:** This field defines the important statuses in your case process. It comes preconfigured with a basic process, but you should modify the values to fit your process. If you're an Enterprise or Unlimited Edition user, you can use this field to distinguish multiple support processes appropriate to the different kinds of cases you want to track.

>> **Case Number:** When you create a case, Salesforce automatically assigns a sequential number used for tracking.

>> **Type:** Use this picklist field to define the type of case. Salesforce presets this list with selections that include Problem and Question, but you can modify the picklist to match your categories.

>> **Case Reason:** Use this picklist field to specify the reason the case was opened. Many companies track this field to identify areas of customer service that they can improve. Of course, you can also modify this list to suit your needs.

>> **Case Origin:** Use this field to record from which channel the case originated — for example, by phone, email, or web. Many companies report on this field to understand and improve the methods by which customers interact with service and support agents.

>> **Internal Comments:** When editing a case, use this field to jot brief comments to communicate internal messages, as needed. Customers or people outside your company will not see this field by default. However, internal comments that are marked Public may be viewed by clients in the Customer Portal, if you have it enabled.

You may also hear the term *case feed.* The case feed borrows functionality from Salesforce's Chatter feature so that users can better collaborate around resolving a particular case. If your organization has Chatter feed tracking enabled on the Case object, your Case record detail will look a little different than that of other standard objects. Internal discussions about a case appear on the Feed tab, next to the Details tab, which contains field details, as shown in Figure 13-2. This layout is meant to give agents quick access to Chatter discussions about the case or record details, with a minimum of page scrolling.

FIGURE 13-2: Viewing case details when Chatter is enabled on cases.

You'll also notice that related lists still appear on the Details page as they do on any other standard record page. The left side also has quick links to the related lists, again so agents can quickly navigate to information. Speed is critical when interacting with a customer, and Salesforce provides as much information as possible to an agent without having to click off the screen to get to the right details.

Creating a Case

One of the main responsibilities of an agent is handling new inbound inquiries. Writing notes on a little sticky square that you attach to your monitor may not be the best way to track information, especially if you have terrible handwriting. In the following sections, we discuss how to begin the case management process in Salesforce so that the right information is tracked for the right customers.

Validating the contact

The first step in creating a case is validating the company and contact information to see whether any special circumstances or SLAs exist. This is less of a technological innovation than a general business best practice. You can't have just any random person taking up your precious time, can you? This information should reside in custom fields on the account record. For example, to do this in response to an inbound call, log in to Salesforce and follow these steps:

1. **Type the company name (or account number — whatever your company uses to identify its customers) into the search bar on the top of the home page and then click Search.**

   The Search Results page appears. You should see the account name listed.

   If the account name is not listed, you should have some business processes in place to determine how to verify that the person or business calling in is, indeed, a customer.

2. **Click the Account Name field.**

   The Account record appears. Verify the business's information on this record that helps you identify that you're allowed to support this company. You might verify an address or an account number. You should confirm those processes first before using cases.

3. **Look at the Contact detail list to locate the person with the problem.**

   Again, depending on your company's policies, you may or may not have specific customer contacts authorized to call you for support.

4. **Click the Contact Name field.**

   The Contact record appears. Verify information on this record that helps you identify that this person is permitted to call for support. If the contact record doesn't already exist, create a new contact record. For more information, turn to Chapter 9.

Entering new cases

After you qualify the customer, you have to associate a case to each new issue you receive. Because cases are associated with contacts, the best, most reliable way to create case records is by starting from the relevant Contact detail page. From the Contact detail page, you can add a case either by using the Create New drop-down list on the sidebar or by clicking the New button on the Cases related list. The result is the same in both situations, and you automatically prefill the Contact lookup field. By doing this, you can always find your case, and your case activities will be listed on the overall Contact detail page.

To create cases by using the best practice, follow these steps:

1. **From the Contact detail page, click the New button on the Cases related list.**

   The Edit mode of a new case appears.

2. **Fill in the fields as much as you can or as required.**

Notice that the Contact field is prefilled with the contact you were working from.

3. **When you're done, click one of the following buttons:**

- *Save:* Brings up the Case detail page.

- *Save & Close:* Saves the current case info and automatically takes you to the Close Case detail page, as shown in Figure 13-3, where you select the appropriate closed case status and add additional details. Use this page to quickly resolve an issue.

![Close Case screen showing Case Edit with Case Information section: Status "Closed", Case Reason "Installation", Internal Comments "Ask to receive cell phone photo of cord; could be caused by rodents." Solution Information section: Submit to public solutions checkbox, Solution Title "Power cord is frayed", Solution Details. Save and Cancel buttons.]

FIGURE 13-3:
Closing a case.

- *Save & New:* Saves the current contact info and automatically opens a new, blank contact record.

- *Check Spelling:* Checks the spelling of the contents of the Description field.

TIP

To clone a case, click the Clone button at the top or bottom of the case record. If it's the day of a new product or feature release, and many customers are reporting the same problem, the Clone button will come in handy for you. Just remember to still skim the new copy that was cloned, to make sure you change certain fields (like the Contact), to be relevant for each customer. This is similar behavior across other records in the Salesforce family.

TECHNICAL
STUFF

You can also set up Salesforce to generate a new case from an email sent to a specific address (like support@yourcompany.com), also known as the Email-to-Case feature. You have a few options, depending on your company's email requirements. Or, you could always have a Web-to-Case form set up (similar to the Web-to-Leads form that we discuss in Chapter 15). For details on how to set up Email-to-Case, read *Salesforce Service Cloud For Dummies*.

Managing Cases

As a service or support agent, one of your key goals as a case owner is to address and resolve many customer issues as quickly as possible. Ideally, the need for speed is balanced with some defined processes to ensure a sense of order. Over time, your caseload will build up as different cases take different lengths of time to resolve. You'll work off the Cases home page, which you access by clicking the Cases tab at the top of the page. There you'll be able to see the most recent cases and adjust your views so that you can see the cases that are most relevant to you. For example, maybe you handle all the Platinum requests for the West Coast and just want to see those. In the following sections, we discuss how to manage your growing caseload.

If your company has several agents resolving cases for a variety of products and services, your administrator may set up *case queues* to automatically funnel cases to the right pairs of eyeballs. For example, you may use your website to collect both product and billing inquiries. Case queues would allow support agents to grab new cases from the product queue, while accounting operations staff can monitor the billing queue. Queues ensure that everyone has an equal chance at the latest cases.

Case queues are accessed from the same location as case views — the Case View drop-down list on the Cases home page.

To choose a case from a queue, follow these steps:

1. **From the Cases home page, select the view that corresponds to a queue that you're supposed to monitor.**

   The list page appears.

2. **In the Action column of the case list, select the check boxes for the case records that you want to accept and begin working on.**

   If you don't see an Accept hyperlink, you're probably looking at a list view instead. See Chapter 17 for more information on list views.

3. **Click Accept to take ownership of these cases.**

   You've now claimed these cases from the general pool of new cases.

Communicating the Outcome

After you research your case and find the right solutions for it, you must communicate this resolution to your customer before you officially mark the case closed. Make sure that your administrator has created appropriate case resolution emails for your support team.

Responding with standard email templates

Standard email templates allow you to merge your attached solutions into the body of an email template, which you then send to your customer. This increases the efficiency with which the support team can answer questions. For information on providing a response to a customer using an email template, turn to Chapter 5.

Closing a case

After you resolve your case and successfully notify your customer, it's time to close the case and move on to the next one. One of the key advantages of Salesforce is its easy-to-use reporting system (more about that in Chapter 23). Additional information is collected after you close a case, so support executives can use the collective feedback to continuously improve the customer experience.

To close a case, follow these steps:

1. **From the case record, click the Close Case button.**

   Alternatively, if you're on the Edit page for the case record, click Save & Close.

   The Close Case page appears in Edit mode.

2. **Select the appropriate closed case status and add any internal comments, if needed.**

   Other fields are shown based on your company's customizations.

3. **Click Save when you're finished.**

Solutions are a feature that is no longer being enhanced by Salesforce.com. Service Cloud does allow the ability to create and apply canned responses to cases, to reduce repetitive typing by agents for commonly reported issues. If you want to learn more about options available, check out *Salesforce Service Cloud For Dummies*.

Chapter 14

Diversifying Your Support Channels

C ase management is the heart of any support strategy, and Salesforce Service Cloud highlights this by giving you the tools to provide excellent customer service through a wide range of channels. In an increasingly connected social world, conventional (and more operationally expensive) service channels such as call centers can no longer be the only source of service.

Today's consumer seeks immediate service around the clock through a variety of devices and channels, without listening to hold music or repeating the issue to multiple reps. The modern customer leaves public feedback, making the customer's experience critical to your company's image and success.

No matter which channel(s) your business employs, Service Cloud gives you the tools to successfully support your multi-channel strategy to deliver consistently high-quality customer support anytime and anywhere.

In this chapter, we lay out how to prepare for your multi-channel strategy. We talk about some of the more popular support channels and show you how you can better direct your customers to self-service options. Then we take a quick look at how Communities play into your multi-channel approach to servicing your customer base.

Preparing Your Salesforce Service Cloud Strategy

As is the case with any new endeavor, you need to put some time and thought into a viable strategy to set you up for success. In order to prepare for some of the great Service Cloud features available to you, think about what you want to get out of this project. Are you having problems keeping your customers happy? Are you looking to reduce cost? Increase profit margins? Maybe you just want to reduce call agent attrition and make their lives easier? Identifying these reasons upfront will help you plan where you're going with your implementation.

Planning the implementation

As a support executive, if you want to get Service Cloud working for you, you need to do some careful upfront planning. After you think through your processes, you can customize cases either by yourself or with your Service Cloud administrator.

TIP

Here are some tips to think about before you get started:

>> **Define and prioritize your service and support objectives.**

>> **Identify and acknowledge your key challenges.** Try to identify the biggest ones first.

>> **Start with the end in mind.** The best way to customize your application is to decide what you want to measure first.

>> **Map out your key processes.** If you're a Visio whiz, use that tool. If not, grab a marker and diagram your key processes on a whiteboard or flip chart. For different types of support issues, think about the similar and different types of information that you want your reps to capture.

>> **Figure out the best approach for your business.** You have many different ways to tackle a business issue with Service Cloud — some of these approaches work better than others.

>> **Assess how much of your support efforts you and your team can share with your customers.** If your users would welcome this sort of change, you may want to set up the community.

>> **Keep it simple.** Don't sacrifice your objectives just to keep things simple. The more complexity you build, the greater the risk that people won't use the application.

TIP

For cases, as with other objects, Service Cloud provides some common design elements that let you customize the record. As you consider customizing cases, keep in mind that you should strive for ease of use, relevance, and data that can help you manage your support executive job while allowing your agents to efficiently manage theirs. (See Chapter 17 for the how-to details on adding new fields, customizing page layouts, adding record types, and other design tricks.)

Identifying your support channels

When you've decided that you want to provide multiple channels for your customers to get the support they need, you need to do some upfront work to determine which channels you'll support, as well as how it all comes together. By offering various avenues through which your customers can get to your agents, you'll quickly learn that in doing so you are not only increasing customer (and call center employee) satisfaction, but also reducing expenses as call volumes decrease.

Which support channels do you currently have? Make a list of what you have and compare it to your desired future state. When you're ready, read on.

Delighting Customers with Multi-Channel Support

Multi-channel support is an obvious boon to any organization with loyal customers. Offering your customers various means to reach the same end, issue resolution, has two key benefits:

» **Increased customer satisfaction:** Customers can interact with your business the way they want to.

» **Decreased operational cost:** Providing answers via multiple avenues keeps call volume down and your agents focused on more complex cases.

Where in the past each channel lived in its own silo (marketing owned social data, call center managers oversaw daily call volumes, and IT departments managed web traffic), Service Cloud offers a holistic view of customer activity and real-time analytics into the utilization of each channel. Now executives and key decision-makers have visibility into channel popularity and can nimbly pivot toward more frequently used channels and divest from those left in the dust. Agents see customers' preferred method of contact and engage with them the way they like.

Let's take a look at some of the features Service Cloud has to help you connect with your customers via multiple channels.

Web-to-Case

In addition to using the phone, your customers may want to reach you directly from your website. With the Web-to-Case feature in Salesforce, your customers fill out a brief form on your company website that automatically creates a case in Salesforce for agents to start working. You can quickly generate a standard HTML form to put on any page; when the customer clicks Submit, the form is sent to Salesforce's servers, which converts the information to a case. This is one of the fastest ways a customer can submit an inquiry, and one of the easiest ways to increase agent productivity and response time.

Web-to-Case is a certain choice for customer service because customers immediately navigate to a company's website when they have problems or need help. To be sure, Web-to-Case does have a few limitations and you do need to do some upfront prep work before diving in and implementing it. We go over those details in a bit. But Web-to-Case is one of the most common tools businesses use to automate case creation directly from their site, and after setting it up, you'll see how easy it is to do in Service Cloud.

NOTING WEB-TO-CASE LIMITATIONS

Before jumping in and discussing how Web-to-Case works and how to set it up, let's talk about a few of its limitations to keep in mind:

- **5,000 cases per 24-hour period:** If the number of cases entered via Web-to-Case exceeds 5,000, Salesforce sends an email to the address associated with the default case owner containing the additional case details. Salesforce queues these additional cases in a pending request queue and then submits them when the 24-hour period is over. If your organization requires the ability to capture more than 5,000 cases via web daily, submit a request to Salesforce.com customer support to increase the limit.

- **No attachments:** At this point in time, Web-to-Case does not support adding attachments.

- **No rich text:** Adding rich text area fields on Web-to-Case forms is possible, but the information captured within them is saved as plain text when the case is created in Salesforce.

- **No spam filters:** Salesforce accepts it all and does not natively filter out spam, although you can set up validation rules and workflows to filter out cases that appear to be spam.

Preparing for Web-to-Case

TIP

Ensure the following before enabling Web-to-Case to make the setup as smooth as possible:

>> **Create an email template for the customer.** Make sure you have an available default email template that your customers receive when they submit a case. Include a case number or confirmation number that the customer can reference. (See Chapter 4 for more information about email templates.)

>> **Create active case assignment rules.** Build assignment rules to assign a case to a default user or queue. If you don't have active assignment rules or if the case doesn't meet their criteria, the owner of a web-generated case will default to the owner indicated in your organization's support settings. (See Chapter 5 for more on setting up assignment rules.)

>> **Customize support settings.** Use support settings to select a default case owner that serves as a net for those cases that do not meet your assignment rule criteria. To do this, choose Setup ⇨ Customize ⇨ Cases ⇨ Support Settings, click Edit, and in the Default Case Owner field select the desired user or queue.

Now you're ready to set up Web-to-Case for your organization.

Enabling Web-to-Case

To set up Web-to-Case, you must first enable it for your organization. Choose Setup ⇨ Customize ⇨ Self-Service ⇨ Web-to-Case, and follow these steps:

1. **On the Capturing Cases from Your Website page, review the listed steps and then click the Generate the HTML link.**

2. **Move the fields you want to display on the Web-to-Case form from the Available Fields column to the Selected column by clicking the Add arrow.**

3. **Enter the URL to which the user returns after submitting the form, and click Generate.**

   Most web forms direct users to a thank you/submitted page or a support home page.

4. **Copy and paste the provided HTML code on your website or into a page hosted on your web server, and click Finished.**

   If this step seems too technical for you, copy and paste the code into an email and send it to someone on your web services or IT team.

TIP

When the web form is up and running, test the form by filling it out, and clicking Submit, and ensuring it routes to the appropriate party in Salesforce and captures the information entered.

Your organization is now able to auto-generate cases via a simple HTML web form that integrates directly into Service Cloud.

Email-to-Case

Service Cloud allows agents to quickly and efficiently manage cases through email as well. By sending an inquiry to an email address set up for your support team, Salesforce automatically creates a case in Salesforce and auto-populates relevant case fields, including any attachments the customer sends. If the sender's email address matches a Contact's email address in Salesforce, Email-to-Case will associate the new case to that Contact record, as well as the Contact's Account record. What's more, agents can reply to the email directly from the case, capturing the entire email thread and customer interaction in one place.

Computer telephony integration (CTI)

The more traditional support channel, the telephone, is not going away anytime soon. Service Cloud supports phone inquiry efficiency in call centers, which is just as important as more modern channels. CTI — technology that facilitates the interaction between or integration of telephone and computer — is commonly used in call centers. It comes in many shapes and sizes but generally reaches the same objective: enabling agents to respond to customers as quickly and effectively as possible with very little needed from the customer.

Live Agent Chat

Another way Salesforce allows your customers to reach you without picking up the phone is through chat. Live Agent Chat is a native chat application that is the quickest way to get in front of your customer and at the lowest cost to you. How customized you want your Live Agent Chat to be is up to you. It can range in complexity depending on that decision.

REMEMBER

In order to implement the feature, you have to enable Live Agent, create Live Agent users by giving them access to it, and customize it according to your preferences and settings.

Enabling Live Agent

To enable Live Agent for your organization, choose Setup ➪ Customize ➪ Live Agent ➪ Settings. Then select Enable Live Agent and click Save.

If the Live Agent menu does not appear under Setup, contact Salesforce.com Support to enable this feature in your organization.

After enabling Live Agent for your organization, you must either create or modify pre-existing user records to provide the relevant Live Agent permissions necessary for them to do their jobs. There are different aspects of Live Agent permissions that are enabled in different places.

Adding Live Agent users

In order to have individual users work as Live Agents and support your customers through chat, they need some minor adjustments to their user records. Choose Setup ➪ Manage Users ➪ Users, and then follow these steps:

1. **Click Edit to the left of the user who will be a Live Agent.**

    Alternatively, click the New User button and create a new user.

2. **On the user record, check the Live Agent User check box.**

3. **Click Save.**

If you can't find the Live Agent User check box, your organization needs to buy more Live Agent feature licenses.

Granting Live Agent users the right permissions

You've checked the Live Agent User check box on the agent's user record, but that's only half the battle. You also have to ensure that your agents have the permissions necessary to accomplish the tasks your company has set out for them. You can accomplish this in one of two ways:

>> **Profiles:** Create or enhance a specific profile to contain these specific permissions bundled within it and assign your Live Agent users to it.

>> **Permission sets:** Create a Live Agent permission set that contains only Live Agent permissions and assign them to the relevant users.

How do you know which option to take? Look at the number of users. Do you have 20 Live Agent users or 3? If your number of Live Agent users is small, add a permission set. Otherwise, create a new profile for your Live Agent users. Just be wary of creating too many profiles — administrating an environment with a large number of profiles can quickly become difficult.

ADMINISTRATIVE PERMISSIONS

All Live Agent users need to have the API Enabled permission.

STANDARD OBJECT PERMISSIONS

The object-level permissions necessary for your Live Agents depend in part on the features you're implementing. For example, if agents need to see visitor and transcript records, they'll need (at the very least) Read permissions on the Live Chat Visitors and Live Chat Transcripts objects. In order for them to create Quick Text, users need full access (Create, Read, Edit, Delete) permissions on the Quick Text object, while seeing Live Agent Sessions requires at least Read permissions on that object.

REMEMBER

Managers or supervisors may need a higher level of permissions, such as Edit, in order to modify records that agents are working on.

Adding Live Agent skills

After setting up your Live Agent users, add Live Agent skills if your company segments agents into different skill groupings. For example, your customers are normally routed to a first-tier customer service representative for common issues (for example, resetting passwords, making address changes, paying by phone, and so on), but more complex problems are directed to second-tier engineers (for technical assistance and troubleshooting). In this case, you would create two skill sets to segment those agents into the appropriate skill groups.

In Salesforce, you can identify and segment your agents' skills and then assign those users to the appropriate skill set so that Salesforce routes your customer requests accordingly.

To create a skill in Salesforce, choose Setup ⇨ Customize ⇨ Live Agent ⇨ Skills, and then follow these steps:

1. **Click the New button.**

2. **Name the new skill.**

3. **Assign users and profiles to the skill.**

   You can assign both individual users that have the skill, as well as entire profiles.

4. **Click Save.**

The skill you've just created appears on the screen, with its name and its assigned users and profiles.

Assigning Live Agent configurations

Live Agent configurations are packaged pieces of functionality to manage Live Agent in the Salesforce console. They're also used to control the Live Agent Console, but this feature is no longer available for new Live Agent customers.

Like Live Agent skills, Live Agent configurations are assigned at the user or profile level and are responsible for toggling certain settings in the console, such as

>> The number of simultaneous chat sessions an agent can have

>> Notifications and sounds when the agent has a new chat request

>> Whether an agent can transfer the chat to another agent or even receive files through the chat window

You can assign different Live Agent configurations to different users and profiles, based on the agent's level of experience or expertise. Consider a new agent that is still training: That agent should probably be grouped in a configuration that allows no more than three chats at any given time. Similarly, you can assign a seasoned agent on your team a configuration that allows for up to seven chats at once. You may want to disable chat transfer for some users while giving this configuration to others.

Creating Live Agent deployments and chat buttons

If you're planning to implement Live Agent Chat, your website visitors need a clearly visible button on your site that indicates help is available if they need it. Chat buttons for Live Agent are what customers should click when they want to initiate a chat with one of your agents.

TIP

Talk to your IT or web team before implementing chat buttons. To customize them, you need to have a Force.com site set up or use some custom code.

You can put multiple chat buttons on your page or deployment, with each button mapped to a specific skill that you've already created. In this way, clicking an Internet Issues button will not route you to the same agent as clicking a Telephone Connectivity button.

Assuming you've already set up a skill or two, start building your button by choosing Setup ⇨ Customize ⇨ Live Agent ⇨ Chat Buttons & Invitations, and then follow these steps.

1. **Click the New button.**

2. **From the Type picklist, select Chat Button.**

3. In the Name field, enter a name for your new chat button.

4. The Developer Name field should auto-populate with the same name you provided in the Name field.

   The field will have underscores instead of spaces because it's an API name.

5. Choose a routing type from the picklist.

   This setting determines how customers are routed to various skills:

   - *Choice:* An inbound chat enters a queue, and any agent assigned the appropriate skill can pick it up.

   - *Least Active:* Automatically routes the inbound chat to the least active agent (measured by number of open chats) that is assigned the appropriate skill.

   - *Most Available:* Routes the inbound chat to the most available agent (measured by chat capacity minus number of open chats).

6. Associate specific skills with the button by selecting one or more skills in the Available Skills column and clicking the Add arrow to move them into the Selected Skills column.

7. Select the language for the text in your chat window.

8. In the Push Timeout field, enter the time agents have to answer inbound chats before the chats are rerouted.

   This only applies to you if you selected Least Active or Most Available from the Routing Type picklist in Step 5.

9. Fill in the remaining fields in the Basic Information section.

   If you have a Force.com site to use for button customizations, enter the information in the Chat Button Customization section.

10. Click Save.

   The button detail page is displayed with generated chat button code you can copy and paste into your site's HTML.

Deployments are places on your site where you deploy Live Agent Chat. You create deployments in much the same way as buttons. Like button creation, deployments also require copying and pasting provided code on each web page where you'll be deploying Live Agent.

There are more customization options for Live Agent that are not outlined here, but now you have the basics down and you're ready to start chatting with your customers!

DIRECTING CUSTOMERS TO
SELF-SERVICE OPTIONS

You'd be surprised by how many customers would prefer to get the answers themselves (if they only knew where to go), rather than call you. One of the most obvious benefits to implementing a multi-channel approach to your customer support business is that customers can help themselves.

Whether you implement Live Agent Chat to allow customers to contact your reps from your website without waiting on hold, or set up a community for customers to search frequently discussed questions or issues, you can allow your customers to solve their own issues, decreasing call volume to your call centers.

Salesforce Communities are branded online spaces for employees, customers, or partners to connect. You can choose to reveal a subset of your Salesforce data to partners, for example, so that they can help you work a deal. Alternatively, you can share files or answers to FAQs with your customers to help them help themselves. See Chapter 12 for more information on setting up a community for your channel partners.

You can also improve your agents' response times so that they don't have to constantly retype repetitive solutions, and your call center managers can track topic trends to provide feedback to product and marketing teams.

Customer service is more important than ever before to secure loyal consumers. As excellent customer service becomes an expectation and not a luxury, consumers are becoming more demanding than ever. Companies need to be proactive and can no longer afford to be reactive. One of the most effective ways to do this is by making your service about your customer.

Let your clients choose the way they want to get in touch. Provide different options for your customers to receive consistent service, regardless of where they are or what time it is. This is the essence of true customer support and is the purpose of offering a multi-channel strategy.

5
Generating Demand with Marketing Cloud

Chapter 15

Creating Campaigns with Marketing Cloud

Companies want to increase revenue by spending marketing dollars intelligently. However, because of the disconnect between sales and marketing teams, managers have a harder time executing campaigns, let alone tracking and measuring the results of their marketing programs. Now, more than ever, marketing departments have to prove that they're contributing to the sales funnel instead of being regarded as a cost center. Marketing executives have to show that their marketing spending is resulting in new customers. If this sounds familiar to you, campaigns in Salesforce can help you manage and track your marketing programs more effectively, helping you manage your customer acquisition costs, bring in more qualified leads, and contribute more to sales.

A *campaign* is any marketing project that you want to plan, manage, and track in Salesforce. The higher-level goal is to create something (a content piece or an event, for example) that generates demand for your product or service. Depending on your current or planned strategies, types of campaigns include trade shows, search engine marketing, email marketing messages, online promotions, webinars, online events, and print advertising, although this is by no means a complete list.

In this chapter, you find out how to create and manage campaigns, segment target lists, execute campaigns, track responses, and analyze campaign effectiveness.

REMEMBER

To administer campaigns, you must be a system administrator or a user with permission to manage campaigns (that is, a marketing manager type). See Chapter 21 for details on configuring your user information and profile to manage campaigns.

Understanding Campaigns

Available for users of Professional, Enterprise, or Unlimited Edition, the Campaign module in Salesforce is a set of tools that you use to manage, track, and measure your marketing programs. Its foundation is the campaign record, which can be manually or automatically linked to lead, contact, and/or opportunity records to provide real metrics on campaign effectiveness.

A campaign record comes standard with a set of fields that help you manage and track your campaigns. Here are the fields used most often to measure campaign effectiveness:

>> **Campaign Name:** This is the name of your marketing project. Choose a name that's readily obvious to sales reps and other users whose leads or contacts might be included in the campaign. For example, if you send monthly email newsletters, you might distinguish each campaign by month, as in "Administrators Newsletter — May 14" and "Support Agent Newsletter — June 15."

>> **Type:** This drop-down list includes the types of campaigns that you run within your marketing mix (Direct Mail, Email, and so on).

>> **Status:** This drop-down list defines the statuses of a campaign. Salesforce provides a simple default drop-down list of statuses to measure a campaign's progress, from the initial planning stages to completion. By using this field, you and others can make sure that the campaign is on track.

>> **Start Date:** This date field tracks when a campaign begins.

>> **End Date:** This date field tracks when a campaign ends.

>> **Expected Revenue:** This currency field estimates how much revenue the campaign will generate.

>> **Budgeted Cost:** This is the amount that you have budgeted for the marketing project.

>> **Actual Cost:** This is the amount that the project actually cost.

>> **Expected Response:** This percentage field is your best guess of the response rate of a campaign. For example, if your email campaigns typically receive a 2 percent response rate, you might use this value to benchmark the effectiveness of the campaign you'll be tracking in Salesforce.

>> **Num Sent:** This is the amount of people targeted in the campaign. For example, if you executed an email campaign to 10,000 email addresses, that would be your Num Sent.

>> **Active:** This check box marks whether a campaign is active. If you don't select it, the particular campaign doesn't appear in reports or on related lists and other campaign drop-down lists on lead, contact, and opportunity records.

>> **Description:** This field allows you to describe the campaign so that other users who want more detailed information on the campaign can get a solid snapshot.

TIP

Depending on your marketing processes, terminology, and goals, you or your system administrator should modify the drop-down list values and change the fields on the record. (See Chapter 17 for details on customizing Salesforce.)

If you're a marketing manager, you can plan and manage the majority of your campaign preparation inside Salesforce. You can

>> Lay out your entire marketing plan of projects.

>> Build the basic framework and business case for a project.

>> Define statuses and success metrics for campaign responses. *Success metrics* measure how you determine whether the campaign was worth your company's time, money, and effort.

>> Develop a detailed project plan so that important tasks get accomplished.

In the following sections, we show you where and how to accomplish these tasks.

Depending on the volume and variety of campaigns your company runs, and how complex your lead qualification strategies are, you may be using a separate cloud-based marketing automation product. Many of them provide integrations with Salesforce through AppExchange packages. It's key to understand Salesforce terminology for concepts associated with the Campaign object, because there may be slight differences in semantics with what another vendor may use.

Creating a new campaign

To create a campaign, log in to Salesforce and follow these steps:

1. Select the Campaign option from the Create New drop-down list on the taskbar.

A New Campaign page appears, as shown in Figure 15-1.

FIGURE 15-1:
Fill in the campaign record.

2. Fill in the fields as much as possible or as required.

If you manage marketing programs for your company, you should see few surprises in the campaign fields. See the preceding section for a summary of the standard entry fields.

3. When you're done, click Save.

Optionally, you can click Save & New if you have more than one campaign to create and want to immediately start on the next one.

After you save your final campaign, the campaign page reappears with the information you entered, as well as additional system-generated fields that automatically update as your company makes progress on a campaign.

TIP

You can associate campaigns to a parent campaign and see the aggregate performance statistics in one place. For example, our Salesforce.com For Dummies, 6th Edition Launch Event could be a parent campaign to other campaigns such as Email Drop, Banner Ad, and Dreamforce book signing. To group campaigns into a campaign hierarchy, have your Salesforce administrator add the Parent Campaign field to your Campaign page layout. You can then use that field to associate child campaigns with a parent. See Chapter 17 for more information on page layouts.

Modifying the member status

A *campaign member* is a lead or a contact who's part of a specific campaign. Depending on the type of campaign you're running, you can modify the campaign to have a unique set of member statuses. For example, the member statuses that you track for an email campaign (Sent, Responded) are typically different from those of a trade show that you're sponsoring.

To customize member statuses for a specific campaign, follow these steps:

1. **Go to the campaign record and click the Advanced Setup button.**

The Campaign Member Status page for your campaign appears. When you first begin to create campaigns, Salesforce creates a default set of member status values of Sent and Responded.

2. **In the Member Status Values related list, click the Edit button.**

The Campaign Member Status page appears in Edit mode, as shown in Figure 15-2.

FIGURE 15-2:
Editing the Campaign Member Status.

3. **Modify statuses by entering a new value in the Member Status column.**

For example, if you're sponsoring a booth at a conference, the preregistrants list is part of the package, and if you want to invite attendees to visit your booth, you might add member statuses of Registered, Invited, Attended, Visited Booth, and Met at Show.

4. **Select the check box in the Responded column to classify a status as responded.**

   This field tracks the Expected Response Rate field against the actual response rate.

5. **Use the Default column to select a default value.**

6. **Click Save.**

   The Campaign Member Status page reappears with your changes.

Building Target Lists

One of the biggest challenges that marketing managers face is developing the right target lists for a campaign. *Target lists* are the lists of people you're targeting in your campaign. Depending on the type of campaign that you're planning, your lists might come from different sources, such as rented or purchased lists from third-party providers or existing lists of leads and contacts already entered in Salesforce. If your target list is composed of the latter, you can create your target list directly from the Salesforce Reports tab and associate specific campaigns to those leads and contacts, or you may add leads and contacts directly to specific campaigns.

Using rented lists

With a rented list, your options are limited. Depending on the circumstances, sometimes you don't know who's on the list because the list is controlled by the vendor. Other times, you agree to limited use terms, such as one-time usage. In these circumstances, simply use the external list as the target list instead of importing the list into Salesforce.

TIP

You can use Salesforce to improve the quality of rented lists. Many third-party vendors look for duplicate names, confirm that they all point to the same person, and then help you merge them into one file. They do this by comparing their database against your customer database when they're generating the record count for a rented list. As long as you can trust the vendor, you can quickly use Salesforce to generate a file of your existing contacts to compare. By getting rid of duplicates first, you can stretch your marketing dollars by making sure that you're not paying for contacts you already have. And if you're doing a mixed campaign of rented and owned lists, you stand a better chance of not upsetting a customer with duplicate mail.

Importing new campaign members

If you own or purchase a list and intend for your teams to follow up on all the records, you can import the list into Salesforce as lead records and automatically link the records to a campaign. Here, we show you how to select a list on your computer to import, mass–associate various characteristics to the list (such as the lead source or campaign), perform the import, and verify that your settings came through.

To import a list and attribute it to a campaign, follow these steps:

1. **On the campaign record, click the Advanced Setup button, verify that the member statuses are accurate, and then return to the campaign record by clicking the Back button in your browser.**

2. **Click the Manage Members button.**

   A drop-down list appears.

3. **Choose the Add Members – Import File option.**

   The Campaign Member Import Wizard starts.

4. **Choose the right-pointing arrow (>) next to the Leads option.**

   This kicks off the Import Wizard. Indicate what kind of data you're importing (Leads).

5. **Select what you what type of import you want to do.**

   You can choose to add new records, update existing ones, or both. In this example, select Add New Records. The selected option expands.

6. **If your import included leads that may already be in Salesforce, choose an option for the Match Lead By picklist.**

   You can confirm an existing record by matching on the lead's name, its email, or a Salesforce unique ID.

7. **(Optional) Use the drop-down list to select a lead source that the imported leads will be associated with.**

8. **(Optional) Use the next drop-down list to select an assignment rule.**

9. **(Optional) Select the Use Assignment Rule Settings to Send Notification Emails to Record Owners check box.**

10. **By default, these imported leads will be assigned to the campaign that you were on before invoking the Import Wizard.**

11. **(Optional) Select the Trigger Workflow Rules and Processes check box if you want workflow rules and processes to kick in on these records.**

12. **Prepare your file, following the instructions that the wizard gives you.**

Here are the main steps to perform:

a. *Add and fill in a column for Member Status unless all records will use the default member status.*

or

Add and fill in a column for Lead Owner unless you'll be the owner or you're applying lead assignment rules.

b. *Save the file in a* .csv *format on your computer.*

13. **In the wizard, click what type of** .csv **file you want to upload.**

A Choose File dialog box appears. Leave the Character Code option as is.

14. **Locate your file and click Open.**

The dialog box closes, and the filename appears in the field.

15. **When you're done, click Next.**

The Edit Mapping step of the wizard appears, where you confirm the mapping of the Salesforce field to the correct column in your uploaded file.

16. **Map the fields by comparing the rows in the Mapped Salesforce Object column against the corresponding CSV Header column.**

Salesforce will try to do some automatic mapping in an attempt to save you some time. If a mapping is incorrect, click Change in the Edit column for the row you want to fix. If a row didn't map automatically at all, click Map in the Edit column to establish the mapping yourself.

A pop-up window appears listing the Lead's fields. Select a field to confirm that you want that field mapped with the corresponding .csv header, and click Map.

17. **When you're done, click Next.**

The Review & Start Import step of the wizard appears.

18. **Review and confirm your selections, how many fields you've mapped, and how many fields on the** .csv **that you haven't mapped. When you're done, click the Start Import button.**

A confirmation window pops up. Because large files may take a while, you'll be emailed when your import has finished. Your new campaign members will appear under your campaign record, which you can access from the Campaign tab.

Targeting existing members with the Integrated Campaign Builder

Assuming that your company has already imported users' leads and contacts, you can build your target lists directly in Salesforce in three ways:

>> Associating existing leads and contacts en masse to a campaign

>> Adding members from custom reports

>> Adding members from a List View

After you link your desired leads or contacts with a specific campaign, you can begin to target them.

Adding members from a campaign record

To associate existing leads or contacts with a campaign you're planning, start by making sure that you can see the leads or contacts via a List View. See Chapter 17 for information on creating List Views. You can add as many as 200 leads or contacts per List View page. Then follow these steps:

1. **From the specific campaign record, click the Manage Members button.**

   A picklist appears.

2. **Select the Add Members – Search option.**

   In this example, we add existing leads. The Manage Members Wizard appears.

3. **In the Manage Members Wizard, do the following:**

   a. *From the Add Members subtab, in the Choose Member Type to Search section, confirm that the Leads radio button is selected.*

      This is the default.

   b. *Specify the Filter Criteria.*

      You may use an existing view or create new criteria now to get the leads you want for this campaign.

      If you're not yet sure what subset of leads to use, step back and give this some thought. Emailing all the leads in your database may not be a wise decision.

TIP

4. **Click Go after you select your criteria.**

   The search results appear below the filter criteria.

5. **Select the check box next to the appropriate leads that you want to be added to this campaign, as shown in Figure 15-3.**

FIGURE 15-3:
View leads to
associate with a
campaign.

REMEMBER

6. **Click the Add with Status drop-down list to immediately select and associate the member status with those selected leads.**

    Your selected leads now appear on the Existing Members subtab.

    Don't worry. If your itchy trigger finger got you to add some members before you were ready, you can use the handy Remove button to disassociate the members from this campaign and start over again.

7. **Repeat Steps 2–6, selecting new views, as needed.**

8. **Click the Back to Campaign:** *Campaign Name* **link below the Manage Members page name when finished.**

    The campaign record reappears.

Adding members from a custom report

As many as 50,000 leads or contacts in a single lead, contact, or campaign report may be associated with a campaign. To add existing members by running a report, follow these steps:

1. **From the Reports home page, click a custom report of the leads or contacts that you'll be targeting. (See Chapter 23 for more information on creating custom reports.)**

    A Reports page appears, as shown in Figure 15-4.

2. **Click the Add to Campaign button.**

    The Add Members Wizard appears.

3. **Select an existing campaign for the Campaign field. Use the Lookup icon to search for your match.**

FIGURE 15-4:
Add report
members to a
campaign.

4. **After a campaign is selected, choose the appropriate status from the Member Status drop-down list, as shown in Figure 15-5.**

FIGURE 15-5:
Selecting the
member status
for report
members.

5. **Use the radio buttons to toggle whether you want the existing member statuses to be overridden by this member status.**

   The default is to not override existing member statuses.

6. **Click Add to Campaign to continue.**

   Step 2 of the wizard appears with a status message of your attempt.

7. **Click Done when you've verified the information.**

   You're returned to your custom report page.

Adding members from a view

If you've followed our example to this point, from any lead or contact view page, you can add members to campaigns. Note that the capability to add members to campaigns from any lead or contact view page allows only marketing managers to select and add members one page at a time, so it's best for adding a small amount of members. If your view is more than one page, you have to advance to that page and then add members. To add a member from a List View, make sure that the view has already been created and follow these steps:

1. **At the view's results page, select the check box next to the appropriate member names that you want to add to your campaign.**

   In Figure 15-6, we add some contacts to a campaign.

FIGURE 15-6:
Add list members
to a campaign.

2. **Click the Add to Campaign button after your members have been selected.**

   The Add Members Wizard appears.

3. **Select an existing campaign for the Campaign field. Use the Lookup icon to search for your match.**

4. **After a campaign is selected, choose the appropriate status from the Member Status drop-down list.**

5. **Click Add to Campaign to continue.**

   Step 2 of the wizard appears with a status message of your attempt.

6. **Click Done when information has been verified.**

   You return to your view page.

Executing Campaigns

Depending on the type of campaigns you're running, you might execute those campaigns online, offline, or in combination. And, based on the complexity of the campaign and your resources, you can use Salesforce to assist with the execution parts of your campaign.

Delivering an online campaign

If you send email campaigns as part of your marketing strategy (and who doesn't nowadays), you can use Salesforce for elements of the execution. Those elements may include

>> **Exporting an email list** from Salesforce for delivery to your email execution vendor or internal resource

>> **Building a web form** to capture leads as part of your email's or webinar campaign's call to action (see the later section "Using Web-to-Lead forms")

>> **Using standard email templates with merge fields** so that you can control the look and feel of your messaging

You can use Salesforce to deliver and track mass emails, but Salesforce Sales Cloud wasn't originally designed or intended to be used for large-scale, mass email marketing. Some Salesforce customers use the mass emailing tool for small campaigns.

TIP

Salesforce Marketing Cloud and several email automation vendors have integrated email execution tools with Salesforce's Sales Cloud. With this integration, marketing managers can more seamlessly deliver larger volumes of email campaigns and track it in the cloud. The costs and functionality vary across the email marketing vendors, so check out the options on the Force.com AppExchange directory at www.appexchange.com. Search using the keyword *email* or talk with your account executive for more information on how Salesforce Marketing Cloud could help.

Executing an offline campaign

If you execute offline campaigns, you can also use Salesforce in a variety of ways to simplify the process. How you use Salesforce depends on the type of campaign, but here are some suggestions:

>> **If you're sponsoring a conference:** Set up an online registration form for your booth computers to capture information on attendees who visit your booth.

>> **If you're sending out direct-mail pieces:** Use Salesforce to generate lists for your fulfillment vendor.

Tracking Responses

After you launch a campaign, you can use Salesforce to track responses. In Salesforce, you have three basic types of tracking mechanisms, which we describe in the following sections.

TIP

To track responses on a campaign, you need to be able to view the Campaign related list on lead and contact records. If you can't view this list, see Chapter 17 on customizing page layouts or ask your system administrator for help.

Using Web-to-Lead forms

Whenever we help clients with using Salesforce, we take a look at their Contact Us web page. If it's filled with a bunch of email addresses (like info@mycompany.com), we immediately recommend that they get Web-to-Lead up and running. After all, a company with a website using Salesforce in this day and age should take advantage of capturing information via an online form.

Web-to-Lead is a Salesforce feature that enables your company to easily capture leads from your websites and automatically generate new leads in Salesforce. With Web-to-Lead, you can collect information from your websites and generate as many as 500 new leads daily. Say that you already have a registration or lead form on your public website. With Salesforce, you can — in minutes — generate HTML code that your webmaster can apply to your existing form. Then, when people fill out the form on your website, the information is routed instantaneously to users in Salesforce. By using Web-to-Lead, your reps can follow up on leads in a timely manner.

Specifically for campaign tracking, you can also create forms for specific landing pages designed for a unique campaign to capture information on a campaign member who responds.

Before you can capture leads from an external web page, though, you need to enable Web-to-Lead, add any additional custom fields to your lead record, generate the HTML code, and add the code to a web page. Of course, involve your web team and web designers to test and review the page before it goes live.

Enabling Web-to-Lead

All Salesforce customers can capture leads from web forms. First, check whether you need to turn it on for your company.

Log in to Salesforce and follow these steps:

1. **Choose Setup ⇨ Customize ⇨ Leads ⇨ Web-to-Lead.**

The Web-to-Lead Setup page appears. Under Web-to-Lead Settings, make sure that Web-to-Lead is enabled. You can tell by looking for the Web-to Lead Enabled check box. If it's selected, you're good to go. If not, go to the next step.

2. **If Web-to-Lead isn't enabled, click the Edit button.**

The Web-to-Lead Settings edit page appears.

3. **Fill out the fields on the page.**

Salesforce provides three fields:

- *Web-to-Lead Enabled:* Select this check box.

- *Default Lead Creator:* Use the Lookup icon to select the default creator for when a lead is generated from a web form. You usually select the user who manages marketing campaigns for your organization.

- *Default Response Template:* Select a default email response template. You don't need to have one, but it's a good practice to reply to leads so that they know you got their request.

4. **When you're done, click Save.**

The Web-to-Lead Setup page reappears.

Generating HTML

You can use a tool in Salesforce that takes the guesswork out of generating HTML code for your web forms.

To generate a general or campaign-specific Web-to-Lead form, log in to Salesforce and follow these steps. (If you just finished the steps in the preceding section, click the Create Web-to-Lead Form button on the Web-to-Lead Setup page, and you'll arrive here.)

1. **Choose Setup ⇨ Customize ⇨ Leads ⇨ Web-to-Lead.**

A Web-to-Lead Setup page appears.

2. **Click the Create Web-to-Lead Form button in the Web-to-Lead Settings section.**

The Web-to-Lead Setup page appears.

3. **In the Create a Web-to-Lead Form section, customize which fields you want to include on your Web-to-Lead form.**

Click a field name in the Available Fields column, as shown in Figure 15-7, and then click the Add arrow button to add that field from the Available Fields column to the Selected Fields column. Conversely, remove fields from the

Selected Fields column by similarly clicking a field name in the Selected Fields column and then clicking the Remove arrow.

REMEMBER

Balance selecting enough fields so that they help you route the lead to the right person with the patience level of the prospect filling out the form.

FIGURE 15-7:
Creating a Web-to-Lead form.

4. **In the Return URL field, enter a return URL (if known) and then click the Generate button at the bottom of the page.**

   The return URL corresponds to the landing page that appears after the lead has submitted his information online. If you don't know whether you have one, or which one to use, check with your marketing manager and your web manager. When you click the Generate button, a page appears with HTML code inserted in a box, as shown in Figure 15-8.

FIGURE 15-8:
Generating basic HTML for your Web-to-Lead form.

REMEMBER

If you're creating a web form specific to a campaign, create the campaign first, and make sure that you selected the Active check box for that campaign record. By doing this, you can select the fields for Campaign and Campaign Member Status, which enables you to track the specific campaign.

5. **Copy and paste the HTML code into a text file and send it to your webmaster.**

6. **Click Finished when done.**

   You return to the Web-to-Lead Setup page.

Viewing and testing the form

You can view and test the HTML code as an actual form by using your favorite web publishing application and a browser.

To view and test the form, follow these steps:

1. **Open a new file in your favorite web publishing program.**

   Popular programs include FrontPage, Dreamweaver, and HomeSite. You can even use Notepad or TextMate.

2. **Copy and paste the HTML code in the HTML mode.**

3. **Save the web page in HTML format (not .txt) on your computer.**

4. **Open a browser and choose File ⇨ Open to open the web page.**

   A web form appears with the lead fields that you selected. The form is relatively unformatted, but your webmaster can apply code to make the form fit with your desired look and feel.

5. **Fill out the basic form and click the Submit button.**

   If you inserted a return URL, that page appears. If not, a page appears that displays the information that was sent to Salesforce.

6. **Log in to Salesforce and click the Leads tab.**

7. **Select Today's Leads from the Views drop-down list.**

   The leads list for today appears. If the test lead isn't listed, click the Refresh button in your browser until the test lead appears.

8. **Click the test lead's link under the Name column to validate the information from your test lead.**

   The lead record appears and displays the information that you submitted. Don't forget to delete the test lead record after you're comfortable that everything's working!

9. **Scroll down to the Campaign related list.**

   You should see a link to the campaign and the default member status. If you selected the Campaign Member Status field when generating the HTML code, you can apply a member status to all leads derived from the web form.

Manually updating member statuses

If your campaign is designed to have recipients respond by phone or email, your reps can manually update records as they interact with campaign members. Reps might have to create lead or contact records first if you didn't build your target list from Salesforce. For example, if you rent a third-party list for an email campaign, the respondent may not yet be recorded in Salesforce.

To manually update a lead or contact responding to a campaign, follow these steps:

1. **In the sidebar Search, search for the lead or contact.**

   See Chapter 3 for details on using Search.

2. **If you can't find the lead or contact record, create it.**

   See Chapter 5 for details on creating records.

3. **Go to the specific lead or contact record page.**

4. **Click the Edit button, make any changes to the record, and click Save.**

   For example, you might use the fields to enter additional information supplied by the respondent.

5. **Use the related lists to log any related information or future activities.**

Adding a member to a campaign

In those circumstances when your target list was built externally, reps need to add the member to the campaign.

To manually add a member to a campaign, go to the lead or contact record and follow these steps:

1. **In the Campaign History related list, click the Add to Campaign button.**

   A Lookup box appears.

2. **Select the appropriate campaign view from the Search Within drop-down list to narrow your options, and use the search bar to find a campaign within that view.**

   The Search Results page appears.

3. **Click the campaign name.**

   The New Campaign Member page appears.

4. **Select the appropriate member status from the Status drop-down list and click Save.**

   The Campaign Member detail page appears.

Updating the status of a current member

If the lead or contact is already linked to the campaign in Salesforce, you'll want to update the member status when he or she responds.

To update member status manually, go to the lead or contact record and follow these steps:

1. **Scroll down the page to the Campaign History related list, and click the Edit button next to the relevant Campaign Name.**

   The Campaign Member Edit page appears.

2. **Use the Status drop-down list to change the status and then click Save.**

Mass-updating campaign statuses

If leads or contacts that are part of a campaign respond in a batch, you can do a mass update of campaign members. For example, if you sent an email campaign to existing contacts and received a batch of online registrations as responses, you could perform a mass update. The following sections tell you two ways to update statuses: in a campaign or in a report. Sometimes you'll be working directly out of a campaign. Other times you may be running a specific report that isn't campaign related (for example, an existing "Northern California Active Customers" report), but you may want to update the status of people who turn up in that data set.

Mass updating all member statuses in a campaign

To mass update campaign statuses for all contacts or all leads in a campaign, log in to Salesforce and follow these steps:

1. **Click the Campaigns tab and select the specific campaign whose members' statuses you'd like to update.**

2. **Click the Manage Members button.**

   A picklist appears.

3. Select the Edit Members – Search option.

The Manage Member page appears, with the Existing Members subtab selected.

4. Use the filter criteria, as needed, to narrow the members that you want to update.

You can also manually select which members to update by selecting the check box next to their names in the results.

5. Select members to be updated for this campaign, as shown in Figure 15-9.

You may select up to 200 members to update.

6. Click Update Status to apply the new status to your selected members.

A status bar displays the results of the operation. You may continue updating by selecting new views, or click the Back to Campaign: *Campaign Name* link when done.

FIGURE 15-9: Updating existing campaign member statuses in bulk.

Mass updating all member statuses in a report

To update the status of several members at once, follow these steps:

1. Click the Reports tab and scroll down to the Campaigns Reports folder from the left sidebar.

2. Click the Campaign Call Down Report link.

A page appears, allowing you to select a specific campaign.

3. **Use the Lookup icon to choose a campaign and click the Run Report button.**

   A Campaign Call Down Report for your campaign appears.

4. **Click the Add to Campaign button.**

   The Add Members Wizard opens.

5. **Confirm the campaign in the Campaign field. Use the Lookup icon to search for your match.**

6. **After a campaign is selected, choose the appropriate status from the Member Status drop-down list.**

7. **Use the radio buttons to toggle whether you want the existing member statuses to be overridden by this member status.**

   The default is to not override existing member statuses. However, if your goal is to update all statuses of members in this report, choose to override the status.

8. **Click Add to Campaign to continue.**

   Step 2 of the wizard appears with a status message of your attempt.

9. **Verify the information and click Done.**

   You return to your view page.

TIP

You may also mass-update campaign statuses for contacts or leads in a campaign by updating the information in a .csv file first and then importing it. For example, a trade show exhibitor may give you a file of all show attendees that you can cross-reference with leads that you invited. After you know which of your invitees actually attended, you may import this file into Salesforce. Just make sure to add and edit a column for Member Status (unless all records will use the default status) and have a column for Lead or Contact ID. Then click the Manage Members button, click the Update Status – Import File link, and follow the guidelines to update the campaign history. See the "Importing new campaign members" section, earlier in this chapter, for more information.

Chapter 16

Driving Sales Effectiveness with Salesforce Content

I f you, as a sales or marketing manager, expect to get the most out of your sales reps, you have to put the best tools at their fingertips. Aside from a desk, chair, phone, and some caffeine, reps need accurate and compelling documentation: sell sheets, white papers, case studies, and so on. All too often, however, sales documents reside in multiple places: network drives, emails, laptops, and so on.

If your reps are losing business because they can't access the right documents, take advantage of Salesforce Content, which you can use to store the latest sales collateral in an easy-to-use, searchable library. And as long as your reps have an Internet connection, they can access Content, even if they're sitting in an airport in Omaha, Nebraska.

What does an easily accessible library mean? If you're a sales rep or manager, this means spending more time in front of your customers and less time chasing information. If you're in marketing or product management, you can better control the message to customers with the confidence that sales reps are providing customers with the most up-to-date information available. And regardless of your role, you can individually store documents in your own personal folder.

In this chapter, we show you how to use Salesforce Content, as well as how to search for documents so that your reps can put them to work to sell more effectively.

Understanding Salesforce Content

Salesforce Content is more than just the place where files are stored in Salesforce. With Content, you get a full content management system that allows you to collaborate, manage, and share material that's stored anywhere on the web. Because it's part of Salesforce, Content can take advantage of all the other features of Salesforce, such as custom fields, sharing, validation rules, and even Apex triggers.

For companies that need to organize a large amount of current documents, Content allows you to search document contents, notifies you when content is updated, and tracks user feedback. All these features help to further increase your sales and marketing teams' productivity. Best of all, Content is built into Salesforce, so it's waiting for you to use as soon as you're ready.

Anyone who has ever managed a document repository can tell you that repositories need to be maintained to remain effective. If you sell a variety of products, for example, your product sheets need to be updated as specs change, deleted if you retire products, and added as you release new products.

And even though Salesforce provides easy-to-use tools to help you manage the workload of document control, keeping a large volume of material up to date can still be a daunting task.

If your company is committed to using Salesforce as the central repository for every department's content, you may want to consider using Salesforce Content for the following reasons: increased collaboration, document tagging, deeper search capabilities, and notification of content changes.

TIP

Before users can interact with Salesforce Content, they have to be granted permission to access that feature. Choose Setup ⇨ Administer ⇨ Manage Users ⇨ Users, and then edit the users that you want to have maintaining your content management system. Make sure that the Salesforce CRM Content User check box is selected for those users.

Creating Libraries

If you want Salesforce Content to be a highly effective sales tool for your staff, you have to organize your content so that people can easily find it. By using libraries, you can sort files into logical groupings.

We've seen many different and effective approaches to organizing libraries in Salesforce. Some companies like to separate content by product family; others prefer to take a vertical approach. The only right answer is the one that works for your company, so make sure that you spend some time deciding on a naming convention for your libraries. The My Libraries list on the Libraries home page will grow over time, so a clean and intuitive naming convention will help prevent a cluttered appearance.

The following is a list of common libraries that work for many organizations:

>> Hardware

>> Sales presentations

>> Product data sheets

>> Case studies

>> Professional services

>> Salesforce training

To create a library, you must first have the Create Libraries permission. (If you're not sure you have it, you can quickly find out by seeing whether you get past Step 1 in the following list. If you're not able to get past Step 1, ask your administrator to help.) To continue, click the Libraries tab to go to the Libraries home page and follow these steps:

1. **Click the New button under the My Libraries heading.**

   A New Library Wizard appears.

2. **Type a name and description for the library.**

3. **When you're done, click Save and Close.**

   The Library Name page appears, and you may begin contributing new content to your new library. You can return to your library at any time by clicking the Libraries tab and looking at the My Libraries list.

REMEMBER

As you plan your content strategy, keep in mind that not all sales documents need to be in Salesforce Content. Some may be better suited as attachments on an account record; others you may not even want to have in Salesforce. As a general rule, files that may be reusable or have wide applicability are good for Salesforce Content. Documents that relate to a specific record are typically more relevant as attachments on record detail pages.

Adding Content

Adding content to a library — also known as *contributing content* — is simple. To upload a new document, follow these steps:

1. **Click the Libraries tab in the Content app and then click the Contribute button.**

   The Contribute Content page appears.

2. **Click the Choose File button and browse your hard drive for the file that you want to upload.**

   Salesforce Content automatically uploads the file you select.

TIP

You can add a website link to refer people to an online video or to information stored on your intranet by clicking the Do You Want to Link to a Website Instead link.

After Salesforce Content uploads your document, it asks you to describe and publish your content, as shown in Figure 16-1.

FIGURE 16-1:
Contributing new content in Salesforce.

TIP

3. **Give your content a descriptive title.**

   Follow standard naming conventions within your company.

4. **Select the Publish to a Shared Library radio button to store this file in a library.**

5. **Select the appropriate library from the drop-down menu.**

6. **If you're not the file's author, select another user from the Author drop-down menu.**

7. **(Optional) Add tags to this document if you want to identify it with words that may not be used in the standard library definitions.**

   Separate tag words with commas. Be sure to use words that people would commonly search for when looking for this document. We recommend that you only allow a subset of content users to determine what tags should be used, if you want to use tags as an alternate way to better filter for content. Otherwise, you risk having redundancy of tag words (like *datasheet* and *data sheet*), which reduces their effectiveness.

8. **Click Publish when you're done.**

TIP

If you have some content that you want to share with two different groups, like sales and marketing, instead of creating a new library just to house their shared documentation, you can associate content with the two libraries by following these steps:

1. **Return to the Libraries home page.**

2. **Select a document from the Top Content section.**

3. **On the Content details page, click the Edit button.**

4. **Select the Library Actions option and then click the Share with Another Library suboption.**

5. **Highlight additional libraries with which to share this document and click the Publish button.**

Editing Content

After you contribute content to Content, you may need to update its details in Salesforce. Search for and go to your Content record from the Content tab and follow these steps:

1. **Click the Edit button.**

   The Edit drop-down list of options appears.

2. **Select the Edit Content Details option.**

The Edit Content window appears.

3. **Update the title and description.**

TIP

You can also upload new versions of files when changes have been made offline by selecting the Upload New Version option.

4. **(Optional) Add tags to this document if you want to identify it with words that may not be used in the standard library definitions.**

Separate words with commas. Be mindful of making the tag word too broad or too specific.

5. **Click Save.**

Anyone subscribed to this Content record will be notified of any new versions that are uploaded.

TIP

You can subscribe to a Content record by clicking the Subscribe button at the top of the record. You'll get an email anytime someone updates the file, along with an explanation of what changed.

Finding Content

You can search for content from the search box located on the Content home page. Click the Content tab to go to the Content home page and then follow these steps:

1. **In the search box, type search terms, as shown in Figure 16-2.**

Optionally, check the filter check boxes to only search within a subset of all your Content. Filters include standard attributes like the content's file format, or the author. This can also include everyone's tag words, which is why we recommend an organized approach to creating tag words.

REMEMBER

In addition to searching filenames, Salesforce Content searches the actual text contained in files of the following formats: rich text format (RTF); UTF-8 encoded TXT; HTML; XML; Adobe PDF; and Microsoft Word, Excel, and PowerPoint files.

2. **Click the Go button.**

The page reappears with a list of Content results based on your search.

FIGURE 16-2:
Search for
content in
Content.

3. **Select the appropriate check boxes for the file(s) you're looking for, and then click the Download button to save copies to your computer.**

Alternatively, click the Title of Content record to see a preview of the file prior to downloading, as shown in Figure 16-3.

FIGURE 16-3:
Preview content
before
downloading.

TIP

While your content is a work in progress, you can leverage the Files tab to combine the features of Chatter and Salesforce Content. You'll be able to share with specific co-workers or groups, collaborate and get feedback, and upload revisions. When you're ready to publish, head over to the Libraries tab and show off your work.

Learning about Files

The main purpose of Salesforce Files is to upload, store, and collaborate on files in the cloud. Using files, you can collaborate with other users in Salesforce by posting them to your Chatter feed or within records directly.

TIP

The maximum size for a file in Salesforce is 2GB, but only 100MB if you're uploading it via Salesforce1, the Salesforce mobile app.

You can upload multiple files simultaneously, directly from your local drive, into Salesforce's drag-and-drop interface on the Files home page, which you can see in Figure 16-4. You can upload every type of file — from PowerPoint presentations to videos, as well as PDFs and Excel documents.

FIGURE 16-4:
Using the Files home page interface.

You can also preview, download, follow, and share the file, directly from the list by clicking the bottom arrow on the file of your choice.

TIP

Files in the file list can come from a few places. Files uploaded to Content will appear in your list, as will a file that was attached or posted within the Chatter feed.

Finally, you can download Salesforce Files Sync to sync your files between your local drive and Salesforce.

Understanding Documents

Prior to the addition of Salesforce Content, you could store files in Salesforce on the Documents tab. Although not as robust as Content, the Documents tab is still available and useful in many ways. For example, you can host images referenced in email templates, custom apps, fields, and even Force.com sites on the Documents tab. These files typically don't change often and definitely don't need to be collaborated on, so you can continue to store them by clicking the Documents tab.

You can also think of the Documents tab as a place where system administrators house files. However, if you need the ability to preview files, collaborate on them with Chatter, or store larger files, those files belong in Salesforce Content.

Creating folders in the Document Library

To create a document folder, you must first have the Manage Public Documents permission. (If you're not sure you have it, you can quickly find out by seeing whether you get past Step 1 in the following list. If you're not able to get past Step 1, ask your administrator to help.) To continue, go to the Documents tab and follow these steps:

1. **Click the Create New Folder link under the Document Folders heading.**

   A New Document Folder page appears.

2. **Type a name for the folder in the Document Folder field.**

3. **Use the Public Folder Access drop-down list to select the access rights.**

4. **Click the radio buttons to select who should have access to the folder.**

5. **When you're done, click Save.**

   The Folder Name Documents page appears, and you may begin adding new documents to your new folder.

Adding documents

Before reps can begin using documents in Salesforce, you or someone in your company must first add the documents to the Document Library.

REMEMBER

When uploading documents, the file size limit on any individual file is 5MB. For some companies, this may be the average size of a PowerPoint presentation or a PDF file with graphics, so plan accordingly.

To add a document and upload its file, log in to Salesforce and follow these steps:

1. **Click the plus sign at the top to the right of your tabs and then select Documents.**

   An Upload New Document page appears.

2. **Type a name for the file in the Document Name field.**

   TIP

   If you want the document name to be an exact match of the filename, leave this field blank. After you select the file, the filename automatically populates the empty Document Name field.

3. **Select the For Internal Use Only check box only if you want this document to be confidential.**

   If you select this check box, you don't alter access to the document, but you flag your end-users not to send the file outside the company.

4. **Select the Externally Available Image check box only if you're uploading an image that you'll be sending in HTML email templates to people who should view it without having to log in to Salesforce to see it.**

   For example, logos or letterhead footers should have this box selected.

5. **Use the Folder drop-down list to select a folder.**

   If you haven't yet created the appropriate folder, or you don't have read-write access to the correct folder, you can first store the file in the My Personal Documents folder and refile the document later.

6. **In the Description field, type a brief description of the document.**

7. **In the Keywords field, type keywords that will help your end-users find the document.**

   Salesforce provides a Find Documents search tool on the Documents home page, so you should select keywords that you think your users will enter.

   For example, if you're adding a case study, you might enter keywords that include relevant products, customer names, challenges, and so on that sales reps could use for cross-referencing.

8. **Under the Select the File step, the Enter the Path radio button is selected by default, so you just need to click the Browse button to select the desired file.**

   A Choose File dialog box appears.

9. **Select a file from the folders on your computer and click Open.**

   The dialog box closes, and the document path is entered in the File to Upload field.

10. **When you're done, click Save.**

When the upload is completed, the document record page reappears in Saved mode with information on the document and a link to view the document.

Using documents

After you create documents in Salesforce, you can use them in various ways in the course of your selling. You can search for documents from the Documents home page or browse through your document folders. You can leverage an image that was uploaded from the Documents tab, in Email Templates. If you're an administrator, you can also customize the logo in the upper-left corner of Salesforce with an uploaded image, as long as it's at most 20KB and 300 pixels wide by 55 pixels high.

DIFFERENTIATING BETWEEN DOCUMENTS, CONTENT, AND FILES

If you're not sure where to store a file, that's okay. Here's a simple recap: Use the Documents tab to store images used in Email Templates and not to attach to records. Use the Files tab for collaborating on works in progress. Use Salesforce Content for publishing approved material throughout the business and delivering them externally. Use attachments for attaching files to records.

6

Mastering Basic Salesforce Administration

IN THIS CHAPTER

Customizing page and search layouts

Managing record types

Using dependent picklists

Setting workflow processes

Reviewing the Process Builder

Summarizing Actions

Chapter 17

Performing Common Configurations

If you're just beginning your implementation, Salesforce comes preconfigured with a number of common fields in simple layouts for each of the tabs. You could buy your licenses, log in, and without any customization, start using it to track your customers. So, why are no two instances of Salesforce likely to be identical?

The answer is a key ingredient to your success: The more Salesforce is customized to your business, the more likely your company will use it effectively and productively . . . as long as you lay a strong foundation (and using this book will help)!

If you're an administrator or a user with permission to customize Salesforce, you have a universe of tools to design Salesforce to fit the way you do business. And you don't need to be a technical wizard to make these changes. With common sense, patience, and a little help from this book, you can customize Salesforce on your own in a way that will allow Salesforce to scale as your business matures. If you're an end-user, you, too, have some basic customization tools you can use to more efficiently navigate Salesforce, and see the records that matter the most to you.

REMEMBER

You may hear the phrase *Force.com* used when talking about Salesforce's customization capabilities. That's the umbrella term used to describe everything under the Setup link, where all the many Salesforce customization features are located. It's described as the foundational platform that makes Salesforce and its many custom applications possible.

We could write another book if we tried to address each feature. In this chapter, we show you how to perform all the core customization options, including creating fields and rearranging layouts. We discuss certain customizations that end-users should be familiar with. Then, for companies that have Enterprise or Unlimited Edition and have complex needs, we show you how to develop custom page layouts, build record types that link to custom profiles, and use the Process Builder to map your business process right into Salesforce.

Discovering the Power of Customization

All your customization tools are conveniently accessible from the Customize menu located under the Build heading of Setup in Salesforce. Navigating the Customize menu is simple when you understand some basics. If you have administrative permissions, log in to Salesforce and do this now:

1. **Choose Setup ⇨ Build ⇨ Customize.**

   The Customize page of Setup appears, and the sidebar expands to display headings for the various objects that can be customized (see Figure 17-1). Under the Customize heading on the sidebar, you see a few select headings for other areas of Salesforce (such as Call Center and Self-Service), which can also be customized.

2. **Toggle the arrow buttons or headings that correspond to the major tabs, such as Accounts, Contacts, and Leads.**

   The sidebar expands with the different customization features available under each heading. These are all the things you can do when customizing a standard tab. Notice that although certain headings have more features, most of the headings have links to common customization features, such as Fields, Page Layouts, Search Layouts, Buttons and Links, and in certain editions, Record Types and Processes.

3. **Click the Fields link under a tab-related heading (like Accounts) on the sidebar.**

   A Fields page appears based on the selected tab heading. This easy and consistent navigation will help you through the customization.

FIGURE 17-1:
Expanding the
customization
sidebar.

TIP

If you hadn't noticed, the tab names listed under the Customize header aren't in alphabetical order. The list used to be much shorter back in Salesforce's infancy. Over time, more features and tabs (also known as *objects*) were created. You don't have to keep scrolling to find where a certain object header is listed. Just use the Quick Find/Search bar in the upper left of the left sidebar (see Figure 17-2). When you type a tab name or feature setting name, links containing those words appear.

FIGURE 17-2:
Using the Quick
Find/Search bar
to find account-
related settings.

Quick Find / Search... ⓘ 🔍
Expand All | Collapse All

Breaking down basic elements

When diving into customization, keep in mind these five basic elements of Salesforce:

>> **Records:** Records are the high-level data elements that capture information that's determined by its corresponding object (such as accounts, contacts, and opportunities) that are stored in the Salesforce database. Think of records like the skin that resides on top of your skeleton, both of which are objects. Each tab corresponds to a type of record. Records consist of fields that hold information specific to that particular record. If you think of the Salesforce database as a filing cabinet holding all your company's information, a record is like a type of form that you house in your filing cabinet. Alternatively, think of a driver's license as a record. There are fields and information on it that, altogether, are used to describe you.

>> **Page Layouts:** Page Layouts allow you to control how a page is displayed to users. Different users (like those in marketing and sales) may need to see some common fields on a Contact record, while also focusing on other fields relevant to just their departments. Different page layouts help different teams see fields that are most relevant to them, which helps with adoption and increased usage of your CRM system.

>> **Search Layouts:** This feature allows you to control how search results are displayed to users. It corresponds to the organization of columns that are displayed on a Search Results page, lookup dialog page, or record home page in Salesforce.

>> **Processes:** This is an option for some objects, allowing you to build various sales, marketing, and service processes in Salesforce that you want your reps to follow.

>> **Record Types:** Record Types allow you to offer certain business processes and subsets of drop-down lists to users based on their profiles. Not to be confused with a type of record (such as an account or contact), a record type, when used with page layouts and profiles, can make only some of the drop-down list values available to users within a profile. For example, an enterprise sales rep with a longer sales cycle may need to track more opportunity stages of her sales cycle, compared to a general business rep whose high-volume transactions only require tracking of a few opportunity stages.

Customizing for relevance

Prior to customizing Salesforce, your CRM project team should conduct a series of business process reviews with functional representatives or stakeholders of the teams that will be using Salesforce. In those meetings, not only should you map out current and desired processes, but you should also ask sets of leading questions that will impact the design of fields, records, objects, layouts, and more. Key questions should include

>> How do you define your customer?

>> What information do you want to collect on a contact?

>> Whom do you expect to fill out this information? Is that realistic?

>> How do you know that you have a qualified lead?

>> What do you want to know about an opportunity?

Use the answers to construct a list of standard and custom fields per object that you believe should be in Salesforce. That spreadsheet should include columns for field name, field type, field values, justification, and so on, and you should review it with your project team prior to customization.

When customizing, keep it simple at the beginning. Don't add or keep a field unless you ultimately believe that you or someone else will use it. You can always build additional fields in the future, especially if you build momentum based on early user adoption success.

TIP

When you create custom fields, fill in the Help and Description fields for them, too. This is often overlooked and results in future generations of employees often scratching their heads as to a field's usefulness. Custom fields get created over time and names sound familiar (but may be obvious in their differences when you create them), and this tacit knowledge rarely gets passed on. Consider the Help text as your future self, training the next new sales rep, marketing manager, service agent, and so on. Use the Description field to give a little more background to which group requested this field and to what they were trying to report with this data.

Building and Editing Fields

When it comes to customizing Salesforce fields, one word describes the experience: *easy*. The hard part is confirming why you want it, who will be realistically filling out the information that you want to capture, and whether this information will be easily reportable when hundreds or thousands of records have this data. The more relevant you make the record fields to your actual business, the better the user adoption batting average and the higher the likelihood of hitting a home run.

Adding fields

All editions of Salesforce allow you to add fields, but some versions allow you to add significantly more fields than others. For example, if you have Group Edition, you can add 100 custom fields per object; with Enterprise Edition, you can create up to 500 per object.

To add a field, click the Setup link in the upper-right corner of Salesforce and follow these steps:

1. **Click any tab-related heading under the Customize heading on the sidebar.**

   The options under the selected heading appear.

2. **Click the Fields link under the heading.**

   The Fields page for the tab appears, displaying a list of standard fields at the top and a list of custom fields and relationships at the bottom.

3. **Click New in the Custom Fields & Relationships related list.**

   Step 1 of the New Custom Field Wizard appears. Data types with descriptions of each of them appear in a list, as shown in Figure 17-3.

FIGURE 17-3: Choosing a new contact custom field's data type.

4. **Select a radio button matching the type of field that you want to create and then click Next.**

   Step 2 of the wizard appears, asking you to enter details about the field you want to create. These two fields are required:

   - A *field label* is what's displayed on page layouts, in reports, and to end-users' eyes (for example, "Reimbursement Date").

   - A *field name* may be the exact same as a field label but must use an underscore (_) as a substitute for a space character. Field names are used as an internal reference by Salesforce and are key for integration (for example, "Reimbursement_Date").

5. **Enter the details and click Next.**

   Step 3 of the wizard appears. The details page varies based on the field type you selected. For example, the settings for a Text Area field are different than for a Currency field.

   If your company's edition is not Enterprise or Unlimited Edition, click Save and you're done. If you prefer, click Save & New to immediately save this custom field and begin creating another one.

6. **For Enterprise or Unlimited Edition, use the check boxes to select the field-level security access and edit rights per profile and then click Next.**

   Step 4 of the wizard appears.

7. **For Enterprise or Unlimited Edition, use the check boxes to select the page layouts that should include this field and then click Save.**

   The Fields page for the selected record reappears.

Viewing and updating fields

On an ongoing basis, situations come up in which you may need to update the properties of a field. For example, management changes or adds statuses, nomenclature changes so that field labels need to change, and so on.

To view and update your fields, choose Setup ⇨ Build ⇨ Customize. Then click the Fields link under a tab heading under the Customize heading on the sidebar. The Fields page for the selected tab appears, displaying lists of standard and custom fields. From this page, you can do the following:

» **Update a field.** Click the Edit link to the left of whichever field you want to modify.

>> **Change the field type on a field.** Click the Edit link for that field, and then click the Change Field Type button at the top of the Edit page. Step 1 of the wizard appears, and you can follow the steps in the preceding section, starting with Step 4.

WARNING

If data already exists in a field and you want to change its data type, you risk losing that data. Also, not all data types can be converted into a different data type. For more details, click the Help link in the upper-right corner of any Salesforce page and type **changing custom field types** in the search bar.

>> **View the field and its properties.** Click a link in the Field Label column.

>> **Delete a custom field.** Click the Del link to the left of the field, next to the Edit link.

>> **Add values to a drop-down list.** Click the Field Name link in the Label column, and then click the New button in the Picklist Values related list, as shown in Figure 17-4.

FIGURE 17-4:
Adding a new picklist value to a drop-down list.

Picklist Values			New	Reorder	Replace	Printable View	Chart Colors ▾
Action	**Values**	**Default**	**Chart Colors**			**Modified By**	
Edit | Del	AMER	☐	Assigned dynamically			Liz Kao-Dummies5, 1/10/2016 6:44 PM	
Edit | Del	EMEA	☐	Assigned dynamically			Liz Kao-Dummies5, 1/10/2016 6:44 PM	
Edit | Del	APAC	☐	Assigned dynamically			Liz Kao-Dummies5, 1/10/2016 6:44 PM	
Edit | Del	ANZ	☐	Assigned dynamically			Liz Kao-Dummies5, 1/10/2016 6:44 PM	
Edit | Del	LATAM	☐	Assigned dynamically			Liz Kao-Dummies5, 1/10/2016 6:44 PM	

>> **Replace values in a drop-down list.** Click the Replace link next to a field. A Find and Replace Picklist page appears. Make sure to add the new value before trying to replace.

TIP

The Replace feature is really helpful when you have existing records with old values that need to be switched to new values. Take the Lead Status field, for example: You could use the Replace feature to update leads formerly marked as Unresponsive and replace them all instantly with a new value called Nurture. However, check to confirm that this doesn't impact any historical analysis that other teams rely on.

>> **Reorder values in a drop-down list.** Click the field name link in the Label column, and then click the Reorder button in the Picklist Values list.

Replicating your key standard processes

On certain standard records in Salesforce, you use a standard drop-down list to map your business processes.

You'll probably want to put some careful thought into handling each type of record. To define your standard business processes, do the following:

1. **Expand the Customize menu until you see the Fields links for various records (under the Activities heading, refer to the Task Fields link).**

2. **Click a Fields link under one of the records mentioned in Step 1.**

   The Fields page appears with Standard Fields and Custom Fields & Relationships related lists.

3. **Depending on the record you chose, look in the Standard Fields related list and then click the Status or Stage link to modify the corresponding processes.**

   In each circumstance, a field page appears with a Picklist Values related list, listing all the values within the process.

4. **In the Picklist Values related list, adjust your process, as necessary.**

   See the preceding section for details on updating picklist fields.

Understanding custom formula fields

A *custom formula field* is a type of custom field that automatically calculates its values based on the content of other values or fields. For example, if you charge your customers a shipping-and-handling fee based on the total quantity of a product listed in an opportunity, create a custom formula field called S&H that multiplies your total quantity amount with a predefined value.

To create a custom formula field, first define the task at hand. What is it you want to calculate? Then follow up to Step 3 of the numbered list in the "Adding fields" section, earlier in this chapter, and choose to add a Formula field. Then continue with these steps:

1. **At Step 2 of the New Custom Field Wizard, provide a field label and field name.**

2. **Use the radio buttons to select the format that your returned value will take and then click Next.**

   Depending on your selection, Salesforce may ask you how many decimal places you want your returned value to display.

3. **Type your formula in Step 3 (as shown in Figure 17-5).**

Salesforce displays two subtabs — Simple Formula and Advanced Formula — to help you with creating your formula, and adding your formula for Salesforce to process:

- *Simple Formula:* Reveals a subset of merge fields to add to your formula, along with standard math operators

- *Advanced Formula:* Reveals all possible merge fields for your record, provides more operators, and shows you a set of Excel-like function categories that you can use to plug into your formula

To use either, simply move your mouse over the tab that you want to use and click it. The body of that tab appears.

FIGURE 17-5:
Creating a
custom formula.

4. **Click Check Syntax when complete to make sure that your formula is up to snuff; then click Next.**

If you get an error message, go back and check your formula. Salesforce's error messages will tell you if it can't find the fields you're referencing, if you used an incorrect parameter, and so on.

5. **In Step 4, confirm field-level security for your new field and then click Next.**

Because it derives its content automatically, the field will be a read-only field. You just have to confirm who can see it.

6. **In Step 5, confirm which page layout you want to add this new field to; click Save when finished.**

The Fields page for the record reappears.

You don't have to be a math or Excel whiz to benefit from custom formula fields, although those skills sure can help you master it faster. If you're like the rest of us and you'd rather not even figure out the tip on your dinner tab, make sure that you go to the Help section from the upper right of any page in Salesforce and search for *examples of advanced formula fields* for a ton of suggestions on how your organization can benefit from prebuilt formulas grouped by specific topics.

Customizing List Views

If you want special lists for the way that you manage, let's say, your accounts, build custom list views. For example, if you're a new business sales rep who focuses solely on California manufacturing companies and always researches the prospect's website before calling, creating a custom view can help you be more effective because you can build your list of target accounts, define columns, and use that view over and over again.

To build a list view from scratch, using the Accounts object as an example, follow these simple steps:

1. **On the Accounts home page, to the right of the View drop-down list, click the Create New View link.**

   The Create New View page appears.

2. **Name the list view in the View Name field.**

   For our fictitious California manufacturing example, you might call the view California Manufacturing Prospects.

3. **Select the appropriate radio button to filter your results quickly by owner.**

4. **(Optional) Filter by additional fields.**

   A basic criteria query is made up of three elements:

   - *Field:* Select a field on which to search. One example is the Type field.

   - *Operator:* Select an operator for your filter. That sounds complicated, but it's easier than you might think. Taking our example, you'd select Equals from the drop-down list.

   - *Value:* In the third field, type the value that you want in the filter. For our example, you'd type **Prospect** because, for this example, you go after only new business.

5. **Select the columns that you want to be displayed.**

   Although Salesforce's preset views take common fields, such as Phone and Billing State/Province, you can display any of the account fields that you're permitted to see on your custom list page. In our example, you'd add another column for the Website field.

6. **Decide whether you want others to see your custom view.**

   This choice might not be available to you. If it is, select the appropriate option, depending on whether you want to share your view with others. If you choose to make it visible to certain groups of users, you can search for and select groups and roles of users who will see the view.

7. **When you're done, click Save.**

   A new list view appears based on your custom criteria. If you don't get all the results you anticipated, you might want to recheck and refine the search criteria. For example, if your company has a habit of using postal abbreviations (NY) or the full spelling for the State field (New York), this habit impacts results.

TECHNICAL STUFF

By default, each filtering criteria for your list view is joined together with AND parameters. If you want to get fancy with your search criteria, click the Add Filter Logic link to use a combination of AND and OR filters.

Working with Records

After you add records into Salesforce, you can make changes to them to reflect the natural evolution of your business and its processes. For example, opportunities may progress, stall, or fade away. Territories change, salespeople leave, or more are brought in. In the following sections, we cover common practices you perform on records: reassigning, cloning, and editing them. We also explain what related lists are, and why they're key to your holistic view of your customer.

Reassigning record ownership

You might find that after you set up a record in Salesforce (let's use an opportunity record in this case), you need to give that record to the right person. In sales organizations, management may have decided to reshuffle sales territories (again). Or your sales teams might be set up in a hunter/farmer configuration, in which you reassign closed opportunities from new business reps to account managers after a certain time has passed.

If you want to reassign a record, open the detail page for that page. In this example, we use an Opportunity record. Follow these steps:

1. **To the right of the Opportunity Owner field, click Change.**

   The Ownership Edit page appears, as shown in Figure 17-6.

FIGURE 17-6:
Reassigning an
opportunity.

2. **Select the user to whom you're assigning the opportunity.**

3. **(Optional) Select the Send Notification Email check box.**

   The recipient gets notified of the reassignment via email.

4. **When you're done, click Save.**

   The opportunity record reappears. The Opportunity Owner field has changed
   to the assigned user.

Cloning records

If you commonly create records that are similar to each other, use the cloning
feature to reduce unnecessary retyping. For example, if you're an account manager who creates work order opportunities for additional purchases from the same
customer, you might want to clone an existing record and change the details.

To clone a record (we'll use an opportunity in our example), go to the record that
you want to clone and follow these steps:

1. **Click the Clone button at the top of the record.**

   A new Opportunity Edit page appears, prefilled with all the data from the
   previous record.

2. **Modify the fields as necessary.**

   Pay close attention to content in required fields such as Close Date, Stage, and
   Opportunity Name because the information prefilled in those fields might be
   incorrect for the new opportunity. Review data in other fields to ensure that
   the information is applicable to this new opportunity.

3. **When you're done, click Save.**

   An Opportunity detail page for your cloned opportunity appears.

Updating records

In the course of working with your records, you inevitably collect information that you want to save directly in that record. To update your record (in this case, we'll use the opportunity as an example), do the following:

1. **Click the Edit button on the opportunity.**

   You can also hover your mouse over the specific field on that record that you want to edit. If a pencil icon appears to the right of the field, double-click the field to edit it. (If you see a padlock icon instead, that means the field is not editable, on purpose. Move along and pick another field to update.)

   To quickly access and edit related records, scroll down to the related list section of the browser page, and click Edit to the left of the desired related record. The Edit page for that record appears.

2. **Update the fields, as necessary, paying particular attention to keeping fields such as Amount, Close Date, and Stage up to date.**

   Nine times out of ten, you'll be editing fields that play a key role in your company's reports. By keeping your information up to date, you and other users can leverage good data when running their analyses.

3. **When you're done, click Save.**

   The opportunity reappears in Saved mode. The fields that you edited are changed.

TIP

For the opportunity record, you can keep track of certain critical updates to your record by using the Stage History related list. Anytime you or one of your team members who has read-write access to your record modifies the Stage field, you can quickly scan this at the bottom of the opportunity record page to see who modified the record and when. Other types of objects can also track the history of changes made to specific fields that you determine. From the Help section, search for *set history tracking* for more information.

Using related lists

Related lists. Say it three times so you don't forget the term. By designing the page with related lists, Salesforce enables you to gain 360-degree customer visibility and ensure that more detailed information is only a click away. For example, if you open an Account detail page for one of your major customers and scroll down below the record fields, you can see multiple contacts, activities, opportunities, cases, and so on listed as links from organized related lists. From these related lists, you can quickly open or edit the specific related list record. And if you don't see these links, you have work to do.

Creating Dependent Picklists

If you find your picklist values building up and affecting the user's experience, you should consider using *dependent picklists* to show values in one list based on what's selected in another list. For example, you could create a custom picklist field called Reason for your opportunity record and offer two sets of reasons, depending on whether the opportunity was won or lost.

Creating these lists is a two-step process. In our example below, we will use a standard field, "Stage" on the Opportunity, and the custom field mentioned above, "Reason":

1. **Identify which two fields you want to use when building your dependent picklist.**

    Think about which fields will dictate the drop-down list for what other fields. The field that determines another field's values is the *controlling field* and can be a standard or custom picklist or a check box. The field that's dependent on the controlling field to determine its displayed values is the *dependent field*. We cover this step in the "Adding fields" section, earlier in this chapter.

2. **Tell Salesforce about these two fields and their roles in this relationship.**

    That's what we cover in this section.

To define field dependencies, follow these steps:

1. **Expand the Customize menu until you see the Fields links under the appropriate tab (under the Activities heading, refer to Activity Custom Fields).**

    The Fields page appears.

2. **Click Field Dependencies in the Custom Fields & Relationships related list.**

    The Field Dependencies page for your record appears.

3. **Click New.**

    The New Field Dependency page appears in Edit mode.

4. **Select your controlling and dependent fields; then click Continue to determine what gets filtered.**

    A field can be dependent on just one controlling field. However, that dependent field may also act as a controlling field to daisy-chain together several dependencies.

5. **At the Edit Field Dependency page, select which dependent list items are visible for which controlling field values, and then click Include Values.**

   If your controlling field has several items in its drop-down list, you might have to click the Next link to see additional columns. You can also select multiple values at once by Shift-clicking to select a range of adjacent cells or Ctrl-clicking to select cells that aren't adjacent.

6. **(Optional) Click the Preview button to see a pop-up window demo your dependent picklist.**

7. **Click Save.**

   The Field Dependencies page returns with your new dependent picklist listed.

REMEMBER

Record types allow certain people to see the same subset of picklist values every time. Dependent picklists allow a user to see different subsets of picklist values based on what they choose in the controlling field.

Customizing Page and Search Layouts

Wouldn't it be great if you could take the fields on a record and rearrange them like jigsaw puzzle pieces on a page until they fit just right? Sounds too good to be true, but with Salesforce, you can do just that and more.

Use page layouts to modify the position of fields, custom links, and related lists on Record detail pages and Edit pages. While you're modifying a page layout, you can also edit field properties to determine which fields should be required or read-only.

And with Enterprise and Unlimited editions, you can create multiple page layouts and assign them to profiles, record types, or a combination of both. By doing this, you can ensure that different users are viewing just the right information to do their jobs.

Modifying a page layout

If you have permission to customize Salesforce, you can modify page layouts at any time. We typically recommend that you create some or the majority of your proposed custom fields first before rearranging them on the layout.

To edit a page layout, click the Setup link in the upper-right corner of any Salesforce page and follow these steps:

1. **Click any tab heading under the Customize heading on the sidebar.**

The selected heading expands with links to customization options.

2. **Click the Page Layouts link under the tab heading.**

The Page Layout page for the selected tab appears.

3. **Click the Edit link next to a page layout that you want to modify.**

A Page Layout editor appears, with the editor at the top and a sample layout below it (see Figure 17-7).

FIGURE 17-7:
Viewing the Page
Layout editor.

4. **Choose from the following options to edit the layout using the nifty drag-and-drop user interface:**

- *Arrange fields, buttons, custom links, related lists, and more.* By default, you see fields that go into the detail section for that record. Select other options to edit from the left sidebar of the layout editor. If you have a lot of fields to wade through, use the Quick Find search bar in the layout editor to quickly locate a field. If it's grayed out, it means that it's already on the layout — clicking it will take you to it. If the field isn't grayed out, you can then click and drag it from the main body of the layout editor to desired locations on the sample layout.

- *Rearrange existing fields.* Hover over them in the sample layout to highlight them, and then click and drag them to the updated destination on the layout. A dark bar shows you where the field will "land" after you drop it.

- *Modify field properties.* Hover over a field on the sample layout, and then click the wrench icon to the right of the field. In the pop-up window that appears, use the check boxes to modify Read Only and Required settings and then click OK.

- *Organize the record with sections.* Hover over a section header and click its wrench icon. Alternatively, click the + Section button in the main body of the layout editor and drag it to where you want it to appear in the sample layout. In the pop-up window that appears, type a name for the section, use the drop-down lists to adjust basic settings (such as columns), and then click OK.

   For example, on an account page layout, you might want to build a section named Strategic Account Planning to organize fields for account planning. When you click OK, the window closes.

5. **To preview the layout, click the Preview As button in the layout editor.**

   Select which user perspective you want to view. A window appears with sample data displayed in the layout as it's currently modified. In the preview window that opens, review the layout and click Close.

6. **When you're satisfied with your layout changes, click Save in the layout editor.**

   The Page Layout page for your selected record reappears.

Assigning layouts to profiles

After you create custom page layouts, you can assign your layouts to profiles. By doing this, users will view detail pages based on their profile and associated page layout.

To assign layouts to profiles, click the Setup link in the upper-right corner of any Salesforce page and follow these steps:

1. **Click any tab heading under the Customize heading on the sidebar.**

   The selected heading expands with a menu of options.

2. **Click the Page Layouts link under the tab heading.**

   The Page Layouts page for the selected tab appears.

3. **Click the Page Layout Assignment button at the top of the Page Layouts list.**

   A Page Layout Assignment page appears with a list of current assignments.

4. **Click the Edit Assignment button.**

   The page reappears in Edit mode.

5. **In the Page Layout column, highlight one or multiple cells by clicking the links.**

Ctrl+click or Shift+click to select multiple cells.

6. **From the Page Layout to Use drop-down list, choose the page layout that you want to assign to the selected profiles.**

7. **When you're done, click Save.**

The Page Layout Assignment page reappears, displaying your changes.

Changing search layouts

If you've ever seen some search results and wished that they showed a few more column headers, you're in for a treat. Search layouts allow you to determine which standard or custom fields appear as headers in multiple types of search features for your organization:

>> Search results from the sidebar or advanced search

>> Lookup dialog boxes that pop up a window when you click the Lookup magnifying glass next to a field

>> Lookup phone dialog boxes that pop up a window when you click the magnifying glass icon on a SoftPhone dial pad, which then allows you to make calls from your computer

>> Recent Records lists that appear on a tab's home page

>> Search results filter fields for narrowing searches

Additionally, you can choose to show or hide standard and custom buttons in a list view page.

To change a search layout, follow these steps:

1. **Click any tab heading under the Customize heading on the sidebar.**

The selected heading expands with a menu of options.

2. **Click the Search Layouts link under the tab heading.**

The Search Layouts Page for the selected tab appears.

3. **Click the Edit link next to any of the search features you'd like to change.**

The Edit Search Layout page for the chosen search feature appears.

4. **Move fields from the Available Fields column to the Selected Fields column using the Add and Remove arrows, as needed. Select or clear any standard or custom buttons that you'd like to have on your list view.**

5. **Click Save when finished.**

   The Search Layouts page for the selected tab reappears.

Using Record Types

If you're using Enterprise or Unlimited Edition, you can use record types to make subsets of drop-down lists, which are available to specific sets of users. For example, if you have two sales teams — say, one that sells into healthcare services and another that sells into retail verticals — both teams might share common picklist fields on an account record but with very different values. With record types, you can customize accounts so that the same Industry field displays retail sectors for one group and healthcare services verticals for the other. When you provide record types to your users, the big benefit is that you make common drop-down lists easier to fill out and more relevant.

You can build record types to support all the major records in Salesforce, including leads, accounts, opportunities, and so on. Before users can take advantage of the record type feature, though, you need to first create the record types and then assign them to profiles. The good news is that with the Salesforce Record Type Wizard, you can perform both actions in a series of guided steps.

TIP

Before creating your record types, check that you first added all values to a master picklist field (drop-down list). (See the section "Viewing and updating fields," earlier in this chapter, for details on editing drop-down lists.)

To create a record type, click the Setup link in the upper-right corner of any Salesforce page and follow these steps:

1. **Click any tab heading under the Customize heading on the sidebar.**

   The selected tab heading expands.

2. **Click the Record Types link under the tab heading.**

   The Record Type page for the selected tab appears.

3. **Click the New button.**

   Step 1 of the New Record Type Wizard appears, as shown in Figure 17-8.

FIGURE 17-8:
Creating a new
record type.

4. **Complete the fields at the top of the page.**

   Most are obvious, but here are three important pointers:

   - *Existing Record Type:* Choose from this drop-down list to clone from another record type. The new record type will inherit all the drop-down list values from the existing record type. You can then modify it later.

     If you choose not to clone, the record type automatically includes the master drop-down list values for both custom and standard fields. That's okay — you can edit the drop-down lists later.

   - *Business process:* On a lead, opportunity, case, or solution record type, select the business process from the drop-down list. See the preceding section for details.

   - *Active:* Select this check box if you want to make the record type active.

5. **Select the check boxes in the table to make the new record type available to different profiles.**

   If you ever need to modify the assignment of record types to profiles, you can do this from the Record Type Settings section of a profile page. Simply scroll down the profile page until you see the Record Type Settings section, click the Edit link next to a record type, and follow the easy steps on the page that appears. (See Chapter 19 for details on updating profile settings.)

6. **When you're done, click Next.**

   Step 2 of the wizard appears.

7. **Use the drop-down lists to select the page layout that different profiles will see for records of this record type.**

   You can apply one layout to all profiles or assign different layouts to different profiles.

8. **When you're done, click Save.**

   The new Record Type page appears with a section called Picklists Available for Editing, which list the drop-down lists on the record type.

9. **Click the Edit link next to a picklist to modify the values.**

   A Record Type Edit page appears.

10. **Highlight values in the Available Values or Selected Values list box and use the arrow buttons to build the Selected Values list as you want it.**

11. **Select a value from the Default drop-down list, if necessary, and then click Save.**

    The Record Type page reappears.

REMEMBER

If a user will need to make use of multiple record types, remember to add the Record Type field manually to a page layout. For example, if a sales rep sells both generators and engines (and opportunity record types exist for both), providing the Record Type field on a layout allows the rep to switch a generator opportunity to an engine opportunity, if needed. See the section "Customizing Page and Search Layouts," earlier in this chapter, for details.

Managing Workflow and Approvals

How many times have you lost or delayed business because someone forgot to do something in your sales process? With the workflow feature in Salesforce, you can create a rule and associate it to emails, tasks, and alerts that can be assigned to different users. You can also update the value of a field on a record if a certain rule occurs. Enterprise Edition and Unlimited Edition users can use workflow to automate certain standard processes to make sure that important balls don't get dropped. For example, if your sales reps create opportunities that sometimes require special pricing paperwork, you can use a workflow rule to automatically send email alerts and tasks to finance and sales managers, and you can set these alerts and tasks to go out a set number of hours later.

Before creating a workflow process, take a moment to understand some basic workflow concepts:

>> **Workflow rules** are the criteria you set that, when triggered, tell Salesforce to assign tasks or send emails.

>> **Workflow field updates** specify what field is updated on an object when a workflow rule is triggered.

>> **Workflow tasks** are the tasks that a workflow rule assigns to users when triggered.

>> **Workflow alerts** are the email templates that a workflow rule sends to specific recipients. (Before creating a workflow alert, make sure that you've created the email template that you'll be sending.)

>> **Workflow tasks and alerts** may be reused for different workflow rules.

To create a workflow process, first make sure that you can fill in the blanks in this sentence: *When X happens, I want A, B, and C to happen.* X is your workflow rule, and A, B, and C are the field updates, tasks, and email alerts. Choose Setup ⇨ Build ⇨ Create ⇨ Workflow & Approvals to begin.

Creating workflow rules

To create a workflow rule, follow these steps:

1. **Click the Workflow Rules link under the Workflow & Approvals heading on the sidebar.**

If this is your first time, the Understanding Workflow page appears.

2. **Click Continue after reading the overview.**

The All Workflow Rules page appears.

3. **Click the New Rule button to create a new rule.**

Step 1 of the Workflow Rule Wizard appears for your new rule.

4. **Select the type of object to which the workflow rule should apply.**

5. **Click Next to continue.**

Step 2 of the Workflow Rule Wizard appears. To configure your rule, do the following steps:

a. *Enter a Rule Name and optional description.*

b. *Decide when the rule will be evaluated by Salesforce.* The options are only when a new record is created, when the record is created or it's been edited and didn't previously meet the triggering criteria (listed as anytime the field is edited to subsequently meet criteria), or every time the record is created or edited.

> c. *Use the rule criteria to determine what conditions must be met to trigger the rule.* Use the Advanced Options for more complex AND/OR scenarios.

6. Click Save & Next.

The Specify Workflow Actions screen appears.

7. Identify what happens when the workflow criteria is met.

An action can happen immediately, or it can happen a specific number of hours or days before or after certain criteria are met. You can create new actions (see the following section for more information) or use existing ones associated with immediate or time-based workflow triggers.

APPROVAL PROCESSES

Approval processes are a more advanced type of workflow that notify users when an action is triggered, require the user to review and then approve or reject the action, and then set off additional actions. For example, an expense report may follow one route of approvals if it's for $250 or less and another process if it's for an amount more than $10,000. Before setting forth with activating this feature for a certain record, make sure that you think through the following questions:

- Do all records of this type absolutely require approval, or just certain ones?

- Who's allowed to submit records for approval?

- Should a record be automatically approved or rejected in certain circumstances?

- Should any actions take place on the record as it moves through the approval chain?

- Who should be able to edit records that are in the process of being approved?

- Who should approve or reject items? Can that person delegate that privilege to someone else, in his or her absence?

- What should happen when a record has received all necessary approvals?

- What should happen when a record has been rejected?

Although it may be nice to automatically shepherd an approval process through to the right people, make sure that your business process is fairly rock solid. For example, are the bottlenecks you face today in your approval process going to disappear, be reduced, or remain if the process is automated? If a busy executive needs to approve all the expense reports but he doesn't manage his email inbox well, you'll have to carefully set expectations about what efficiency gains you'll get with automated approvals.

Assigning workflow tasks

To create a new workflow task, first go to the workflow rule that you want to associate with this task and then follow these steps:

1. **Choose Setup ⇨ Build ⇨ Create ⇨ Workflow & Approvals ⇨ Workflow Rules and click the Rule Name of the appropriate rule.**

   The Workflow Rule page for the rule appears.

2. **Click Edit from the Workflow Actions related list.**

   The Specify Workflow Actions step appears.

3. **In the Immediate Workflow Actions area, click the Add Workflow Action button and select New Task from the resulting drop-down list.**

4. **Configure the task as you would a regular task, but note the Due Date field.**

5. **Complete the Due Date field so that the created task has a due date that's a number of days relative to a base date you select in the drop-down list.**

6. **Click Save when finished.**

   The Workflow Task page for this task appears. Note that the Rules Using This Workflow Task related list shows the associated workflow rule.

Choose Setup ⇨ Build ⇨ Create ⇨ Workflow & Approvals ⇨ Field Updates to select what field on what object changes when a workflow rule is triggered.

TIP

Using workflow email alerts

To create a new workflow email alert, first go to the workflow rule that you want to associate with this task and then follow these steps:

1. **Choose Setup ⇨ Build ⇨ Create ⇨ Workflow & Approvals ⇨ Workflow Rules and click the Rule Name of the appropriate rule.**

   The Workflow Rule page for the rule appears.

2. **Click Edit from the Workflow Actions related list.**

   The Specify Workflow Actions step appears.

3. **In the Immediate Workflow Actions area, click the Add Workflow Action button and select New Email Alert from the resulting drop-down list.**

4. **Complete the fields to associate an email template with a set of recipients.**

   Note that the recipients may or may not be Salesforce users. And remember that the email template must have already been created.

5. **Click Save when finished.**

The Workflow Alert page for this alert appears.

At the Specify Workflow Actions page, you can also click the Add Workflow Action button to have a new field updated, or an outbound message sent when a certain event occurs.

TIP

Understanding the Process Builder

Now that you've learned about workflow rules as a new Salesforce administrator, you'll find that you can reflect many business process steps in Salesforce with a few clicks, without having to stand in line and wait for programmers to get around to helping you out. For example, you can easily create a workflow to create a "Schedule on-boarding call" task for your success manager, three days after any opportunity over $250,000 reaches the "Closed Won" stage.

There are times when you may have to link several business steps, and find that manually creating workflow rules can get a little tedious. In the preceding example, you may want to instead schedule the sending of an onboarding email two days after any opportunity below $5,000 reaches the "Closed Won" stage.

In this section, we provide a high-level introduction to the Process Builder and its various steps needed so you can, well, build your first process.

Choosing to use the Process Builder

If you find that you have more than one "If this happens, then do that" process that you want to daisy-chain together and automate in Salesforce, consider using the Process Builder. The Process Builder is a more powerful alternative to workflow rules, and is accessed via a point-and-click graphical interface. It lets you build and see all the logical "if this, then that" actions for one business process. The Process Builder is available in Enterprise and Unlimited editions.

Some more commonly requested actions that Process Builder can perform that a regular workflow can't, include the following:

>> Creating a new record

>> Updating a related record in addition to the specific one that kicked off the process

>> Posting a comment to Chatter

>> Submitting an approval

TECHNICAL
STUFF

If you've inherited a Salesforce organization with a lot of custom code and have technical knowledge about Apex, review the details about Process Builder limits and considerations, accessed via Salesforce Help. Click the Help link at the top right of every Salesforce page, and type **process limits and considerations** for more detailed technical reading.

Creating processes

In this section, we continue with our high-level overview of what steps are needed to build a new process.

Before you dive into using the Process Builder, make sure you can sketch out your process as simply as possible. Streamline your process so you can explain, "If X happens, then Y. If X doesn't happen, then evaluate this other criteria and decide to do something."

TIP

If you start hearing yourself describe umpteen subjective exceptions like "Well, sometimes we don't do ABC; instead, we do XYZ if the sales rep doesn't like to do ABC" with no consistent pattern, stop and take a step back. If you can't explain the process using words that can then be reflected in a business process diagram, the technology won't be able to understand you, either.

REMEMBER

The goal of automation is to streamline the execution of repetitive business processes that impact the majority of your use cases, and to accommodate common exceptions. Check that your teams aren't overengineering a solution that is built for exceptions. Consultants and developers may willingly build you something that matches your exact specifications, but making that flexible and scalable in the future to adapt to changing business processes may be more time-consuming (or expensive) than anticipated.

A process starts when a record belonging to an object that you specify is created or edited. For example, a process can be built based on the Opportunity object, which you'll identify. The process can be run the first time a new record is created, or when the record has been created or edited.

Adding process criteria

After identifying the object that will start the process, you'll want to add in your various criteria. Think of these as the "ifs" in the number of if/then conditions that you want to build. You'll add criteria based on conditions that you get to set, either via filter criteria or by writing a formula. You can also set criteria to evaluate nothing, and automatically default to being true, which then executes the actions. An example of some conditions appears in Figure 17-9.

FIGURE 17-9:
Setting conditions
of satisfaction for
your criteria.

If initial criteria are not met, you may create further criteria to address what happens next. If you don't create other criteria and your one criteria's condition isn't met, then nothing happens. Which sometimes is what you want to happen.

Adding process actions

After creating your criteria, you need to define at least one action that occurs if those criteria are true. Actions can happen immediately, and more than one action can happen simultaneously. Depending on certain details (for example, if actions are executed only if specific changes are made to a record), actions can be scheduled to happen a set time in the future.

Activating and deactivating processes

After you've created your process, you'll need to activate it to make it live. If you realize that, after it's activated, you need to make edits to your process, you'll need to deactivate the process. If something is really not going right, deactivate it immediately. If you want to make a more iterative adjustment, clone the process first to make changes, then plan out a smoother deactivation of the outdated process, and an activation of the cloned-and-edited process. Even if a process is deactivated, you won't be able to edit it. This is most likely due to compliance-related reasons.

If you're up for diving into the details of building out your first process, click Help in the upper right of any Salesforce page; then type **process builder** in the search bar that appears in the Salesforce Success Community.

Creating Actions

If your org is using Chatter, you'll see that adding things to the Chatter feed is done by clicking icons and their related names that appear above a comment box, as shown in Figure 17-10. Those icons and their related names are collectively known as Actions.

FIGURE 17-10:
Viewing Actions on a Lead record.

As you and your users begin to adopt Salesforce more, you can really help accelerate user adoption by helping them reduce clicks and page scrolling for their most common tasks with Actions. In this section, we provide a high-level overview of Actions, various types of Actions, and how you can create new ones for your users.

Actions (not to be confused with process actions mentioned in the previous section) can be considered shortcuts to most common repetitive behaviors performed by your users. Actions appear in the top of the home page, or any record detail page for any object for which you have enabled it. Some of the more common terms that you'll hear include the following:

>> **Standard Chatter Actions:** These are the default Actions you see when Chatter is enabled for your org. They allow you to post a comment, share a file, embed a link, create a poll, and more.

>> **Default Actions:** These are canned behaviors that Salesforce has already created, which you can use to get up and running with Actions. Behaviors like logging a call or event, or creating a new contact, can be done from these predefined Actions. You'll have the freedom to decide which standard object records can benefit from this.

>> **Nonstandard Actions:** These are Actions that you create, because they don't already exist as default Actions. They don't require additional programming to create the Action.

>> **Object-specific Actions:** These are default or nonstandard Actions that are used for a specific object's record. This means that details from that related object can be auto-populated in that Action, to reduce manual entry and increase productivity.

>> **Global Actions:** These are Actions that can appear on any page, like the Home or Chatter page, or also on object pages. Unlike object-specific Actions, clicking a global Action creates records that have no relationship with the record from which the Action was invoked.

Figure 17-11 shows an example of global Actions that appear in the Chatter feed of someone's home page, and the various types of common behavior replicated by Actions.

FIGURE 17-11:
Viewing available
Actions on a
home page.

Creating Actions

Knowing where to go to create Actions depends on whether you want to create an object-specific action or a global one. Object-specific actions for standard objects are created from the specific object's section under the Setup ⇨ Build ⇨ Customize ⇨ Object Name ⇨ Button, Links, and Actions link. Object-specific actions for custom objects is also possible from the custom object's detail page under Setup ⇨ Build ⇨ Create ⇨ Objects ⇨ Custom Object.

Creating an action is straightforward, as shown in Figure 17-12. You tell Salesforce what type of action you want performed, what name is displayed for the action, and whether you want to accept Salesforce's default icon. For certain fields, you can assign predefined values, which helps the users reduce the clicks they have to make.

Lead Actions
New Action

Enter Action Information · Save · Cancel

Object Name · Lead · i
Action Type · Log a Call · i
Standard Label Type · Log a Call · i
Name · Left Voicemail · i
Description · i
Icon · Change Icon

Save · Cancel

After you've created the action, Salesforce displays what default fields someone has to fill out when she invokes that action, in the Action Layout Editor. You can move fields around, remove some fields, add some fields — all using the same user interface as the Page Layout Editor, mentioned earlier in this chapter in the "Customizing Page and Search Layouts" section.

REMEMBER

These are actions meant for quick creation and completion. Don't overwhelm the action layout with too many fields.

Adding Actions to page layouts

After creating your Action, you now need to add that button to the page layout for the object on which you want the Action to appear. We discuss how to access page layouts to customize earlier in this chapter in the "Customizing Page and Search Layouts" section. The point is that you can move your Action so that it falls anywhere within the list of other action icons. In Figure 17-13, a default action on the lead record has been moved to the first action.

Hide Feed · Click to add topics

Log a Call · Post · Poll · More ▾ · Follow

Subject · Comments · Followers
Call · No followers.

Name · Related To
Lead · Dave Carroll, Oracle · Opportunity

Log a Call

FIGURE 17-13:
Seeing your
action on the
page.

On the page layout editor, you'll see various Action layout options. *Quick Actions* are synonymous with actions we described in the previous section. They appear within a web browser page of a user's Salesforce Classic UI. Ignore the Salesforce1 and Lightning Experience Actions section — that refers to more advanced customization on a mobile device, or within the Lightning Experience UI.

Chapter 18

Diving Deeper into Standard Object Setup

I n Chapter 17, you get an understanding of the most common configuration options available to you out of the box. If you've read that chapter, you understand what it means to build fields, work with records, use record types, and get even more comfortable with business automation. In Chapter 19, we go over how to further customize Salesforce by building objects and apps that make sense for your particular business model. This chapter, on the other hand, shows you some specific configuration options for standard objects in Salesforce.

As you already know (assuming you've read some of this book before turning to this page), Salesforce comes preconfigured with standard objects and standard fields in simple layouts for each of these standard objects. We cover these objects — such as Accounts, Contacts, Leads, Opportunities, and Cases — in earlier chapters.

In this chapter, we set out to show users common configuration tools and settings as they relate to these standard objects, and what they do for your organization. We cover sales-specific standard object settings, and then discuss settings on marketing-related objects, followed by service settings. By the end of this chapter, you'll have a good idea of which settings can be toggled for specific objects, as opposed to the more general settings that apply across all standard objects in Salesforce.

Configuring Sales-Specific Settings

As you probably already know, Sales Cloud standard objects really center around Accounts, Contacts, and Opportunities. Of course, we can extend that to include a number of other objects. You're probably already raising your eyebrows and wondering about them. However, if we wanted to cover everything, we'd need a lot more blank pages and you'd have a lot more reading to do. Let's get into some of Salesforce's configuration settings that are specific to sales organizations.

Using Account Settings

You use an *account record* to collect all the critical information about the companies with which you interact. If you go to the Setup menu, you'll find some options under accounts that don't appear under other objects. One of those subheadings is Account Settings.

You can use Account Settings to indicate two default behaviors for your organization. The first toggles the organization's View Hierarchy link and the second enables Account Insights.

Showing the View Hierarchy link

In Salesforce, you can create account parent/child relationships to distinguish between departments, subsidiaries, or locations of the same overarching entity you do business with. For example, your APAC sales team can be selling to Goldman Brothers Headquarters in Hong Kong, while your central region sales director attends meetings at the Goldman Brothers office in downtown Chicago. (See Chapter 8 for in-depth information on account parent/child relationships in Salesforce.) The children all roll up to the parent (usually, HQ), and the tiers can be easily viewed in the form of an account hierarchy, as shown in Figure 18-1.

To make this tiered hierarchy visible directly from the account record, you have to enable this setting under Account Settings. To do this, choose Setup ➪ Customize ➪ Accounts ➪ Account Settings and click the Show View Hierarchy link. Now, when you click into an account, you see a link that says View Hierarchy to the right of Account Name, as shown in Figure 18-2.

FIGURE 18-1:
Viewing the account hierarchy.

FIGURE 18-2:
The View Hierarchy link on an account.

This step is important to save time when navigating between large volumes of subsidiaries or locations for a single customer. It allows users to view hierarchies visually, making the tiered structure less theoretical.

REMEMBER

You can't enable this link for a subset of users. When you turn it on, anyone with access to that account can see and click the link.

Enabling Account Insights

Account Insights uses third-party technologies (such as Twitter and news articles) to gather real and recent insights and news information about the account in question. It helps users and salespeople stay up to date on relevant accounts and industries they work with on a daily basis. For example, Account Insights can help a rep know that now is not the best time to reach out to his point of contact at Larry's Laundry, if news articles show that Larry's Laundry is currently under investigation for money laundering.

To enable account insights, choose Setup ➪ Customize ➪ Accounts ➪ Account Settings, select the Enable Account Insights check box, and click Save. Figure 18-3 shows what Account Insights looks like on the account detail page if you have Lightning enabled for your organization. See Chapter 20 for more information on the Lightning interface.

FIGURE 18-3:
Viewing Account
Insights on the
account detail
page.

TIP

You can only view Account Insights in Salesforce1 or if your organization is Lightning enabled.

Building Account Teams

If you work at a large company, you probably know that it takes a team of people to win complex deals and maintain large accounts. The Account Owner field may identify the primary person in charge, but often you need to know whom to go to for a specific purpose, or maybe the account owner is just out sick or on vacation. Account Teams lets you list all the individuals at your company who work with an account and detail their specific role.

To enable Account Teams for your organization, follow these steps:

1. **Choose Setup ⇨ Customize ⇨ Accounts ⇨ Account Teams.**

The Account Team Setup page appears.

2. **Click Enable Account Teams and then select the Account Teams Enabled check box, as shown in Figure 18-4; then click Save.**

The Page Layout Selection page appears, allowing you to select all the Account page layouts to which you want to add the Account Teams related list. If you have account types (and layouts) that never require team collaboration, don't add the related list to these.

3. **(Optional) Select the account page layouts to which you want to add the Account Teams related list and click Save.**

The Account Team Setup page appears, where you can choose to define team roles for your organization.

Account Team Setup

Enable or disable the ability to define account teams and use teams for accounts.

☑ Account Teams Enabled

Save   Cancel

FIGURE 18-4:
Enabling Account Teams.

Now that Account Teams are enabled for your organization, to give credit to your team and make sure that others know whom to call, go to an account record and follow these steps:

1. **Scroll down to the Account Team related list or click the Account Team hover link at the top of the page.**

   If you don't see the Account Team related list, have your administrator activate the feature in Setup.

2. **Click the Add button to add up to five team members.**

   The New Account Team Members page appears, as shown in Figure 18-5.

FIGURE 18-5:
Add Account Team members.

3. **Use the Team Member lookups to select fellow users of Salesforce who work on this account.**

   You can always go back and add more later.

4. **(Optional) Specify the sharing access you want to give for this account, its opportunities, and its cases.**

5. **Select the appropriate role in the Team Role drop-down list.**

6. **Click Save.**

   You're returned to the account record's detail page with your Account Team listed.

You can always define or modify the roles available in the Team Role drop-down list by choosing Setup ➪ Customize ➪ Accounts ➪ Account Teams, and clicking the Team Roles link. You can add new roles, rename existing ones, or just change the order in which they appear in the list.

REMEMBER

These Team Roles also define how they appear on Opportunity teams.

Identifying contact roles on opportunities

Adding contact roles to your opportunities is pretty easy (see Chapter 10). In case you don't remember, contact roles are really a way to specify the role the contact plays on this opportunity or in your business process. In this way, the individual or team that is selling on a given opportunity can better understand the players involved and whom to reach out to. If a business user asks for a new contact role or wants to customize the existing contact roles available on your opportunities, read on.

To customize contact roles on opportunities, follow these steps:

1. **Choose Setup ➪ Customize ➪ Opportunities ➪ Contact Roles on Opportunities.**

   The opportunity contact roles picklist values appear, as shown in Figure 18-6.

FIGURE 18-6: Customizing contact roles on opportunities.

2. **Click the Edit link to the left of the role you want to edit.**

   The edit page appears for the contact role picklist value you selected.

3. **Rename the role in the Opportunity Contact Role field, or select the available check box to make this role the default value.**

4. **Click Save when you're done.**

Now that you've edited the default contact roles for a given opportunity, you're ready to let your sales users select them. To learn how to add them to your opportunities, see Chapter 10.

Tracking different sales processes

The final sales-related setting that we cover is what Salesforce calls *sales processes*. In Salesforce, a sales process determines which opportunity stages are selectable for a given record type. (See Chapter 17 for more information about record types.)

You can create multiple sales processes if your organization has different types of deals that follow different paths to close. In other words, if selling one product line requires more effort, qualification, and stages than another, simpler product, you can use multiple sales processes to accommodate both.

To create a sales process in Salesforce, choose Setup ⇨ Customize ⇨ Opportunities ⇨ Sales Processes, as shown in Figure 18-7.

1. **Click the New button.**

   The New Sales Process page appears.

2. **Type a name for your sales process and a description to make it easier to identify later; then click Save.**

   The Sales Process Opportunity Stages page appears, as shown in Figure 18-8.

3. **Select the Opportunity Stage values for the process by using the add and remove arrows; when you're done, click Save.**

   That's it! You've created your first sales process and added the appropriate stages to it.

FIGURE 18-7:
Using the Sales Processes page to create or maintain opportunity processes.

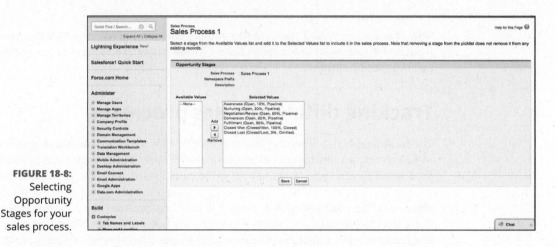

FIGURE 18-8:
Selecting Opportunity Stages for your sales process.

TIP

To use each of your processes, you'll have to associate them to your opportunity record types. When you create or edit an opportunity record type, you'll see a picklist value called Sales Process, where you can select the corresponding process for that opportunity type.

Managing Marketing-Related Settings

Now that you know about sales-specific settings and where to go to enable them, let's talk marketing.

Assigning leads

Nobody wants a database full of leads if they're not assigned to the right people. When you have incoming leads, you have to make sure they're assigned appropriately. To do this, you can set up some assignment rules to automate lead routing, as we show you in Chapter 7. Reassigning leads is easy — we show you how to reassign record ownership in Chapter 17. Use these out-of-the-box Salesforce tools to increase your marketing power and efficiency.

Choosing a default lead owner

Salesforce requires that you choose a default lead owner, so that new leads that come into your system don't fall through the cracks (assuming they don't meet any of your lead assignment rule criteria). The lead owner can be a lead queue, an appointed data steward in your organization, or your system admin, depending on the size of your company and whether you have a governance structure implemented within it.

To select a default lead owner, click Setup and follow these steps:

1. **Choose Customize ⇨ Leads ⇨ Lead Settings.**

   The Lead Settings page appears, as shown in Figure 18-9.

FIGURE 18-9:
Looking at the Lead Settings page.

2. **Click the Edit button.**

   The Edit Lead Settings page appears, with the Lead Queue Settings section at the top.

3. **From the drop-down menu, choose whether you want the type of owner to be a User or Queue, and then click the lookup icon and select the user or queue.**

4. **(Optional) Select the Notify Default Lead Owner check box to send a notification email to the owner inbox when the lead is assigned.**

5. **Click Save when you're done.**

Great! Now you've assigned a default lead owner, so your leads will be auto-assigned to this user or queue when they can't be routed based on other rules and criteria you've established.

Confirming lead conversion settings

Lead conversion is an important process in Salesforce, and we talk a lot about it in Chapter 7. There are three default lead conversion settings you can set up for your organization.

First, choose Setup ⇨ Customize ⇨ Leads ⇨ Lead Settings. You see the second section, Lead Conversion Settings, with three options, as shown in Figure 18-9:

>> **Require Validation for Converted Leads:** Use this option to enforce validation rules when converting leads.

>> **Preserve Lead Status:** This option comes into play if your organization uses record types on the Lead object. If this check box is selected, the Lead Status doesn't automatically change to the new owner's default value during conversion. Use this option if you want to keep the lead status as-is during conversion no matter what.

>> **Enable Conversions on the Salesforce1 App:** Use this option if you want to give users the ability to convert their leads through the Salesforce1 mobile app.

Capturing campaign influence

Campaigns and campaign influence are two cornerstones of marketing. Any marketing department sees the value in capturing the return on investment (ROI) of their campaigns and tying revenue back to their efforts. You can choose to associate influential campaigns to opportunities automatically or manually.

To enable the automatic campaign association to opportunities, follow these steps:

1. **Choose Setup ⇨ Customize ⇨ Campaigns ⇨ Campaign Influence.**

   The Campaign Influence page appears, as shown in Figure 18-10.

2. **Under Enable or Disable Automatic Association, click Enabled.**

   Now, if a campaign is related to a contact role on an opportunity and the opportunity hasn't closed, the campaign will automatically be associated with that opportunity. For example, select Disabled if you prefer to manage and associate influential campaigns manually on a one-off basis using the Campaign Influence related list.

3. **(Optional) Enter a Campaign Influence Time Frame.**

   This allows you to designate the maximum number of days between the date when the campaign was first associated and the date the opportunity was created. For example, if you enter 20 days as the time frame, and one of your contacts becomes a member of a campaign on August 1, the campaign will be considered influential to any opportunity associated with that contact by August 20.

4. **(Optional) Create association rules to add additional criteria that campaigns must meet in order to be automatically associated with an opportunity.**

Setting Customizations for Your Service Organizations

The service side of Salesforce also has some settings that need to be taken into account when setting up cases and other service-oriented objects. Let's jump in and take a look at what we can configure out of the box.

Understanding Support Settings for your cases

Support Settings are fairly comprehensive in Salesforce, and we don't go into every one. However, we do cover the most commonly used settings, and for the rest, you can consult other resources, like *Salesforce Service Cloud For Dummies*, by Jon Paz and TJ Kelley (Wiley), to get the help you need.

To get to the Support Settings, shown in Figure 18-11, choose Setup ➪ Customize ➪ Cases ➪ Support Settings. Here are some common settings:

>> **Default Case Owner:** A required field that defaults to an owner for cases when case assignment rules fail to locate one.

FIGURE 18-11:
The Support Settings page.

Support Settings

The Support Settings specify the defaults and email templates used by the automated support features.

Edit

Default Case Owner	Jon Paz	The default owner of a case when assignment rules fail to locate an owner.
Notify Default Case Owner		
Automated Case User	Jon Paz	The user listed in the Case History related list for automated case changes from: • Assignment rules • Escalation rules • On-Demand Email-to-Case • Cases logged in the Self-Service portal
Case Creation Template	-- None --	Use this template to notify contacts that a case has been created or updated for them.
Case Assigned Template	-- None --	Use this template to notify your users a case has been assigned to them.
Case Close Template	-- None --	Use this template to notify contacts that a case has been closed.
New Cases Visible in Portal	✓	Should the newly created cases be visible in the portal?
Enable Case Comment Notification to Contacts		Use this setting to specify whether contacts who are not members of your Self-Service portal can be notified when a new comment is added to a case.
Notify Case Owner of New Case Comments		Use this setting to notify case owner when a comment is added to a case.
Early Triggers Enabled		Use this setting to enable early triggers on escalation rules.

>> **Automated Case User:** A required field that is listed as the actor in the Case History related list for automated case changes, such as when escalation or assignment rules fire.

It's usually best to have the Automate Case User be a Service Cloud admin or super user.

>> **Show Closed Statuses in Case Status Field:** Select this option if you'd rather not have users fill out information on a separate closed case page layout and you'd prefer to let them just close out a case quickly through the status picklist.

>> **Enable Case Feed Actions and Feed Items:** Select this option to change your cases to the upgraded case user interface. You'll have to also give users access to the Case Feed.

For more in-depth information about these options and others, see *Salesforce Service Cloud For Dummies*.

Defining escalation rules

Escalation rules are criteria and rules you define when you want cases to be automatically escalated. For example, let's say you have three different tiers of support: Gold, Silver, and Bronze. You can create different escalation rules to say that if a case with Gold support isn't resolved within 24 hours, it will be escalated to a support manager.

To create an escalation rule, choose Setup ➪ Customize ➪ Cases ➪ Escalation Rules, and follow these steps:

1. **Click the New button to create a new escalation rule, enter a name for it, and click Save.**

   Don't select the Active check box until you're done with the escalation rule and you deactivate any currently active rules.

2. **Click the new escalation rule you created, and then click the New button in the Rule Entry list.**

   The Rule Entry Edit page appears, as shown in Figure 18-12.

FIGURE 18-12:
Entering rule entry criteria for your escalation rule.

3. **Enter the sort order in which Salesforce will run this particular rule entry.**

   This comes into play when you have multiple rules. Salesforce evaluates each entry in the order you designate and stops looking when it finds a criteria match.

4. **Select criteria for the rule entry.**

   In Figure 18-12, the rule entry indicates three criteria that, if met, will automatically escalate the case. If the case is (a) high priority, (b) a problem (as opposed to an inquiry or feature request type of case), and (c) owned by Tier 1 (or the highest tier of support), the case will be escalated.

5. **Select the business hours criteria for the rule.**

   You can choose to use the organization's business hours, use the case-specific business hours, or ignore them altogether. Business hours help support teams so that you time-based criteria run only during your business hours.

6. **Select how escalation times are set, and click Save.**

Now you've created your first escalation rule! Go into a case, set the criteria you've chosen, and test it out. But first, don't forget to go back and activate the escalation rule.

We've shown you some of the inside tips on object-specific settings in the Setup menu for Sales, Marketing, and Service. Now you have a basic foundation and understanding of where certain settings are toggled for which objects. We encourage you to go in and get your hands dirty. Explore for yourself!

Chapter 19

Building Custom Apps

What if you could modify your business applications in minutes to match the unique ways you manage your customer relationships? How much more productive could you be if you spent less time fighting your technology and more time with your customers?

Force.com is the Salesforce platform you use to customize and create on-demand applications simply by pointing and clicking your mouse on easy-to-use web pages. In fact, with Force.com, you can not only customize your existing Salesforce applications, but also build entirely new applications to fit the way you do business. If you need a little inspiration, you can also install a preexisting solution from the AppExchange directory (www.appexchange.com).

In this chapter, we demystify the Force.com platform and define some basic terms to give you a glimpse of the awesome power of creating custom apps. Then you see how to share your creation on the AppExchange. Finally, we offer simple and critical tips for preparing your deployment game plan.

Understanding Elements of the Force.com Platform

Force.com is the Salesforce.com on-demand platform: a suite of development tools for customizing, building, integrating, and installing business applications — and you don't need to build or maintain any infrastructure yourself to use it.

Force.com is both a collection of customization tools as well as the underlying infrastructure that powers the Salesforce app that you use. The cool part is that, over time, Salesforce.com engineers have exposed parts of their secret sauce so that you can use it, too, and they've also used these customization tools to build additional features into Salesforce.

Briefly, here are some key terms you need to know:

» **Force.com:** The engine that makes Salesforce what it is today. It's the underlying technology that enables you to customize existing applications from the Setup area, create new ones (with or without any programming experience), integrate Salesforce with other company systems, and share these snippets online with others.

» **Apex code:** Another subset of the Force.com platform. The Salesforce procedural scripting language that allows users to write custom logic and create integrations between Salesforce and other systems. If you're technical, you now have the ability to build new objects, create triggers and classes, change the user interface (UI) to handle custom forms and interactions, use a web services application programming interface (API), and all that techno-speak stuff.

» **Visualforce:** Another powerful technical capability that Salesforce provides. You can use it to customize the actual front-end page design and components of your custom application. You're no longer limited to Salesforce's default colors, visual design, and tab layouts.

» **AppExchange:** An online directory where you can quickly browse, try, download, and install apps that can instantly run alongside your existing Salesforce applications.

REMEMBER

Salesforce.com frequently rebrands the names of its various offerings. The preceding terms are the most recent versions as of this book's publication. The underlying functionality, look, and feel that we discuss is still the same as we describe it.

Unless you're a developer (or a glutton for punishment), you don't need to know the technical ins and outs. What you do need to know is that Force.com enables Salesforce administrators to easily customize and extend their existing on-demand applications without extensive involvement from developers. For building applications, which can take months with traditional software, you can point and click to quickly develop new applications in hours or days, completely integrated with your existing Salesforce customer relationship management (CRM) system.

To see all options available to you with building Custom apps, log in to Salesforce and follow these steps:

1. **Choose Setup ⇨ Build.**

   The Build page appears. This page highlights all the features and functionality available to help you customize, build, share, and integrate your CRM.

2. **On the sidebar menu, notice the menu items below the Build header.**

   This chapter focuses on the tools listed under the Create header. We cover the Customize header in Chapter 17. We don't discuss Develop because that's a more technical discussion, and we promised you "no code required."

Preparing Your Custom App Strategy

Force.com places so much potential at your fingertips that just like a kid in a candy store, you may have the urge to just jump in and start building custom objects and tabs — a baptism by fire. Although that method is appetizing in theory, it's a quick way in reality to get a stomachache, especially if your business grows and more people start entering information in Salesforce. Resist that impulse until you review these simple steps for planning your strategy for on-demand applications:

1. **Define and prioritize objectives.**

   Your wish list doesn't need to be very involved, but it should spell out the who, what, when, why, and how.

2. **Build a plan.**

   With agreed-upon objectives, take your project down another level and lay out a plan to address the most pressing objectives.

3. **Determine the most suitable approach.**

   You have many different ways to tackle a business issue with Force.com — some better than others.

   - *Use the discussion boards* at the Salesforce Success Community website (`http://success.salesforce.com`) to check existing or upcoming functionality. You may not need to build a unique solution.

   - *Browse the AppExchange* to see whether any available prebuilt applications meet your general requirements.

4. **Keep it simple.**

   Don't sacrifice your objectives at the expense of simplicity — although at the beginning, simple is often better.

5. **Start with the end in mind.**

   If a custom app seems like the right strategy, figure out what it is that you want to measure. Understand how well your solution may scale (or not).

TIP

A great way to design your application so that it takes full advantage of relationships is to simply draw it out on a piece of paper or a white board. Your design doesn't have to be fancy or complicated, but it should define the standard and custom objects you need and how they should be linked.

Creating Custom Objects

Once you have a plan, you'll have to know how to create its building blocks. In this section, we tell you how to create custom objects and relate them to each other.

Building your custom objects

Typically, you create a custom object to house a discrete set of information that's different from what is contained in other standard objects. For example, an Opportunity object contains opportunity information. A Custom Expense object contains information about expenses that's unique from the typical purpose of other standard objects.

If you want to build a home, you have to add the basic building blocks first. The same analogy applies to custom apps and objects. For example, if you want to build a recruiting application, you may decide that you could use the Contacts object for applicants and need to build custom objects for Job Postings and Interview Feedback because they're distinct blocks of data.

To set up a new object, follow these steps:

1. **Choose Setup ⇨ Build ⇨ Create ⇨ Objects.**

The Custom Objects page appears. This page, your starting point for creating an object, is where all your custom objects are displayed.

2. **Click the New Custom Object button.**

The New Custom Object page appears.

3. **In the Custom Object Information section, type the basic details for your object.**

You usually just need to fill out the Label and Plural Label fields. This will then automatically populate the Object Name field. Labels are what your end-users see (like "Time Off Request"). The object name is what Force.com sees (like "Time_Off_Req") in case you need to have another system (or another part of Salesforce) talk to it.

4. **Complete the Enter Record Name Label and Format fields.**

The record name appears on page layouts, related lists, lookups, and search results. This is what you use to differentiate one record of this object from another. Depending on the type of object you're creating, you may want to switch the data type from Text to Auto Number.

Here's how to tell when to use text versus auto numbers:

- *Text:* The name has some intrinsic value.

- *Auto numbers:* You're creating an object that will relate to other standard objects in a fundamental way. Auto numbers are useful for sequenced business documents, such as invoices, purchase orders, IT tickets, and timecards.

5. **Select the custom object's optional features.**

With simple pointing and clicking on your part, Force.com allows you to select your custom object's features that are identical to many of the features found on standard objects, such as tracking activities, allowing reporting, or tracking its field history.

6. **Leave the Deployment Status as In Development so that only you can see it, instead of all the other Salesforce users within your company.**

TIP

We recommend making sure that you can explain the business process around using the new object *before deploying it* to help guide correct adoption.

Select the Deployed button if you're ready for your users to begin using it. If you wait to deploy the object, return to this screen by choosing Setup ⇨ Build ⇨ Create ⇨ Objects. Select your object from the list of custom objects, and you return to the custom object detail page.

7. **Select the Launch New Custom Tab Wizard check box and then click Save.**

    The New Custom Object Tab Wizard starts. See the section "Adding a tab to a custom object," later in this chapter, for the how-to's on building a new tab.

If you already mapped the custom objects that will be part of your app, create all the objects first before modifying them. This action is especially helpful if you're building relationships between them.

Modifying custom objects

Designing your custom object is as simple as modifying a contact record or adding to a contact record's related lists. If you need to change the basic settings, simply click the Edit button at the top of the Custom Object page for the object, and the Edit Custom Object Wizard reappears.

If you want to customize your new object, you can point and click through the related lists on the page.

Certain Setup features — including custom profiles, multiple page layouts, record types, workflow, and field-level security — are available only in the Enterprise and Unlimited editions.

Building relationships

One primary reason for building applications with Force.com is to create a single, integrated, one-stop shopping experience for your users.

The key to those linkages is building custom relationships between objects. For example, if your company wants to manage account planning in Salesforce, you want to create a relationship between the standard Account object and a custom object for the Account Plan.

To build a relationship, follow these steps:

1. **Choose Setup ➪ Build ➪ Create ➪ Objects.**

    The All Custom Objects page appears.

2. **Click the desired custom object under the Label column.**

    The Custom Object page appears.

3. **Click the New button in the Custom Fields & Relationships related list (see Figure 19-1).**

    The New Custom Field Wizard appears.

Dummies Publication
New Custom Field

Help for this Page

Step 1. Choose the field type
Step 1

Next   Cancel

Specify the type of information that the custom field will contain.

Data Type

○ None Selected
Select one of the data types below.

○ Auto Number
A system-generated sequence number that uses a display format you define. The number is automatically incremented for each new record.

○ Formula
A read-only field that derives its value from a formula expression you define. The formula field is updated when any of the source fields change.

○ Roll-Up Summary ⓘ
A read-only field that displays the sum, minimum, or maximum value of a field in a related list or the record count of all records listed in a related list.

○ Lookup Relationship
Creates a relationship that links this object to another object. The relationship field allows users to click on a lookup icon to select a value from a popup list. The other object is the source of the values in the list.

○ Master-Detail Relationship
Creates a special type of parent-child relationship between this object (the child, or "detail") and another object (the parent, or "master") where:
  • The relationship field is required on all detail records.
  • The ownership and sharing of a detail record are determined by the master record.
  • When a user deletes the master record, all detail records are deleted.
  • You can create rollup summary fields on the master record to summarize the detail records.
  The relationship field allows users to click on a lookup icon to select a value from a popup list. The master object is the source of the values in the list.

○ External Lookup Relationship
Creates a relationship that links this object to an external object whose data is stored in an external data source.

FIGURE 19-1:
Create a new custom field or relationship.

4. **In Step 1 of the New Custom Field Wizard, choose the type of relationship with another object.**

   Force.com supports two types of custom relationships: Master-Detail and Lookup. They're both one-to-many relationships.

   REMEMBER

   A Lookup relationship links one object to another. The representative custom field will have a little magnifying glass icon next to it so that you can "look up" a value from that related object to associate with another object. Master-Detail (also known as parent-child) relationships are a special type of association: The relationship is required for the detail. If you delete the master record, its related children are also deleted.

   The two relationships look the same in the UI — as a lookup field with a magnifying glass on the right side and as a related list on the related object.

   But here are two big differences:

   • **Master-Detail relationships cause the cascade deletion of child records to occur when the parent record is deleted.** For example, if you delete an account, all related child records are also deleted.

   • **In a Master-Detail relationship, the detail record inherits the Owner and sharing rules of the master record.** Detail objects are dependent on their masters. In Lookup relationships, however, they don't transfer sharing rules — they're completely independent.

   When in doubt, start with the Lookup option.

   TIP

5. **Click Next to continue.**

6. **In Step 2 of the wizard, select the other object that you want to relate your object to.**

   You can create as many as 40 Lookup relationships and up to two Master-Detail relationships with a custom object.

7. **Click Next to continue.**

8. **In Step 3 of the wizard, enter the label for the lookup field.**

   As a default, Force.com prefills the fields with the name of the object you selected, although you can change it.

9. **Click Next to continue.**

10. **If you have Enterprise or Unlimited Edition, set the field-level security in Step 4 of the wizard. (If you don't, skip to Step 14 because you won't be able to set field-level security.)**

    If you chose the Master-Detail option, the security is set for you because it must be available within field-level security. If you chose the Lookup option, select the appropriate check boxes to control visibility and edit rights to the field.

11. **Click Next to continue.**

12. **If you have Enterprise or Unlimited Edition, in Step 5 of the wizard, select the page layouts in which you want to display the field.**

    Suppose that you're creating an expense application. You may want the rep's layout to be different from the manager's layout.

13. **Click Next to continue.**

14. **In Step 6 of the wizard, deselect the check boxes if you don't want the custom object to appear on the related list of the selected object.**

    For example, if you're linking expenses with accounts, you may not want a long list of expenses showing up on an account record.

15. **When you're done, click Save.**

    The Custom Object page reappears, and your custom relationship is displayed in the Custom Fields & Relationships related list.

TIP

Build your relationships before loading any actual data.

Remember that between two objects, you can have only one object that allows the Master-Detail relationship, so the other object has to be a Lookup relationship. A standard object also can't be the child of a Master-Detail relationship.

TECHNICAL
STUFF

If you're drawing out your entity relationship diagram and find that you need two objects to have a many-to-many relationship with each other, build a junction object between the two. The junction object will act as a bridge between two objects, to give the impression of two Master-Detail relationships.

Here are some other ways that you can modify custom objects to fit your company's business processes:

>> **Creating fields:** With Force.com, you can quickly add fields to your custom object, much like you can with a standard object, such as an account or a contact. See Chapter 17 for more information on creating custom fields.

>> **Changing layouts:** After or as you build fields, feel free to start rearranging the page layout for the object record. Often, that's one of the easiest ways to get a pulse on what's missing from your record. See Chapter 17 for more information on editing page layouts.

>> **Customizing related lists:** After you add your Lookup relationships and custom fields, you're ready to start customizing your related lists. Force.com allows you to modify the columns that are displayed in a related list.

REMEMBER

Don't forget this step because without customizing this section, your users don't see much in a related list. When you add the right columns, though, the related list becomes a powerful tool for your users. By customizing the columns displayed in a related list, users can quickly see a summary of relevant information from a record's detail page. See Chapter 17 for more information on customizing related lists.

Creating Custom Apps

After you sketch the basic requirements for your new application, and built the objects that you need, you're ready to begin assembling this into an app. The custom app is much like a container, into which you associate your objects and tabs.

TIP

To see an example of custom apps that others have created, visit the AppExchange (www.appexchange.com) and browse apps by category. Apps created by Force.com Labs are those that came from Salesforce.com's own employees.

Choose Setup ⇨ Build ⇨ Create to get to a powerful set of customization tools that can empower your business faster than the status quo of traditional software solutions.

Setting up a custom app

REMEMBER

Many companies want internal branding for their business applications. Before you can apply branding like this, though, you have to first add the logo to a public folder on the Documents tab. (From any page, click the Documents tab; create a new public folder that's easily identifiable, like *Logos*; and click the New Document button from within that folder.) Make sure that the image is a GIF or JPEG file smaller than 20KB. Ideally, use a horizontal image. If it's larger than 300 x 55 pixels, Salesforce will scale the image to fit the space.

To add the custom app, choose Setup ➪ Build ➪ Create and then follow these steps:

1. **Click the Apps link in the sidebar.**

   The Apps page appears. You see a list of your standard Salesforce apps, plus any custom apps you created.

2. **Click the New button above the Apps list.**

3. **In Step 1 of the New Custom App Wizard, select what type of app you want to create, and click Next.**

4. **In Step 2 of the wizard, enter a label and description for your app, and click Next.**

   The name you type in the label field appears on the Force.com Apps pull-down menu.

REMEMBER

5. **In Step 3 of the wizard, assuming that you want to apply your branding, insert a logo from your Documents tab, and then click Next.**

   You have to first add the logo to a public folder on the Documents tab.

   The logo will appear as the header whenever a user selects the custom app from the Force.com Apps menu. Of course, if you don't want to brand the app, you can leave the current Salesforce-provided image.

6. **In Step 4 of the wizard, select the tabs that will make up your app, and then click Next.**

   You do this step simply by clicking tabs from the Available Tabs box and using the arrow buttons to create your list of Selected Tabs.

   If you haven't created all your custom tabs yet, don't worry. As you create custom tabs, you can associate them with your custom or standard apps. (For all the details, see the section "Creating custom tabs," later in this chapter.)

7. **In Step 5 of the wizard, select the check boxes to assign the app to different user profiles.**

   You want to make sure that the right apps are available to the right people in your organization.

REMEMBER

8. **When you're done, click Save.**

   The Apps page reappears, and your new custom app now appears in the list.

Creating custom tabs

With Force.com, you can create two primary types of custom tabs: custom object tabs and web tabs. They look just like the standard tabs that your users already use, and you can build the tabs in less than a minute — piece o' cake.

Adding a tab to a custom object

If you read through the section "Building your custom objects," earlier in this chapter, you've probably already built a custom tab. Sometimes, however, you build a custom object and decide later to add the tab.

REMEMBER

Don't over-tab your application if it's not necessary. Ask yourself: "Will my users need all the object's data available from a central area?" If the answer is yes, you may need a custom tab.

To build a custom tab, follow these steps:

1. **Choose Setup ⇨ Build ⇨ Create ⇨ Tabs.**

   The Custom Tabs page appears.

2. **Click New in the Custom Objects Tab related list.**

3. **In Step 1 of the New Custom Object Tab Wizard, select the object from the picklist, and then use the Lookup icon to choose a tab style.**

   The tab style affects both the color of the tab and the icon associated with a custom object record under Recent Items.

4. **In Step 2 of the wizard, select the desired tab visibility for your user profiles.**

   With the radio button feature, you can control tab visibility of your profiles.

5. **In Step 3 of the wizard, select the apps to which the new custom tab will be available.**

   This step makes it simple to associate custom tabs with just the right apps for your users.

6. **When you're done, click Save.**

   The Custom Tabs page reappears with your new custom tab listed.

Building a web tab

In the normal course of a day, your users frequent other websites as part of their jobs — to access an intranet, to arrange travel plans, to use an internal web-based application. . . . The list goes on. Why not make it easier for users to get to your business-related sites? With Force.com, you can build web tabs that access web applications and Visualforce.

TECHNICAL STUFF

We don't go into the details of Apex code or Visualforce because they require coding, but imagine that you have a particular form to which your teams are emotionally attached (a client profile form with four columns, for example). With Visualforce and the help of an experienced developer, you can display your data in Salesforce in unique formats and keep everyone happy. To manage these features, choose Setup ➪ Build ➪ Develop.

To create a simple web tab, follow these steps:

1. **Choose Setup ➪ Build ➪ Create ➪ Tabs.**

The Custom Tabs page appears.

2. **Click the New button in the Web Tabs related list.**

3. **In Step 1 of the New Web Tab Wizard, click a button to select a layout.**

4. **In Step 2 of the wizard, define the display properties for the content, and then click Next.**

In this example, we show you how to create a URL-based web tab for news labeled News. Select a Tab Type to tell Salesforce if this tab's content is coming from a URL or a dynamically generated URL. Type in a relevant Tab Label and choose a Tab Style.

5. **In Step 3 of the wizard, enter a URL, add any additional merge fields, and then click Next.**

Embedding merge fields is easy after you get the hang of it. For example, this URL is the standard search results URL from CNN:

```
http://http://www.cnn.com/search/?text=salesforce
```

We copied and pasted the URL in the Button or Link URL box. Then we used the merge field tool for {!Org_Name} and put that in place of salesforce in the URL so it looked like this:

```
http://www.cnn.com/search/?text={!Org_Name}
```

6. **In Step 4 of the wizard, click the drop-down lists to control which user profiles can access the tab, and then click Next.**

7. **In Step 5 of the wizard, check the box next to whichever custom apps you want to contain this web tab, and then click Save.**

Understanding the AppExchange

As customers, employees, and partners began building custom applications (or *apps*), some bright person came up with an idea: Wouldn't it be great if other customers like you could simply try, download, and install these custom apps without having to build them on their own? iTunes uses the web to distribute music, so why shouldn't enterprise applications work the same way?

Enter AppExchange, the website owned and operated by Salesforce.com where you can try, download, and quickly install apps that can extend the value of Salesforce to meet your unique needs. You can even use the AppExchange to share your custom apps.

Of course, the biggest benefit beyond how much easier your life will be is the impact on your users. The AppExchange marketplace isn't just about easy sharing — it's about your employees using integrated business apps with all your information in one place.

REMEMBER

Customers, partners, and Salesforce.com personnel can all provide AppExchange with applications. Many of them, particularly the ones published by Salesforce.com employees (a.k.a. Salesforce Labs), are free to install and use. Others, such as the ones provided by partners, may have a fee associated with them.

Downloading music and videos from the web is something we take for granted nowadays. But downloading enterprise apps? Wow, that seems like a whole 'nother animal.

Yet, when you get down to it, AppExchange is still about the exchange of a package of goods from one party to another. As with many innovations, getting the most out of a new system usually amounts to understanding some basic terms and knowing your limits before jumping in.

Here are a few key terms you should know before you get started:

>> **Installation:** The process by which you download, install, and deploy a custom app from AppExchange.

>> **Publishing:** The process by which you package a portion of your customizations and make them available, either publicly or privately, on AppExchange.

>> **Managed package:** An AppExchange package created and maintained by a verified third-party vendor. Unlike unmanaged packages, whose components you can modify and customize, managed package components have limited customization capabilities. This allows vendors to provide you with an upgrade path that'll leave you successful instead of stuck in the mud because you changed something that's not supported by a newer version.

And here are a few more things to keep in mind:

» Although anyone can try out the AppExchange, to install and share apps, you must have a Salesforce instance and have administrative rights to that instance. (Did we just hear a sigh of relief?)

» You can publish many types of AppExchange components, not just custom apps, on AppExchange. You can exchange custom links, dashboards, Visualforce code snippets, and more.

» Some apps are self-contained — *native* — in Salesforce. They were built with Force.com and don't depend on other external applications. Other custom apps are *composite.* Such apps may look and feel like Salesforce apps but connect with other services not owned by Salesforce.com. *Caveat emptor* (let the buyer beware).

Familiarize yourself with AppExchange at www.appexchange.com, and then try out some apps before you decide whether you want to use them.

If you want to install a custom prebuilt app, you can do it with a few simple clicks. This process amounts to downloading the package, installing the app into your instance of Salesforce, and deploying it to all or a portion of your users.

REMEMBER

A *package* refers to all the components that make up the custom app. A package may include custom tabs and objects, custom links, custom profiles, reports, dashboards, documents, and more.

To install a custom app, follow these steps:

1. Click the Get It Now button on the app's detail page in AppExchange (at www.appexchange.com).

2. Click the Log In to the AppExchange button to log in using your Salesforce credentials.

This identifies who you are. If you've already got Salesforce open in another tab in your browser, you'll move to the next step. Make sure you enter the information that reflects which org you want to install the app into.

3. Choose whether you want to continue the installation of the app in your production or sandbox.

Larger organizations may have customizations that need to be tested with this package. A sandbox that is practically an exact copy of what you have in your live system is a good place to kick the tires without the potential of impacting your business if something goes wrong.

If you don't have access to a sandbox, install the app in your production environment, but make sure you make it visible just to system administrators first until they've thoroughly tested the installation.

4. **Review the list that appears, which tells you what you'll be installing and where.**

   Salesforce makes this as transparent an installation as possible. You can see if the app is free or not, what the subscription model is, and where it's being installed.

5. **Check the box to confirm that you've read the terms and conditions, and then click the Confirm and Install button to continue.**

6. **Enter your Salesforce login and password again for the org in which you want to install the app.**

   The Package Installation Details page appears in Salesforce.

   If you're experimenting with the AppExchange for the first time, you may want to consider using the Sandbox Edition or a free Developer Edition instance to install, customize, and test the custom app.

7. **Examine the details of what's getting installed by clicking the View Components link and the API Access link.**

   This page summarizes the custom app's details, including objects, fields, tabs, reports, and dashboards.

   Make sure that you examine the contents of a package thoroughly before proceeding. Understand the package's API access to various objects, including details of what permissions the package will have on what objects.

8. **Select a radio button to choose the audience that you'll be installing this package for: admins only, all users, or certain profiles.**

   We recommend that you start with first testing this out to admins only. Then you can think about who has access to edit and view the contents of the app before you're ready to deploy it live. If you want to install the app for select profiles, the Select Specific Profiles details appear on the same page.

9. **Specify the level of access for each profile.**

   The access levels here determine the layout assignments, field-level security, and other fun stuff such as editing permissions for the custom objects in the package. Access levels set here don't affect those of any existing objects you have. Determine which profiles have no access or full access.

10. **Click the Install button.**

    A progress page appears as installation begins. An Install Complete page appears after the installation finishes. Bet your traditional software can't create a whole new app that fast!

11. **Click Done.**

At this point, you can choose to deploy the app immediately to users or further customize it. We suggest that you click OK to confirm the download and begin prepping some dummy data before you deploy this to users.

The Installed Packages page appears. If you check out the upper-right corner, you'll notice that the Force.com Apps menu now contains a listing for your new app.

REMEMBER

After you install the app, you can use Force.com to modify its tabs, objects, and other customizations, just as though you had built the custom app yourself. Even though you've installed the app as we recommend in Step 8 earlier, it's not available to nonadministrators until it's deployed.

IN THIS CHAPTER

Getting acquainted with the
Lightning Experience user interface

Deciding whether the Lightning
Experience is right for your company

Preparing to switch to the Lightning
Experience

Chapter 20

Introducing the Lightning Experience

Salesforce has been struck by lightning! No, not really, silly. But figuratively, its new Lightning branding describes several new or revamped features that provide a more modern visual experience for users used to the look and feel of common consumer-like apps like Twitter and Facebook. Lightning features are also built to more easily adapt to how information is displayed and interacted with on tablets and mobile devices. More Salesforce users will be experiencing the tool on devices other than the web browser on a computer, and Salesforce wants to empower administrators to build solutions that are compatible with an increasingly mobile workforce.

In this chapter, we provide an overview of the Lightning Experience, which provides a different end-user experience from the one that has evolved more than 15 years ago when Salesforce first debuted. The changes are relevant most noticeably on the home page, object home pages, records, and reports and dashboards. The look and feel that is the default interface, and that we display in the rest of this book's figures, is called Salesforce Classic.

As of the publication of this book, the Lightning Experience and its compatibility with Salesforce Classic customizations continues to evolve. In this chapter, we tell you where you should go for more information to help assess if your company is ready to make use of the Lightning Experience. If the answer is yes, we help you prepare to make that leap.

Navigating the Lightning Experience Interface

In this section, we highlight what an end-user sees when he logs in to a Salesforce instance that's chosen the Lightning Experience user interface.

Walking through the home page

The Lightning Experience was designed after extensive research and feedback from Salesforce's user base. The majority of Salesforce's primary users are part of some sales function, so this revamp focuses heavily on providing concise information to a more sales-oriented user.

When you first log in to Salesforce, you see the home page, as usual. However you'll know when you're in the Lightning Experience because the navigation menu that takes you to other objects is on the left side of the browser, as showing in Figure 20-1.

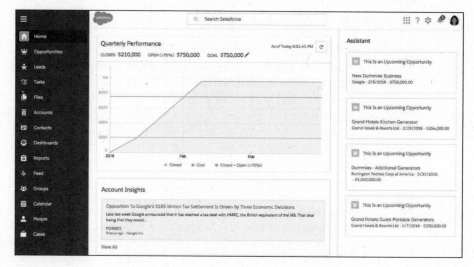

FIGURE 20-1:
The home page in the Lightning Experience.

The Global Search bar prominently appears in the top center of the page, so you can easily find records. Also, when you move your cursor into the search bar and click, a list of your most recently accessed records shows up, as shown in Figure 20-2.

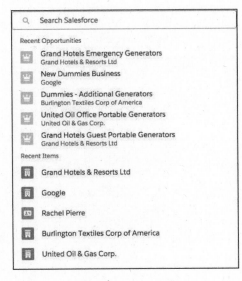

FIGURE 20-2:
The Global Search
bar in the
Lightning
Experience.

The right-side of the home page is where the Assistant lives. This right sidebar area serves up records based on several criteria, including those that have past due dates, activities to address today (like contacting a Lead), and Opportunities that are scheduled to close in the future, or ones that haven't had any interaction with you in a while. It's meant as a place to quickly understand which activities and deals you should focus on.

The top-middle portion of your home page is taken up by a very noticeable quarterly performance chart. This gives you a quick visualization of your goal this quarter, the amount of money you've already closed, which ones are still open with a greater than 70 percent chance of successfully closing this quarter, and your total potential upside.

Below the quarterly performance chart is the Account Insights area, which can provide quick news highlights about accounts relevant to you. The information is aggregated by Data.com.

Below the Account Insights section are two final sections, Recent Records and Top Deals, as shown in Figure 20-3. Recent Records provides a shortcut to your most recently accessed records. Top Deals helps a seller (or sales manager) remember her top potential moneymaking opportunities, so she can better focus her sales activities.

FIGURE 20-3:
The Account
Insights, Recent
Records, and
Top Deals
sections of the
Lightning
Experience
home page.

Monitoring activities on a record

When you click a record, you see its details and any activities or collaborative discussions related to that record. Consider this a workspace for this record, from where you can manage all interactions. The presentation of a record's details begins with highlights about a record, in the top portion of the page. In Figure 20-4, you see an example of an Opportunity detail record, with basic information on the top.

The next section might be the Sales Path, which is unique to Lead and Opportunity records, and which we discuss later in this chapter. For now, we focus on the other sections that foster driving action.

On any detail record page, you see information grouped initially in three buckets — Activity, Collaborate, and Details — to reduce the amount of vertical page scrolling to get to the most pertinent information. Depending on the type of record, these sections may be in the main part of a detail page or in the right-hand column. The behavior will be consistent across objects, and that's what we want you to learn.

The Collaborate section is where your collaborative Chatter feed interactions appear (see Chapter 6 for more information on Chatter). The Details section displays more fields related to this specific record. The Activity section is the default one that appears, with a subset of composer tabs below it that allow you to immediately compose activities related to this record, like log a call, create a new task or event, or send an email.

FIGURE 20-4:
Managing all aspects related to a specific Opportunity record.

When you're working in Salesforce, it should be about driving action to move a deal forward. The things you're logging in Salesforce should correlate to that.

Below the Activity section, you see the activity timeline. This includes tasks and events that haven't been completed yet and are grouped under the Next Steps area. Below that is a Past Activity section, which shows your activity history or previous actions taken.

Tracking all your deals on the Opportunity kanban board

Lightning Experience provides an option to display your Opportunity list views in the format of a columnar kanban board, where each column represents a certain Opportunity stage and applicable deals in that stage.

Kanban refers to an engineering process originally used in Japan by Toyota that optimized inventory levels. The general system of moving a card through various stages, represented visually by columns, until its completion, has been adopted in other industries because it provides a visualization of progressing to a goal.

To visualize your opportunities on a kanban board, as shown in Figure 20-5, follow these steps:

1. **From the navigation bar on the left side of the screen, click Opportunities.**

   A list of recently viewed Opportunities appears.

2. **Click the downward-pointing triangle to the right of the Recently Viewed Opportunities list name.**

   A list of standard and custom list views appears.

3. **Select a list view so that it displays on the screen.**

4. **On the right side of the list view header area, click the icon that looks like a small grid.**

   The Display As drop-down list appears.

5. **Select Board from the Display As drop-down list.**

   The list view changes to a kanban board, where each opportunity is represented as a card, nested under its current Opportunity stage. The board also shows a summary of all Opportunity Amounts for that particular stage.

6. **(Optional) Move an Opportunity to a different stage by hovering over its card, and then clicking and dragging it to its updated column.**

   The Opportunity's stage is updated, and the sum of the Opportunity Amounts in the affected columns changes to reflect the move.

FIGURE 20-5:
Viewing an Opportunity kanban board.

Accessing apps with the App Launcher

In the upper-right corner of any Lightning Experience page is a small icon that looks like a 3 x 3 gray grid. That's the App Launcher icon. Clicking the App Launcher icon takes you to the App Launcher page, shown in Figure 20-6, which shows all the various apps that your Salesforce instance has installed.

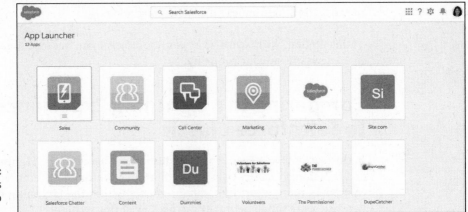

FIGURE 20-6: Launching apps from the App Launcher.

REMEMBER

Apps in Salesforce can mean a collection of custom objects that you've chosen to group together, or that have been provided by a third-party via the AppExchange. For more information on creating custom apps, check out Chapter 19.

You can click and drag an app "card" so the cards are displayed in an order that represents the apps that you access most frequently.

Clicking an app card shows the brief description of the app, and then the various object names grouped under it, which you can also click to get to that object's home page. Also, because the Lightning Experience continues to evolve, this app page will specify which objects are not yet supported within the Lightning Experience's look and feel. Clicking those not-yet-supported objects will open a new browser tab, in the Salesforce Classic display, so you can still continue to be productive.

Considering Lightning for Your Organization

You may be hearing all this talk about the Lightning Experience, while your company currently uses Salesforce and lives in the Salesforce Classic world. At some point, people may be looking to you for your opinion on whether Lightning Experience is the magic bullet for your organization.

In this section, we discuss what you should evaluate in order to make some educated decisions at your company.

Comparing the Lightning Experience to Salesforce Classic

In this section, we cover some key differences between the Lightning Experience and Salesforce Classic. Over time, there may be more differences as Salesforce.com pours more effort into enhancements within the Lightning Experience, but here are some fundamental differences as of this writing:

>> **The home page has been updated.** The navigation options have moved to the left of the screen, the main focus of the page is on the quarterly performance chart, and the Calendar and My Tasks sections have been consolidated and replaced by the Assistant. The experience today is deliberately focused on a user with sales responsibilities.

>> **Home page tabs have moved.** The navigation to various objects used to look like tabs, and then over time looked like headings, but the *tab* name always stuck around. Whatever you call them, they've now moved to the left of the screen, where the object name can be reduced to just its icon, and the navigation bar's width can shrink, too, to allow the most efficient use of your browser window.

>> **The Chatter feed is now nested in its own subsection.** In Salesforce Classic, the Chatter feed is at the top of the record's page. Lots of collaboration can turn into lots of posts that users have to scroll past to get to the record details. In the Lightning Experience, the Chatter feed is tucked within the Collaborate subtab, which is accessible from the "top of the fold" view in a browser. The feed's details are just a click away if you want to see them, and not taking up valuable visual real estate otherwise. See Figure 20-7 for an example of the Collaborate subtab on an Opportunity record.

FIGURE 20-7:
Collaborating on an Opportunity record.

>> **Record details are now nested in their own subsection.** Similar to the Chatter feed, a record's details can often span many pages. A record's details are nested under a Details subtab.

>> **Sales Path provides guidance on Leads and Opportunities.** To help coach users within a sales organization and foster proper usage of Salesforce, leads and opportunities can now offer a Sales Path. This gives sales trainers and managers a narrative of what a user should accomplish in a particular stage of his process. This can include what fields should be filled out, instructions, and links to resources. Of course, this means your business has to have some business process to reflect within the system! For an example of a Sales Path item, see Figure 20-8.

FIGURE 20-8:
Receiving guidance while along the Sales Path.

TIP The Lightning Experience will continue to evolve and more features will be supported in this user interface. Because Salesforce.com averages three updates a year to its product, a lot can happen within a year! To stay up to date on what features are supported, click Help from the upper-right section of your Salesforce Classic interface. Search for the keywords *compare Lightning Experience and Salesforce Classic* for a grid of features by object, and what's supported in each.

Assessing your organization's readiness

The devil's in the details, and you should be familiar with your organization's configuration before diving in deeper.

Primarily, the Lightning Experience is focused on making your sales users even more efficient. If you have a lot of users outside of sales that are heavy users of Salesforce, consider their experience if you were to debut the Lightning Experience to your sales users.

Also consider how defined your business processes are today. If your sales reps aren't expected to log calls or activities, and they're not being too consistent with when they're adding opportunities or updating their stages, the Lightning Experience's benefits may not be fully realized by your users.

Does your Salesforce instance use a lot of custom code? You'll need to have your developers confirm if what they've built is supported in the Lightning Experience. This area is evolving quickly, so it's best to check the Salesforce Release Notes to confirm.

Planning Your Lightning Deployment

If you think your organization is ready to convert to the Lightning Experience, you'll want to ensure you have some processes confirmed first in order to make use of the user interface. In this section, we discuss a few areas that, with a little planning, can prepare your users for a richer experience when they join the Lightning Experience.

Determining sales path tips

Though training your new sales reps can help them sell more productively, many companies don't invest in a person or people to help with sales learning and development. Sometimes this is due to companies not having a disciplined sales process to teach their salespeople. Other times, a process may be in place, but sales management doesn't believe in it and, thus, doesn't support reps' adherence to it.

Though the Sales Path feature in the Lightning Experience won't magically create a business process for you, you can time the enabling of Lightning Experience with sales training on a new process.

You'll want to define the names of your sales stages, and list expectations of what milestones are accomplished at each stage. Are there specific fields that need to be filled out before progressing to the next stage of the opportunity life cycle? Is there access to presentation templates or marketing material applicable to that stage? Map all those out so you can reflect them in the Sales Path.

TIP

Because this feature is also available for the lead life cycle, you can also collect processes and steps for your inside sales or sales development teams.

Benefitting from account insights

What are the approximate sizes of the typical companies that buy your products? Are they Fortune 500 companies publicly traded on a U.S. stock exchange? Are they small private businesses, or perhaps private companies that make as much revenue as some public-company peers?

The answers here will be unique for your business, and can determine if you enable the Account Insights functionality. Larger companies that get reported on in the news will show up in this section; the mom-and-pop shop down the street probably won't (unless it comes up with a social media campaign that goes viral).

Choosing a pilot group

If you're still a bit hesitant about rolling out the Lightning Experience to your organization all at once, nominate a sales team to act as your pilot group. People naturally feel uncomfortable with change, so taking baby steps in your organization can allow you to take a more measured approach to deployment. With a smaller set of initial adoptees, you'll be able to gather feedback and provide more focused help to users, so the transition doesn't seem so intimidating.

Turning on the Lightning Experience

Now that you've gathered all your processes, and you've identified your pilot group, it's time to turn on the Lightning Experience. This section walks you through how to enable this from the Salesforce Classic user interface.

To enable the Lightning Experience, do the following:

1. **Click Setup in the upper-right corner.**

   The Force.com home page appears.

2. **Click Lightning Experience in the left sidebar.**

TIP

If you don't see Lightning Experience, type the phrase **Lightning Experience** in the Quick Find/Search bar that appears at the top of the left sidebar.

The Lightning Experience home page appears.

3. **In the Enable These Recommended Features First section, review the features mentioned and enable or set up any that are listed.**

Make sure you've reviewed any feature's Tell Me More link first, and that you've collected information from your stakeholders on relevant business processes that may need to be mapped into the tool.

4. **In the Decide Who Can Use Lightning Experience section, click Set Up Permissions if you want to pilot this to a subset of users.**

The Permission Sets page appears where you can create a permission set to apply to any user who will be using the Lightning Experience. For more information on permission sets, make sure to go online to www.dummies.com/extras/salesforcedotcom to read our Web Extra on this topic.

5. **In the Enable the New Salesforce Experience section, toggle the Lightning Experience slider to the right, where the label will change from Disabled to Enabled.**

6. **Click the Setup link.**

You'll see a progress page as you magically transform to the new experience.

Switching between the Lightning Experience and Salesforce Classic

Now that you're in the Lightning Experience, what if you change your mind and want to go back to the Salesforce Classic world? In the old days before Salesforce and the cloud, anyone asking this would get a raised eyebrow and a gentle "deal with it" response from her IT department.

Fortunately, the folks at Salesforce.com remember the pain of those old days, and they've worked to ensure that users in the Lightning Experience can quickly change back to the Salesforce Classic user interface if desired.

To switch from the Lightning Experience to Salesforce Classic, do the following from the Force.com home page:

1. **In the upper-right corner of the page, click the far-right icon that represents you.**

If you've got a Chatter profile photo uploaded, that'll be what you see.

Your username shows up, along with links to your profile and personal settings. You'll also see a link to switch to Salesforce Classic, as shown in Figure 20-9.

FIGURE 20-9:
Changing from
the Lightning
Experience to
Salesforce
Classic.

2. **Click Switch to Salesforce Classic.**

Your Salesforce Classic home page appears.

IN THIS CHAPTER

Managing users over time

Planning your sharing model

Building profiles to determine access

Defining your role hierarchy

Delegating administrative duties

Chapter 21

Accessing the Right Data with User Permissions

How can Salesforce be customized for your company so each user sees only pertinent information? You've come to the right chapter.

For administrators or members of your customer relationship management (CRM) project team with the right privileges, Salesforce allows you to easily configure your system so that users can access and share information according to your goals. With Salesforce, you have a variety of ways to control access and sharing of data, from system-wide sharing rules to assigning profiles. And, if you have Enterprise or Unlimited Edition, you have industrial-strength flexibility, even to the point of field-level security.

In this chapter, we show you all the steps you can take (or should consider) for configuring Salesforce to ensure that users see only what they need to see. We discuss concepts around creating the role hierarchy, assigning profiles, determining field-level security, creating users, and setting up your sharing rules.

Understanding User Administration

When Salesforce.com supplies user licenses for your organization, administrators can add users into Salesforce. You don't have to create the roles and profiles before you add users, but we recommend doing so because Role and Profile are important fields when you're creating a user record. In this section, we discuss various ways of creating users and managing them.

Not sure what roles and profiles are, but want to get started quickly? At least review the "Defining the Role Hierarchy" and "Reviewing the standard profiles" sections later in this chapter, so you understand what the out-of-the-box permissions allow.

Creating a new user

To add users, click the Setup link and follow these steps:

1. **Click the Users link under the Administer ⇨ Manage Users heading on the sidebar.**

   A users list page appears.

2. **(Optional) Use the View drop-down list if you want to select from standard or custom list views of your users.**

   Salesforce presets your views with three standard options: All Users, Active Users, and Admin Users.

3. **Click the New User button to add users one at a time.**

   A New User page appears in Edit mode.

   To enter a list of users that need to be created (instead of one at a time), click the Add Multiple Users button instead.

4. **Complete the fields, paying close attention to selecting appropriate Role and Profile values.**

   Select the Generate New Password and Notify User Immediately check box at the bottom of the New User page if you want the user to immediately receive an email with her username and temporary password. If you're in the midst of an implementation, we recommend deselecting this check box and doling out passwords when you're good and ready.

WARNING

If your company is just starting out with Salesforce, be cautious and don't give all your new users the System Administrator profile. Future generations of users at your company will thank you for taking a prudent approach to configuring things in Salesforce, as opposed to allowing too many cooks into the Salesforce kitchen.

5. **Click Save.**

The User detail page appears.

Activating and deactivating users

After you've created a new user, you can activate or deactivate him. Activation means the user is able to log in to Salesforce and start using it. Deactivation means, well, the opposite. There is no concept of deleting a user, which helps with compliance and auditing purposes, as well as avoiding a lot of complications when it comes to historical records owned by and actions performed by that user.

To activate or deactivate a user, click the Setup link and follow these steps:

1. **Click the Users link under the Administer ⇨ Manage Users heading on the sidebar.**

A users list page appears.

2. **Click the Edit link to the left of a user's name.**

The User Edit detail page appears for that user.

3. **Check the Active box, depending on what you want to do.**

If you see a checkmark, that means the user is active. Removing the checkmark means that user is deactivated.

4. **Click Save to save your action.**

You're returned to the user list page.

Freezing users

What if the user you're trying to deactivate is associated with some special settings in Salesforce (like being a default lead or queue owner)? This may take some time as you confirm with business users who the replacement assignee should be. In the meantime, the clock is ticking and you still need to prevent this user from accessing Salesforce. That's when you can freeze a user's record, which disables that user's ability to access Salesforce while you perform related system adminis-trator duties.

To freeze a user, click the Setup link and follow these steps:

1. **Click the Users link under the Administer ⇨ Manage Users heading on the sidebar.**

   A users list page appears.

2. **Click the name of the user you want to freeze.**

   The user's detail page appears.

3. **Click the Freeze button.**

   You're returned to the user detail page, and the button name changes to Unfreeze. To unfreeze that user record, click the Unfreeze button.

Establishing Data Access Concepts

Before jumping into the guts of system design, take a minute to review five basic configuration elements. These will help as you begin to think about who in your company should see and edit what in Salesforce.

>> **Users:** These are the specific people who use your Salesforce system.

>> **Sharing model:** Defines the baseline, general access that users have to each other's data. Also known as organization-wide defaults, org-wide defaults, or simply, OWDs. If you already know that certain groups should not be seeing other groups' information, you want to start with the most restrictive sharing model and use things like the role hierarchy and sharing rules to open access to information. It's easier to provide more access than it is to selectively restrict it.

>> **Roles and role hierarchy:** Define who reports to whom in your organization, for the purposes of seeing and editing information owned by others, which aids in running reports. Think of roles as a way to provide *vertical access* to data (that is, up and down a hierarchy). People higher up in the hierarchy are able to report on those below them in the hierarchy. For example, if you're a manager of a team of sales reps, you'll have a role above your team and be able to see all the account, contact, and opportunity data owned by your team. Individual sales reps, however, may not be able to see opportunity information owned by their peers. This doesn't always have to mimic your company's org chart exactly, however. Another example is that a sales operations analyst may not have any direct reports, but must run reports on the entire sales team. This person could share a role with the head of sales, only because of her reporting needs. Each user should have an assigned role within your defined role hierarchy.

TIP

PLANNING USER ACCESS TO ACHIEVE SUCCESS

Put the major stakeholders of your Salesforce solution in a room and ask them one question: "How do you envision people sharing information in Salesforce?" More often than not, you'll get blank stares.

Discuss sharing issues with your CRM project team after you hear about their current CRM processes. Current business processes, explained without any Salesforce jargon from the team, can often help you formulate an opinion based on what you believe would be best for your company. Take into consideration the culture, size, and type of sales organization at your company. Use this opinion to guide the specific nature of your questions.

Now, you *should* ask that question, but we suggest following it up with scenarios. Here are a few ideas to get you started:

- Should a sales development rep be able to see what the CEO sees?

- Should a sales rep be able to view data from other reps? Should one sales rep be allowed to edit another's lead record?

- Do certain groups need wider access than others? For example, does a call center team that supports all customers need more or less access than a team of sales reps? What about a professional services team member who helps during the sales cycle, as well as during the implementation, and answers any postlaunch questions for up to a certain number of days?

- Do you have marketing operations or sales operations staff? How will they be interacting with Salesforce? Should they be able to see everything that VPs of their organizations see, especially because they'll probably be doing all the legwork for them?

- Does a manager require different permissions than a rep, to change information that the rep can't?

- Do multiple people commonly work on the same account or opportunity?

- Do you have any compliance or audit concerns with a fully open or completely private sharing model?

Use these types of questions and their answers to guide your configuration.

>> **Profiles:** Control a user's capability to see and access different fields within a record in Salesforce. For example, service reps will find some fields on an account record more relevant than other fields that may be very important to a marketing operations analyst. To make the service reps' view of the account record more pertinent and less confusing, you could hide certain irrelevant fields from their view by assigning them a custom profile. You must assign a profile to each user.

>> **Sharing rules:** Opens up access to data for specific users or groups of users. Think of this as opening lateral or horizontal access to your data, by giving certain peer groups or individuals this exception.

You use these five elements as the primary levers to deliver the proper level of access and control for your company in Salesforce.

Defining Your Sharing Model

As an administrator or member of your CRM project team, one of your biggest decisions in Salesforce is how users will share information. A *sharing model* controls the level of access that users have across an organization's information, not just up and down the chain. You can use the sharing model with the role hierarchy, public groups, personal groups, and the default access for each role to get pretty specific about what you want people to view or change. You use the organization-wide sharing model and, if necessary, public groups and expanded sharing rules in Salesforce to configure your sharing model.

TIP

For smaller, younger organizations, start with an open, collaborative sharing model, as opposed to a secretive sharing model in which no one knows what anyone else is doing. (A secretive sharing model sounds like any oxymoron, right? Well, it can be because if you don't carefully think about ramifications, you could be back to where you started with giant heaps of information.) If collaboration is one of your goals, a more-restrictive sharing model can have a greater potential negative impact on end-user adoption. You can always change the sharing model in the future if people scream loudly enough. But nine times out of ten, the value of collaboration overcomes the initial concerns with users viewing other users' data.

Setting organization-wide defaults

The organization-wide defaults (OWDs) set the default sharing access that users have to each other's data. Sharing access determines how data created by users in a certain role or public group is viewed by users within another role or public group. For example, you many want your sales operations team to see the dollar value of won opportunities so that they can verify what was booked versus what's listed on the signed contract, but you probably don't want them editing the amount of that won opportunity. If any role or public group possesses data that at least one other role or group shouldn't see, your sharing model must be private; all other levels of openness must be granted as an exception via groups (more on that later).

REMEMBER

No matter which defaults you set to the sharing model, users will still have access to all data owned by or shared with users below them in the role hierarchy.

To configure the organization–wide defaults, click the Setup link and follow these steps:

1. **Choose Administer ⇨ Security Controls ⇨ Sharing Settings.**

   The Sharing Settings page appears, showing org-wide defaults for several objects, as well as specific sharing rules for those objects.

2. **Click the Edit button in the Organization Wide Defaults list.**

   The Organization Sharing Edit page appears.

3. **Select the desired settings.**

   Click some picklists to see the different options. The options are typically Private, Public Read Only, and Public Read/Write. Some objects may have options specific to that object's functionality, like the Calendar object, and the ability you have to set how much information people can see on others' calendars. For example, if you want the most restrictive model, choose the following as your defaults: Private for the major records and Hide Details for Calendar. Some standard objects, like the Lead and Case objects, have extra-special powers and have an additional option, Public Read/Write/Transfer. This assumes that someone working heavily in leads or cases will often need to transfer a lead or case record that isn't owned by him to someone else.

REMEMBER

   Remember what we said about role hierarchy providing "vertical access" to data? A Private sharing setting on an object still assumes that people with a role above yours in the role hierarchy can see and report on those records. Salesforce always, by default, respects the hierarchy structure — sharing settings determine only how peers and those outside your typical chain of command see your data. For more complex sharing scenarios, you can have the option to deselect the ability to grant access to records based on role hierarchy, but, you may want to consult with Salesforce support or a Salesforce Partner before making such a complex change.

4. **Click Save.**

   The Sharing Settings page reappears with your settings listed under the Organization Wide Defaults list.

Granting greater access with sharing rules

By using public groups, roles, or roles and subordinates, you can create sharing rules to extend access above and beyond the organization-wide defaults. For example, if your default sharing model is read-only but you want a group of call center agents to have edit privileges on account records, you could do this with a custom sharing rule.

To add a sharing rule and apply it to your data, click the Setup link and follow these steps:

1. **Click the Sharing Settings link under the Administer ⇨ Security Controls heading on the sidebar.**

   The Sharing Settings page appears.

2. **Scroll down and click the New button next to any of the standard or custom object Sharing Rules lists, as shown in Figure 21-1.**

   All lists operate much the same but relate to different records. A Sharing Rule setup page appears for your selected record.

Sharing Rules

| Lead Sharing Rules | New | Recalculate |

No sharing rules specified.

| Account Sharing Rules | New | Recalculate |

No sharing rules specified.

| Opportunity Sharing Rules | New | Recalculate |

No sharing rules specified.

| Case Sharing Rules | New | Recalculate |

No sharing rules specified.

| Campaign Sharing Rules | New | Recalculate |

No sharing rules specified.

| User Sharing Rules | New | Recalculate |

No sharing rules specified.

FIGURE 21-1: Adding a new sharing rule.

3. **Use the drop-down lists to define the data you want to share and the related roles or groups that you want to share that data with, as shown in Figure 21-2.**

For example, you may want to grant your customer support team read/write privileges to account data owned by all internal users. You can apply the sharing rule based on types of users who own the record, or create other filter criteria.

Setup
Account Sharing Rule

Use sharing rules to make automatic exceptions to your organization-wide sharing settings for defined sets of users.

Note: "Roles and subordinates" includes all users in a role, and the roles below that role.

You can use sharing rules only to grant wider access to data, not to restrict access.

Step 1: Rule Name

Label	Call Center
Rule Name	Call_Center [i]
Description	

Step 2: Select your rule type

Rule Type ◉ Based on record owner ◯ Based on criteria

Step 3: Select which records to be shared

Account: owned by members of | Public Groups �◊ | All Internal Users ◊ |

Step 4: Select the users to share with

Share with | Roles and Subordinates ◊ | Customer Support, North America ◊ |

Step 5: Select the level of access for the users

Default Account and Contract Access	Read/Write ◊
Opportunity Access	Read Only ◊
Case Access	Read/Write ◊

FIGURE 21-2:
Showing a sharing rule.

4. **Click Save.**

The Sharing Settings page reappears with your new rule listed under the appropriate related list.

TIP

When you add a new sharing rule, Salesforce automatically reevaluates the sharing rules to apply the changes to all your records. If your modifications are substantial, you'll be warned with a dialog box that the operation could take significant time, and Salesforce will email you when complete. When you click OK, the dialog box closes, and the Sharing Settings page reappears. Use the Recalculate button in the appropriate related list to manually apply the changes when you've made modifications to groups, roles, or territories.

Setting Up Profiles

In Enterprise and Unlimited editions of Salesforce, you can use profiles to control a user's permission to view and perform many functions. Roles and sharing rules determine which objects a person sees, and whether she can make changes to that object. A profile determines what details a person sees on that object. Depending on which edition you're using, you can use profiles to

>> Define which page layouts a user will see

>> Control field-level access

>> Determine the apps viewed by a user

>> Alter the tabs displayed to users

>> Make record types available to certain users

>> Secure certain login settings

Reviewing the standard profiles

Most editions of Salesforce come with five or six standard profiles, which can't be altered except for the tab settings. The number of standard profiles may differ depending on the types of Salesforce licenses your organization has purchased. Newer organizations can stick to standard profiles and address their company's basic requirements related to user access. If you have Group or Professional Edition, you can't actually view the settings on the standard profiles.

If you have Enterprise or Unlimited Edition, choose Setup➪Administer➪ Manage Users➪Profiles to see your profiles. Otherwise, here's a brief explanation of the more common standard profiles for Salesforce license types and how they're typically applied:

>> **System administrators** have full permissions and access across all Salesforce functions that don't require a separate license. You'd typically grant this level of control only to users administering the system or who play a critical part in configuring and customizing Salesforce.

>> **Standard users** can create and edit most record types, run reports, and view but not modify many areas of the administration setup. If you can't create custom profiles, you'd probably choose to assign sales reps to the standard user profile.

- » **Solution managers** have all the rights of standard users and can review and publish solutions.

- » **Marketing users** have all the rights of standard users and can perform a variety of marketing-related functions, including importing leads and managing public documents and email templates. If your Salesforce edition has campaigns, marketing users can also administer campaigns.

- » **Contract managers** can add, edit, approve, and activate contracts. They can also delete nonactivated contracts.

- » **Read only** is just what its name implies. Users assigned to this profile can view data and export reports but can't edit anything.

REMEMBER

Profiles never conflict with your organization's sharing model or role hierarchy. For example, a Standard User profile allows a user to create, edit, or delete leads, but if your sharing model is read-only for leads, the Standard User won't be able to delete leads owned by others.

TIP

Over the years, Salesforce.com has expanded the types of licenses you can buy, to better accommodate your organization's users and how often and what they need to access in Salesforce. To get the latest comprehensive list with definitions, click the Help link from within any Salesforce page and type **license types** into the search bar.

Creating custom profiles

If you have Enterprise or Unlimited Edition, you can build custom profiles that provide you greater flexibility than the standard permissions granted to users and the layouts that they see. For example, you may want to create a custom profile for your finance team so that only users with that profile can edit check boxes on the opportunity that track whether certain signed forms have been submitted when you close a deal. See Chapter 17 for details on creating custom layouts and record types.

To create a custom profile, you can start from scratch, but we suggest cloning and modifying an existing profile by following these steps:

1. **Choose Setup ⇨ Administer ⇨ Manage Users ⇨ Profiles.**

The User Profiles page appears. You can see which profiles are standard or custom ones based on which ones have the Custom box checked.

2. **Click the Standard User link in the Profile Name list.**

The Profile: Standard User page appears. In practice, you can clone from any of the profiles, but by starting from the Standard User profile, you can simply add or remove permissions.

3. **Click the Clone button.**

   The Clone Profile page appears.

4. **Type a title in the Profile Name field and then click Save.**

   The Profile page for your new profile appears.

5. **Click the Edit button to modify the permissions, as shown in Figure 21-3.**

   The Profile Edit page appears.

Profile Edit
Standard Dummies User
Help for this Page

Set the permissions and page layouts for this profile.

Profile Edit		Save Cancel

Name	Standard Dummies User	
User License	Salesforce	Custom Profile ✓
Description		

Custom App Settings   i = Required Information

	Visible	Default			Visible	Default
App Launcher	☑	○		Sales	☑	◉
Call Center	☑	○		Salesforce Chatter	☑	○
Community	☑	○		Sample Console	☐	○
Content	☑	○		Site.com	☑	○
Marketing	☑	○		Work.com	☑	○

Connected App Access

Chatter Desktop	☐	Salesforce1 for Windows	☐
Chatter Mobile for BlackBerry	☐	SalesforceA	☐
Salesforce1 for Android	☐	Salesforce Files	☐
Salesforce1 for iOS	☐		

Tab Settings

☐ Overwrite users' personal tab customizations

Standard Tab Settings

Home	Default On	Ideas Themes	Default On
Accounts	Default On	Leads	Default On

💬 Chat

FIGURE 21-3:
Previewing a
Profile Edit page.

TIP

Salesforce packs a plethora of possible permissions into a profile page. Some of those permissions aren't obvious; others are dependent on your selecting other permissions. If you have questions as you're working through the Profile Edit page, click the Help for This Page link in the upper-right corner of the page to go directly to the relevant Help documentation. If you place your cursor over the *i* icon, located next to certain Administrative Permissions on the Profile Edit page, rollover text appears with tips on other required settings.

6. **Under the Custom App Setting section, determine which standard and custom apps are visible for a profile and which one is the default.**

   This determines the content of the Force.com app drop-down list.

7. **Under the Tab Settings section, use the drop-down lists to determine the tab settings for your new profile.**

Choose from the three possible options:

- *Default On:* You want a tab to be displayed.

- *Default Off:* You want a tab not to appear while still allowing a user assigned to the profile the choice to turn the tab back on. For example, if you created a profile for sales reps and you want to hide the Contracts tab but give the rep the option to display it, select Default Off on the Contracts field.

- *Tab Hidden:* You want the tab to be hidden without an option for the user to turn the tab back on. For example, if your company isn't going to use cases, you may decide to hide the tab.

REMEMBER

Making a tab hidden in a user's profile doesn't prevent the user from accessing those records (in reports, for example). To prevent a user from accessing a particular type of record altogether, remove the Read permission on that type of data from the Object Permissions sections of the page.

8. **(Optional) Select the Overwrite Users' Personal Tab Customizations check box if you want to overwrite the user's current personal customization settings with the settings for the new profile that you're applying.**

9. **Under the Administrative Permissions header, select or deselect check boxes to modify administrative permissions from the profile.**

Most of these settings are designed for administrators, but some of these may be important, depending on your goals for a custom profile. For example, if you want to build a manager's profile, you may want to retain permissions such as Manage Public Reports and Manage Public List Views so that managers can create public reports and list views for their teams.

10. **Under the General User Permissions header, select or deselect check boxes to modify common user permissions from the profile.**

For example, if you don't want sales reps to be able to export customer data to a file, you could create a custom profile for reps and remove the Export Reports setting.

11. **Under the Standard Object and Custom Object Permissions headers, select or deselect check boxes to modify standard or custom object permissions from the profile.**

For example, if you don't want support reps to be able to modify opportunities, you could create a custom profile for support reps and select only the Read check box in the row for opportunities.

12. **Click Save.**

The Profile page reappears for your new profile. Your new profile will now appear the next time you follow the instructions in Step 1.

13. **Click the View Users button if you want to assign users to the profile.**

A Custom: *Custom Profile Name* list page appears in which you can view, add, or reset passwords for users in the profile.

Defining the Role Hierarchy

Think of a *role hierarchy* as the Salesforce system's data-access trickle-down org chart: If you're assigned to the role at the top of the chart, you have full access to your own data, and that privilege trickles down to the data of everyone below you in the hierarchy — and life is good.

TIP

When you're constructing your hierarchy, don't confuse your actual company org chart with the role hierarchy. Role hierarchy is all about access to data to perform your duties in Salesforce and how you want to organize certain sales-related reports. As such, hierarchies often have fewer layers than a typical org chart. For example, if your executive team will be users, you might simply create a role called Executive Team, assuming that many of those users will have similar trickle-down viewing and editing privileges.

You can use the role hierarchy in Salesforce as a primary method to control a user's visibility and access to other users' data. After you assign a role to a user, that user has ownerlike access to all records owned by or shared with subordinate users in the hierarchy. For example, if you set up a hierarchy with a Sales Rep role subordinate to a Sales Manager role, users assigned to Sales Manager would have read and write access to records owned by or shared with users in the Sales Rep role.

To set up your company's role hierarchy, click the Setup link in the upper-right corner and follow these steps:

1. **Choose Administer ⇨ Manage Users ⇨ Roles.**

The Understanding Roles page appears, and you see a sample hierarchy, as shown in Figure 21-4.

TIP

To select a different sample hierarchy, make a selection from the View Other Sample Role Hierarchies drop-down list.

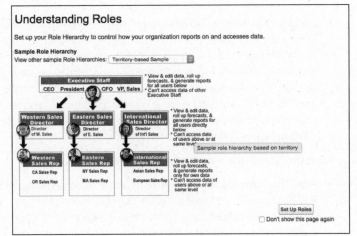

Understanding Roles

Set up your Role Hierarchy to control how your organization reports on and accesses data.

Sample Role Hierarchy
View other sample Role Hierarchies: Territory-based Sample

Sample role hierarchy based on territory

Set Up Roles
☐ Don't show this page again

FIGURE 21-4:
Seeing a sample role hierarchy.

2. **Click the Set Up Roles button.**

   The Creating the Role Hierarchy page appears.

3. **(Optional) To select a different view of the hierarchy, make a selection from the drop-down list on the right side of the page.**

   Salesforce provides three standard views for displaying the role hierarchy: tree, list, and sorted list. For this example, we're opting for the default, Tree view.

4. **In Tree view, click the Add Role button at the place in the hierarchy where you'd like your new role to appear.**

   A Role Edit page appears for the new role.

5. **Complete the fields.**

   The fields are pretty obvious, but here are some tips:

   - *This Role Reports To:* Use this lookup field to define the role's place in the hierarchy. Because the lookup field is based on roles you already created, add roles by starting at the top of your hierarchy and then working your way down, as shown in Figure 21-5.

Role Edit
New Role

Role Edit

Label	Director, EMEA Sales
Role Name	Director_EMEA_Sales
This role reports to	VP, International Sales
Role Name as displayed on reports	Director, EMEA Sales

Save   Save & New   Cancel

FIGURE 21-5:
Creating a new role in the hierarchy.

- *Contact, Opportunity, and Case Access:* Select these options that fit your company's objectives. (You may not see these fields if you have a very public sharing model — more on that in the following section.) You can provide an account owner with read-write access to related opportunities or cases that she doesn't own, has view-only access to, or has no access to. This flexibility comes in handy in heavily regulated industries, in which you might have to prevent an account executive from knowing about certain deals or issues going on with her account.

6. **Click the Save button or the Save & New button.**

   - *Save:* The Role: *Role Name* page appears, displaying the detail information you just entered and listing any users in this role. From the users in the *Role Name* Role detail list, you may also assign existing users to this role or create new users with this role. (Check out the section "Creating a new user," earlier in this chapter.)

   - *Save & New:* A New Role page appears, and you can continue building the hierarchy. Repeat Steps 2–6 until your hierarchy is done.

Using Other Security Controls

Beyond the major configuration settings (such as roles, profiles, and sharing model), as an administrator, you have other settings for managing the use and security of your data in Salesforce. You can find these features by choosing Setup ➪ Administer ➪ Security Controls.

In the following sections, we discuss how to manage field-level access and delegate a subset of administration to others.

Setting field-level security

If you have Enterprise or Unlimited Edition, you have three primary ways to control access to and editing of specific fields: profiles (which we discuss earlier in this chapter), page layouts (Chapter 17 covers these), and field-level settings (stay right here for the details). With field-level security, you can further restrict users' access to fields by setting whether those fields are visible, editable, or read-only.

To view and administer field–level security, click the Setup link and follow these steps:

1. **Choose Administer ⇨ Security Controls ⇨ Field Accessibility.**

   The Field Accessibility page appears, listing all objects.

2. **Click the link for the type of record for which you want to view and manage field-level security.**

   A Field Accessibility page for the selected record type appears, as shown in Figure 21-6. For example, click the Account link if you want to review the security settings on account fields.

Field Accessibility
Account

This page allows you to view Account field accessibility for the following profiles.

Choose a different tab

Choose your view

View by Fields
Use this option to choose a field and view a table of field accessibility for different profiles and record types.

View by Profiles
Use this option to choose a profile and view a table of field accessibility for different record types.

FIGURE 21-6:
Preparing to view field accessibility.

3. **Under the Choose Your View header, click the View by Fields link.**

   The Field Accessibility page appears with a Field drop-down list. If you want to see a different view of this information — in which you get to see one profile and the security levels for all the fields for the selected data type — click the View by Profiles link.

4. **Select a field from the Field drop-down list.**

   The page reappears with a table displaying your company's profiles and the profiles' accessibility to the selected field.

5. **In the Field Accessibility table, click a link in a cell in the Field Access column to edit the profile's field access for a specific record type.**

   An Access Settings page for the selected profile and selected field appears, as shown in Figure 21-7. If you want to modify access for all profiles associated with the page layout assigned to this profile, you can also adjust that here.

6. **Select the check boxes to modify the field-level settings, and then click Save.**

   The Field Accessibility page for the selected record type reappears.

Access Settings for Account Field
Billing Address

The **Billing Address** field is currently **Editable** for the **Standard Dummies User** profile.

[Save] [Cancel]

Field-Level Security:

Profile	Field	Visible	Read-Only
Standard Dummies User	Billing Address	☑	☐

Page Layout:

◉ Remove or change editability of the **Billing Address** field on the **Account Layout** page layout.
◯ Choose a different page layout for the **Standard Dummies User** profile.

Use the checkboxes below to change the page layout settings for the **Billing Address** field on the **Account Layout** page layout.

Page Layout	Field	Visible	Read-Only	Required
Account Layout	Billing Address	☑	☐	

Changes to the **Account Layout** page layout will apply to all profiles that are assigned to this page layout. The table below shows which profiles are currently assigned to the page layout.

Profiles	Account Layout
Analytics Cloud Integration User	✓
Analytics Cloud Security User	✓
Authenticated Website	✓
Contract Manager	✓
Cross Org Data Proxy User	✓
Customer Community Login User	✓
Customer Community Plus Login User	✓

FIGURE 21-7:
Modifying field-level access on a profile.

REMEMBER

If you modify a field-level security setting for a profile by deselecting the Visible check box, this means that the record related to that field is still searchable. The field will never be viewable to a person with that profile, so that person won't be able to create reports or search using it, but he can use reports created by others that leverage that field. So, if an account — say, ABC Corp. — had its Employees field filled out with the number 1001, but that field was not visible to Watson, who has the Standard User profile, Watson could still run a report created by Holmes, who, with a different profile, was able to customize a report looking for all accounts where the Employees field was greater than 1000. In that report, ABC Corp. would be listed and Watson would see ABC Corp., but he would not see the Employees field in the output. Watson would also not be able to customize a report using the Employees field because he can't see it to modify a query.

TIP

If you need to provide someone with similar access to records as an existing user, with the exception of visibility to a few fields, we recommend that you do this via field-level security on a new custom profile, versus removing the field from the page layout. It may not be visible on a page, but that field is still visible elsewhere in Salesforce — like when creating and running reports and list views. Even if you're not strict about a group of people not seeing a field, field-level security can help reduce end-users seeing an overwhelming number of fields that they have to wade through when creating reports.

Delegating administration

As an administrator for your growing world of Salesforce users within your company, you hold the key to who accesses your Salesforce instance. You shouldn't try to cut corners by making everyone system administrators just because you're annoyed each time people bug you to add a new user, or because they get impatient about your asking "Why?" in response to their requests.

Salesforce allows you to delegate some administrative duties to nonadministrators. Delegated administrators can help you create and edit users in roles you specify, reset passwords for those users, assign users to certain profiles, and manage certain custom objects. For example, if your marketing department is growing quickly, you may want to allow a manager in the Marketing Manager role to add new marketing users to Salesforce who need the Marketing User profile.

REMEMBER

With more users and different groups that need access to the same object, be cautious in granting delegated administration permissions to users for specific custom objects. Usually this will result in changes being made that benefit one group at the expense of another, and you're left to diplomatically mend strained relationships. It's your responsibility as a system administrator to have a holistic understanding of how system changes will affect all your users.

To delegate administration, you must first define the groups of users to whom you want to delegate these new privileges. Then you have to specify what you want those newly delegated administrators to do. To define delegated administrators, follow these steps:

1. **ChooseSetup ⇨ Administer ⇨ SecurityControls ⇨ DelegatedAdministration.**

   The Manage Delegated Groups page appears.

2. **Click New.**

   The Edit Delegated Group page for the new delegated group appears.

3. **Enter the Delegated Group Name.**

   In our example, we selected Sales Operations.

4. **Click Save.**

   The Delegated Group page for your new group appears.

5. **Click the Add button in the Delegated Administrators related list to specify which users will belong in this group.**

   The Delegated Administrators page appears.

6. **Use the Lookup icons to find and add users to this group.**

7. **Click Save.**

   The Delegated Group page for your group reappears.

8. **To specify which roles and subordinate roles a delegated administrator can manage, click the Add button in the User Administration related list.**

   The Roles and Subordinates page appears.

9. **Use the Lookup icons to find and add roles that your delegated group may manage.**

10. **Click Save.**

    The Delegated Group page for your group reappears.

11. **Click Add in the Assignable Profiles related list to specify which profiles these delegated administrators may assign to users.**

    The Assignable Profiles page appears.

12. **Use the Lookup icons to find and add profiles that your delegated group may assign.**

13. **Click Save.**

    The Delegated Group page for your group reappears.

14. **Click Add in the Custom Object Administration related list to specify which custom objects and related tabs a delegated administrator may manage.**

    The Custom Object Administration page appears.

15. **Use the Lookup icons to find and add custom objects that your delegated group may assign.**

16. **Click Save.**

    The Delegated Group page for your group reappears.

IN THIS CHAPTER

Understanding your migration options

Executing your migration plan

Organizing your data

Using the right tools to migrate data

Getting help

Chapter 22

Managing Data

I f you're a system administrator, often your greatest headache isn't configuring or customizing the system but getting your data in and maintaining it so that it's useful. Nothing hurts a rollout more than complaints from users that their data isn't in Salesforce, that information is duplicated in several records, or even worse, that the information is wrong. Your end-user adoption suffers if you don't maintain your records after the rollout. End-users love to complain about poor data quality, but they're often not initially motivated to be diligent about putting clean data in there, or they're in too much of a rush to determine sources of truth with other business groups, forgetting that garbage in equals garbage out. If you're not diligent, you can find yourself in the same mess that drove you to Salesforce in the first place.

If data maintenance is giving you nightmares, use the data management tools in Salesforce to easily import leads, accounts, and contacts. If you have in-house expertise or engage a Salesforce partner, you can migrate other critical data (such as opportunities, cases, and activities) by using proven third-party tools. When your data is stored in Salesforce, you can rely on a variety of tools to help you manage and maintain your database.

In this chapter, we first discuss basic options for data import. Then we show you how to use Salesforce tools to manage your data (including mass-transferring, deleting, and reassigning data). Finally, we touch on advanced concepts, such as mass-transferring and mass-deleting your data. Complex data migration and updates of data between your data sources and Salesforce are beyond the scope of this book, but we make sure to point you in the right direction.

Understanding Your Options for Data Migration

Salesforce has easy-to-use wizards that step you through importing your campaign updates, leads, accounts, contacts, and custom objects. If you're a system administrator or you have the right profile permissions, you can perform these tasks for your users. For other legacy data (such as opportunities, cases, and activities) that you want to have in Salesforce, you have to enter information manually or use the Data Loader, which is a data import and export tool that comes with Enterprise and Unlimited editions to automatically migrate data into Salesforce.

Using the Data Import Wizard

The Data Import Wizard for importing leads, accounts, contacts, solutions, and custom objects is conveniently located under the Data Management heading in the Administration Setup section of Setup. It has a user-friendly interface, showing in Figure 22-1, that walks you through importing or updating records.

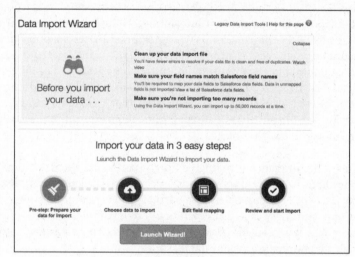

FIGURE 22-1: Launching the Data Import Wizard.

If you're an administrator, you also see links to the import wizard in the Tools section of certain tab home pages. For example, if you want to import your company's leads, click the Leads tab, and then click the Import Leads link in the Tools section. Steps and tips for using the import wizard for different objects' records are detailed in relevant chapters of this book, as follows:

>> **Import leads:** Only a user with the Import Leads permission can perform this operation. See Chapter 7.

>> **Import contacts and accounts:** Salesforce provides one wizard that can take you through importing contacts and/or accounts. Individual users also have the ability to import their personal contacts and accounts. See Chapters 4 and 9.

>> **Import campaign leads or update contacts or leads linked to a campaign:** Salesforce provides a Campaign Member Import Wizard to update marketing statuses for leads and contacts. See Chapter 15.

Investigating the Data Loader

Data migration is a tricky matter. The Data Loader is a small client application that helps bulk-import or bulk-export data in comma-separated value (.csv) format. You access this tool by choosing Setup ➪ Administer ➪ Data Management ➪ Data Loader. With this tool, you can move data into and out of any type of record in Salesforce, including opportunities and custom objects. The Data Loader supports inserting, updating, deleting, and exporting Salesforce records.

WARNING

As someone famous once said, with great power also comes great responsibility. Only use Data Loader if you're comfortable with understanding how objects and records relate to each other. Data Loader is a very powerful tool for nontechnical users. You can export data, import data, and accidentally overwrite and delete a lot of data.

Several vendors also provide proven extract, transform, load tools (ETLs) that enable you to migrate records to (or from) Salesforce, automatically scrub and transform the data based on custom logic that you define, and append those records where appropriate.

TECHNICAL STUFF

Without getting too technical, experts link data by using the Force.com application program interface (API) to enable your technical people to access data programmatically. Force.com (http://developer.force.com) is the platform used to customize or integrate Salesforce to do even snazzier things than what you can do with it out of the box. And before you suffer from jargon overload, a *platform* is basically a collection of rules and commands that programmers can use to tell a program — Salesforce, in this case — to do certain things. To access the Force.com API, though, you must have Enterprise or Unlimited Edition.

Migrating Your Legacy Data

During the preparation phase of your implementation, you need a well-thought-out and well-documented plan for your data migration strategy. That plan needs to include details on objectives, resources, contingencies, and timelines based on the different steps in your plan. In the following sections, we discuss some of the steps that you should consider.

Determining your data sources

The companies we've worked with typically have some type of existing contact management tool, a variety of spreadsheets with other customer data, and often, contact information living in users' email inboxes and productivity applications (not to mention Word documents and sticky notes).

TIP

As you go through your preparation, assess what and how much information needs to be in Salesforce. Here are some tips for this step:

>> **Garbage in, garbage out.** When you move to a new home, you usually look through your old home's closets and decide what to haul with you and what to throw away. Moving data requires the same type of evaluation.

>> **Make a list.** Catalog the different data sources, including what types of records, what range, and how many.

>> **Design a storage plan.** Work with your customer relationship management (CRM) project team to determine where different information should go — and why.

>> **Think about the timing and the sequence of the import.** For example, many companies create user records first, then import accounts and contacts, and finally, migrate and append opportunities.

>> **Keep it simple, if possible.** The more complicated you make the migration, the greater the impact on your timeline. Assess the level of effort versus the potential value of the effort.

Preparing your data

Clean it now, or clean it later. Some project teams like to "scrub" data before importing it into Salesforce. Identifying and merging duplicates makes finding the right record easier. Fixing inconsistencies in your data, such as ensuring that all State/Province fields hold two-character abbreviations, makes reports more accurate.

If your legacy system doesn't make cleanup easy, you might prefer to bring all the records into Salesforce first and then use the Salesforce data management tools to clean data later. The risk is that people with the best intentions may still succumb to human nature and not want to focus on the cleanup effort once the data is already in the new system.

TIP

Regardless of when you do it, cleaning data is not glamorous work, but it's gotta be done, and should be done on a regular basis. Here are a few tips as you prepare your data:

>> **Export to a simple format.** Oftentimes, it's easiest to export data to applications like Microsoft Access or Excel, with which you can delete columns, sort rows, and make global changes.

>> **Strive to use standard naming conventions.** If different data sources refer to accounts by different names (for example, IBM versus International Business Machines), now is a good time to standardize naming. This can help avoid duplicate record creation.

>> **Edit or add fields in Salesforce to support the migration.** For example, if your pipeline reports track margin per opportunity, you need to build a custom Opportunity field to support margin data. Read more about creating custom fields in Chapter 17.

>> **If your existing data source has unique record IDs, migrate those IDs to a custom read-only field.** You can always delete or hide the field at a later stage. Not only can this help you verify the accuracy of your migration, but those IDs might also come in handy for integration (especially if you don't plan to shut down the other data source).

>> **Map your data columns to field names in Salesforce.** For example, the Company field in Microsoft Outlook typically maps to the Account field in Salesforce. Some system administrators even rename the column headers in migration files so that they exactly match field names in Salesforce. Doing this minimizes the migration madness.

>> **Conform your data to fit Salesforce standards** (or the other way around). Each field in Salesforce has certain properties that may include size limitations, decimal points, date formats, and so on.

>> **Add a Data Source column to your import file and map it to a custom field in Salesforce.** By doing this, you can defend where data came from.

>> **Assign the correct owners to records wherever possible.** If you don't have all records assigned, the owner defaults to whichever administrator is executing the migration.

>> **Gain acceptance from stakeholders of the files you've prepared.** At least if you offer them the chance to review, you avoid surprises.

Testing the import

TIP

Test before you execute the final migration. Often, you discover things that you missed or could improve. For example, fields can be mapped incorrectly, or you may just need to create some extra ones. Here are a couple of tips:

>> **Select a small sample of significant records.** The higher profile the records, the better — especially when reviewed by a stakeholder.

>> **Review page layout.** Consider adjusting the page layouts to make validating the data import easier. Put fields in Salesforce in similar screen locations to those of your legacy systems.

Analyzing the test data results

TIP

When your test data is in Salesforce, compare it carefully with your test file to ensure accuracy and completeness. Here are a few tips on how to productively analyze the test data results:

>> Build a custom report that allows you to look at the record data collectively.

>> Open a record, if necessary, and compare it against the import file. Confirm that the record's fields show what you think they should show.

>> Build a custom view from a relevant tab home page to see your imported data laid out in columns on a list page. Users could go to a report, but a view keeps them focused.

>> Validate the data with selected stakeholders to get their feedback and support that the test data results look correct. It's not enough that you think the test import was accurate. Your end-users are the ultimate test.

>> Adjust your process or make changes to the import file or Salesforce based on the results of the test import. For example, maybe you forgot to map a field or the data didn't import correctly because of a field's properties.

Migrating your final data

After you successfully analyze the test data results, you're ready to import your file(s). Yes, that's a simplification of what could be a complicated set of tasks, but the overall process is tried and true.

TIP

Here are a few suggestions for this step:

>> **Communicate expectations with your users.** If you're moving from one system to another, you might have a lapse in which data must be updated prior to going live.

>> **Do it during downtime.** If you have significant data, consider running the migration during nonworking hours. Especially if the system is live for some groups of users already, this may avoid confusion.

>> **Build yourself some cushion for error.** Don't try to execute the migration the day before sales training. Something unanticipated could happen that prevents successful completion.

Validating and augmenting your data

Similar to analyzing results of the test data (see the section "Analyzing the test data results," earlier in this chapter), when the data has been loaded, run reports to validate a cross-sampling of records to ensure accuracy and completeness. If you can, compare screens in Salesforce with those of your legacy system. Make sure that data is stored in the correct fields and that values make sense. If you see an address in a phone field, you need to clean your data or fix your field mapping. Strive for perfectly imported data — but expect less than that, too.

Prior to rolling out Salesforce, take the extra step of manually or automatically updating some records to wow users and drive more success. When giving a demonstration or training, show users these fully entered examples and let them know the potential for Salesforce.

Managing Your Salesforce Database

After you implement Salesforce, you need to make sure that you create processes for periodically updating and backing up your data. If you don't, human error can lead to frustration and heartache. Duplicate records, dead leads, records that need to be transferred when a user leaves the company — these are just a few examples of data that needs to be updated.

Most of the data maintenance tools are accessible from the Data Management heading located under the Administrative Setup heading on the sidebar of Setup. (See Chapter 7 for details on deduplication options.)

Backing up your data

If you have Unlimited, Enterprise, or Professional Edition, Salesforce offers a weekly export service of all your data that you can use to create a backup. Other editions have access to a monthly export, with similar behavior.

To export and back up your data, follow these steps:

1. Choose Setup ⇨ Administer ⇨ Data Management, and click the Data Export link.

The Weekly Export Service page appears.

2. Click the Export Now button.

3. Select the appropriate export file encoding from the Export File Encoding drop-down list and select the check boxes if you want to include files and replace carriage (hard) returns with spaces.

If you live in the United States or Western Europe, you don't have to change the Export File Encoding selection.

4. Specify which Salesforce objects you want to export, or just leave the default Include All Data check box selected.

5. When you're done, click the Start Export button.

The Weekly Export Service: Export Requested page appears. You'll receive an email from Salesforce with a link to a page where you can retrieve zipped .csv files of all your data. You have 48 hours to download your data, after which time the data files are deleted.

6. Click the link in the email and log in to Salesforce, if required.

The Export Service page appears, as shown in Figure 22-2.

You can also access the Export Service page by choosing Setup ⇨ Application Setup ⇨ Data Management ⇨ Data Export.

FIGURE 22-2: Downloading your data export file.

7. **Click the Download link.**

   A dialog box appears, allowing you to open or save your zip file to a location accessible from your computer.

Although not required, we recommend that you schedule a routine data export of your data by clicking the Schedule Export button on the Export Service page (refer to Figure 22-2). This option follows the same steps as an immediate backup, but it also allows you to select when you want your backup to automatically occur.

Mass-transferring records

A sales rep leaves. Sales territories get readjusted. You imported a file but forgot to assign records to the right owners in advance. These are just a few examples of when you might have to transfer records. Salesforce allows you to mass-transfer lead, account, and custom object records — and the processes for all three types are very similar.

When transferring leads or accounts, Salesforce automatically transfers certain linked records on the detail page.

>> **For both leads and accounts:** All open activities owned by the current owner transfer to the new owner.

>> **For accounts:** All notes, contacts, and open opportunities owned by the existing owner transfer to the new owner.

>> **For custom object records:** No linked records are transferred.

To mass-transfer records, follow these steps:

1. **Choose Setup ⇨ Administer ⇨ Data Management ⇨ Mass Transfer Records.**

   A Mass Transfer Records page appears.

2. **Click the Transfer link for the appropriate type of record, depending on your needs.**

   A Mass Transfer page appears with a set of filtering options to help you search for records. You can use the filters to specify the set of data that you want to transfer — for example, all Accounts with San Francisco in the Billing City field.

3. **In the Transfer From and Transfer To fields, use the Lookup icons to find the appropriate users.**

   With leads, you can also transfer to or from queues. See Chapter 7 for details on lead queues.

4. **If you're mass-transferring accounts, select the check boxes to specify whether you want to transfer types of opportunities, cases, and teams.**

5. **Define additional criteria to filter your search by using the drop-down lists and fields provided.**

   You do this by selecting a field from the first drop-down list, selecting an operator from the second drop-down list, and then typing a value in the field. For example, if you want to transfer all of one sales rep's New York City accounts to a new rep, your criteria would be

   - *Field:* City

   - *Operator:* Equals

   - *Value:* New York

6. **When you're satisfied with your settings and filters, click the Find button.**

   The Mass Transfer page reappears with a list of results.

7. **Use the check boxes to select the records that you want to transfer.**

8. **When you're done, click the Transfer button.**

   The Mass Transfer page reappears when the transfer is complete.

Mass-deleting records

If you're the administrator, you may want or need to mass–delete records. A couple of typical examples include deleting dead leads and eliminating accounts that haven't had any activity. Salesforce allows you to mass–delete leads, accounts, contacts, activities, cases, solutions, and products — and the processes are very similar.

To mass–delete records, follow these steps:

1. **Choose Setup ➪ Administer ➪ Data Management ➪ Mass Delete Records.**

   The Mass Delete Records page appears.

2. **Click one of the Mass Delete links, depending on the type of standard record that you want to mass-delete.**

   The Mass Delete Records page appears with a three- to five-step wizard for mass-deleting. The five-step wizard for Accounts is shown in Figure 22-3. The Mass Delete Accounts page has two extra steps based on opportunities that are closed/won or that aren't owned by you. The Mass Delete Products page has one extra step to archive products with line items on opportunities.

FIGURE 22-3:
Select records for mass deletion.

3. **Review the Salesforce warnings in Step 1 of the wizard.**

   Consider what other related records would be deleted and the consequences of that action. For example, deleting an account provides an option to delete its related opportunities. If this includes closed-won deals, this will impact any historical trend reporting covering that time frame.

4. **Back up relevant data by generating a report and exporting it to Excel as part of Step 2 of the wizard.**

   See Chapter 23 for details on building and exporting reports.

5. **Use the filters in Step 3 of the wizard to define criteria for the search.**

   You do this by selecting a field from the first drop-down list, selecting an operator from the second drop-down list, and typing a value in the field.

   You can see an example of this in the preceding section.

6. **Click the Search button.**

   The Mass Delete page reappears with a list of possible records at the bottom of the page. Do the following:

   - *If you're mass-deleting accounts,* you can select the check box in Step 4 of the wizard if you want to delete accounts that have Closed/Won opportunities and/or select the check box to delete accounts with another owner's opportunities.

   - *If you're mass-deleting products,* select the check box if you want to archive products with line items on opportunities.

   - *If you're mass-deleting another object,* proceed to Step 7.

7. **Use the Action column to select records to be deleted.**

8. **When you're satisfied, click the Delete button.**

   A dialog box appears to confirm the deletion.

9. **Click OK.**

   The Mass Delete page reappears, minus the records that you deleted.

Finding and merging duplicates

Salesforce can merge existing duplicate records. The hard part is less about the technology and more about your coming up with some foundational guidelines to determine whether data in a field is accurate. Some companies rely on data that is synced with a specific third-party service, like Dun & Bradstreet or LinkedIn. Whatever you choose, you need to establish a tie-breaking source of truth, because salespeople often find differing data from other sources that they may reference to justify moving that account into their territories. When you've established the guidelines, finding and merging duplicates is possible and can be woven into the part of a regular sales process.

For example, an inbound sales development rep may have to wade through dozens of inbound lead records a day from users who sign up for product trials. One of the data quality steps that should be ingrained in a rep's day is clicking the Find Duplicates button on a lead record to see if the person already exists.

To find duplicate lead records, follow these steps:

1. **From any lead record, click the Find Duplicates button.**

   The Search for Duplicates page for that lead appears.

2. **Check which fields should determine if another record may be a duplicate.**

   Salesforce defaults to looking for duplicates that match by name, company, email address, and phone number. It returns matching leads, contacts, accounts, and opportunities based on the default criteria. If you change the criteria, click Search again to refresh the results.

3. **Check the box to the left of each lead's name that you want to merge.**

4. **Click Merge Leads.**

   The merge page for your records returns, listing all fields for that object, and the contents of each record for those fields. This is where your predefined guidelines come in. Salesforce highlights which fields have conflicting information, and suggests which record should be the master one, as shown in Figure 22-4.

Merge Leads   Help for this Page

Previous Merge Cancel

Select the values that you want to retain in the merged record. Highlighted rows indicate fields that contain conflicting data. The Master Record selected will retain read-only and hidden field values. The oldest Created By date and user will be retained in the merged record. Note: All related records including any campaigns and activities will be associated with the new merged record.

	Dave Carroll [Select All]	David Carroll [Select All]
Master Record	○	◉
Lead Owner	Liz Kao-Dummies6	Liz Kao-Dummies6
Name	◉ Dave Carroll	○ David Carroll
Company	○ Oracle	◉ Oracle Corp.
Title		
Lead Source	Other	Other
Campaign		
Industry		
Annual Revenue		
Phone	(650) 650-6506	(650) 650-6506
Mobile	(510) 555-5555	(510) 555-5555
Fax	(510) 555-5555	(510) 555-5555
Email	dcarroll@merce.com	dcarroll@merce.com
Website		
Lead Status	New	New
Rating		
No. of Employees		
Address	136 Brecon Court Redwood City, CA 94062 USA	136 Brecon Court Redwood City, CA 94062 USA
Product Interest		
SIC Code		
Number of Locations		
Current Generator(s)		
Primary		
Description		

FIGURE 22-4: Evaluating matching duplicate records.

5. **Use the radio buttons on fields with conflicting data to confirm which record is the source of truth for a particular field.**

   Reference your pre-established guidelines.

6. **Click Merge.**

WARNING

   This action can't be undone.

   The merged record appears.

Getting Help with Complex Data Tasks

TIP

This chapter shows you some of the basic operations that you can perform to import and manage your data in Salesforce. For many companies that have more complex data needs, this may be an oversimplification. If you need help with your data, here are some resources you can turn to:

>> **Talk with your customer success manager or account executive.** These folks can help define your needs and point you to the appropriate solution or resource.

>> **Go outside.** If you're looking for outside help, contact a Salesforce.com consulting partner. Your customer success manager or account executive can put you in touch.

» **Check out offerings by partners on the AppExchange.** Go to `www.appexchange.com` and search using the phrase *data cleansing* in the search bar.

» **Talk to developers.** On the Salesforce Developers site (`http://developer.force.com`), click the Community tab to talk to a community of developers who have wrestled or are familiar with your data challenges. These forums are of a technical nature, but if this is what you're looking for, you might find it here.

7
Measuring Overall Business Performance

Chapter 23

Analyzing Data with Reports

How much time do you waste every week trying to prepare reports for your manager, your team, or yourself? You have to chase down the information, get it into a useful format, and then make sense of the data. By the time you do all of that, the information is probably already out of date, despite your best efforts. Have you ever felt less than confident of the details or the totals?

If this sounds like a familiar problem, you can use reports in Salesforce to generate up-to-the-moment data analysis to help you measure your business. As long as you and your teams regularly use Salesforce to manage your accounts, opportunities, and other customer-related information, you don't have to waste time wondering where to find the data and how to consolidate it. Instead, let Salesforce do that work for you.

And unlike other applications in which the business users often have to spend precious time relying on more-technical people to build their custom reports, you can do this all by yourself in minutes, with no geeky programming. With an easy-to-use reporting wizard, you can customize existing reports or build them from scratch.

This chapter includes an overview of the standard reports provided by Salesforce, building reports from scratch, and modifying existing reports to make them your own. Within a report, we take you through the different ways you can filter the report to get just the information that's necessary for creating a clearer picture of your business. Finally, be sure to check out our suggestions on how to keep your reports organized in easy-to-find folders as your universe of reports expands.

Discovering Reports

With reports, you can present your data in different formats, select a seemingly infinite number of columns, filter your data, subtotal information, use color to highlight when certain conditions are met, and embed formulas, just to name a few features. And like other pages in Salesforce, you can quickly find the details. So, for example, you can go from the Reports home page to a lead report to a lead record simply by clicking links.

Navigating the Reports home page

When you click the Reports tab, as shown in Figure 23-1, you'll see a search bar, a Folders navigation tree in the left panel of your browser, and a list of recently run reports within a particular folder in the main panel of this page. Salesforce has functionality on the Reports home page to help you more easily navigate through a large set of reports and dashboards. Salesforce comes standard with a set of predefined reports and folders that are commonly used for measuring sales, marketing, support, and other functions. For example, the Opportunity Pipeline report is an oft-used report by sales individuals and managers to help prioritize which deals to work on.

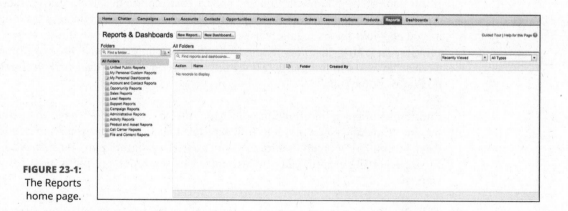

FIGURE 23-1:
The Reports
home page.

TIP

You can't save a custom report in a standard folder. If you're an administrator, consider creating custom folders using the New Report Folder option that's accessed from the little folder icon to the right of the Find Folders search bar in the left-side pane, as shown in Figure 23-2. Organize this according to your important functional areas that ultimately replace these standard folders.

FIGURE 23-2:
Creating a new report folder.

From the Reports home page, you can do the following:

- **Find reports.** Type keywords into the Find Reports and Dashboards search bar, and while you're typing, Salesforce will return matching reports based on the report's name and description fields.

- **Search a folder.** Use the Find Folders search bar or scroll down the Folders navigation pane to quickly locate a particular folder.

- **Create a folder.** If you're an administrator, click the New Folder link as mentioned in the previous tip to create new report folders to house custom reports.

- **Select a folder.** When you click a folder in the Folders pane, the contents of that report or dashboard folder will appear in the main panel. To backtrack, click the All Reports option at the top of the Folders navigation tree in the Folders pane.

- **Filter report lists.** Use the filters on the right side of the main pane, as shown in Figure 23-3, to narrow the number of reports that you see within a particular reports folder.

FIGURE 23-3:
Filtering on Reports.

>> **View recent reports.** Select the Recently Viewed option from the filter drop-down list to match the criteria of what reports you want to see. Click and hold down your mouse button over the Scheduled Items icon (that's its own column heading) to quickly select additional columns to help you more quickly find your report. You can also click and drag column headings to rearrange them or remove them.

>> **Display the report.** Click a report title.

>> **Edit, delete, or export data to Excel.** On standard or custom reports, click the Customize button, the Delete button, or the Export Details button. We talk more about exporting your reports in the "Exporting Reports to Excel" section, later in this chapter.

>> **Create a report.** Click the New Report button to start the Report Builder Wizard.

Displaying a report

When you click a report title or run a report from the wizard, a report page appears based on the criteria that was set. For example, under the Opportunity Reports folder, click the Opportunity Pipeline link. The Opportunity Pipeline report appears, as shown in Figure 23-4. This report, as we mention earlier, is one of the most-used standard reports in Salesforce.

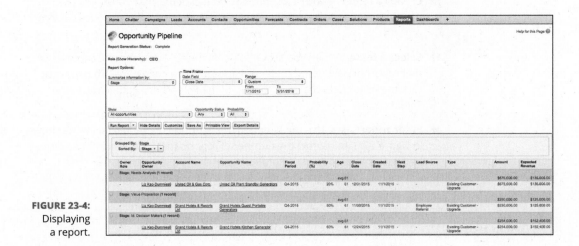

FIGURE 23-4:
Displaying
a report.

A basic report page in Salesforce is broken up into a few parts:

>> **Org Drill Down:** You can use this area at the top of the page to quickly limit results based on role hierarchy. This helps reduce the number of redundant reports that you have to create just to see a slightly different view of the data based on a team's structure. For example, you can use the Org Drill Down to see how the Eastern region team's numbers are faring. You could drill down even further to see how a specific sales rep in the Eastern region is doing, without having to create a separate report. See Chapter 21 for steps on setting up the role hierarchy.

>> **Report Options:** This section is at the top of the page, just below the Org Drill Down. You can use it to summarize, filter, and perform other operations on a report. For details on report options, see the "Filtering Reports Efficiently" section, later in this chapter.

>> **Additional filters:** This optional section is customized by the person building the report, and it allows additional filtering of certain fields that are picklists.

>> **Generated report:** This section shows the report itself. What's visible depends on the construction of the report and what you have permission to see in Salesforce. See Chapter 21 for more details on sharing.

TIP

In the Generated Report section, you can click a column heading to quickly re-sort your report by the selected column.

Developing Reports

Salesforce comes with a huge menu of useful reports, and yet they may not be exactly what you're looking for. For example, if your company has added custom fields on the account record that are unique to your customer, a standard New Accounts report doesn't show you all the information you want to see on recent accounts.

The next time you need a custom report, don't pester the IT geeks. Instead, use Report Builder to build a new report or customize an existing one.

Building a report from scratch

You don't have to be a technical guru to create a report in Salesforce. Just make sure that you can articulate a question that you're trying to answer, and then Report Builder will guide you through the steps for creating a custom report that will help you answer the question.

To create a report from scratch, click the Reports tab and follow these steps:

1. Click the New Report button.

The Create New Report page appears, as shown in Figure 23-5.

FIGURE 23-5:
Defining the objects for the report.

2. Select the report type that you want to report on, and then click Create.

You do this by first selecting the basic category of object from the Select Report Type panel, which displays a list of folders representing key objects. Clicking a folder reveals more specific report types to choose from. The standard report types will give you a visual preview of sample data and how it would look in that report template. The Create button is at the lower-right corner of this page.

When you click Create, the Report Builder drag-and-drop interface appears.

3. Customize your report using the following Report Builder features:

- *Adjust your view and time frame.* Do you want the report to show just records that you own, ones that you and your underlings own, or all records that your role is able to see? What time range do you want the report to cover? Use the picklists in the Show and Date Field section to narrow your results.

- *Add custom filters.* To help further narrow your result set, use the Add drop-down list along the Filters row. For example, you can create a custom filter to show only results where the opportunity amount is greater than $10,000.

- *Drag and drop fields.* Find fields in the left sidebar that may be additional columns that you want to have in your report. Simply click and drag that field name over to the Preview section of the Report Builder and then place that new column among your other headers.

- *Add a chart.* Look for an optional Add Chart button in the Preview pane to add a graphical summary of your results. Use the Chart Editor to choose a chart type, determine what data to represent, and decide how you want that data to be visually presented.

4. **When you're done creating your report, click the Save button.**

   The report saves, and a sample preview appears in the Report Builder Preview pane.

TIP

You can get pretty advanced with filtering options. As long as you can explain to yourself in plain English what criteria you're looking for, you should be able to build a report for it using options under the Filters ⇨ Add drop-down list, as shown in Figure 23-6. For example, if you define strategic accounts as companies that *either* did more than $1 billion in annual revenue *or* had more than 500 employees plus $500 million in annual revenue, you can generate this report. To do this, add your field filters from the Filters ⇨ Add picklist and then choose the Filter Logic option. A field will appear where you can order each filter you have and associate it using AND or OR logic.

FIGURE 23-6:
Adding filter logic to the report.

Customizing existing reports

A fast and easy way to generate reports is to customize an existing report and save it as a new one. For example, if you like the standard Pipeline Report but you want to modify the columns, you can simply work from the existing report.

To customize an existing report, go to the Reports tab and follow these steps:

1. **Find a folder that contains a report that you want to customize; click that folder, and then click a link for that report in the main Reports pane.**

   The report appears.

2. **Click the Customize button.**

   Using the Customize button, the Report Builder page appears. You can then drag and drop interface fields into columns for that report (as discussed in the previous section). A preview of the report appears while you're customizing it.

3. **Continue customizing your report until you're satisfied, and then click the Run Report button.**

   The report appears modified based on your settings from the wizard.

4. **When you're done, click Save or Save As.**

   The Save button replaces the prior custom report. The Save As button saves the new report as a new one. In either case, a page appears to save the report.

5. **Complete the fields and click Save.**

   The Reports home page appears, with a link to your new report.

CREATING CUSTOM REPORT TYPES

The Report Wizard is pretty darn thorough. At the same time, your company's quant jocks may want to perform even more advanced reporting than what's offered in the standard Report Wizard. Or you may want to simplify the number of fields that your report users see when they go through the wizard. Professional Edition, Enterprise Edition, and Performance Edition administrators can create custom report types (CRTs) to address both of these needs.

For more advanced reporting capabilities, in techno-speak, CRTs let you change the joins on the table. So, if you have a Projects object and want to report on all accounts with projects and project team members, you can create a CRT and determine which fields show up in your Select Columns to Total step. For more information on setting up CRTs, go to the Help & Training section within Salesforce and search for *create a custom report type*.

Filtering Reports Efficiently

Over time, you'll develop core reports that have the columns that you want in a format that makes sense to you. One of the huge benefits of reporting in Salesforce is that you can use existing reports on the fly and apply report options to filter or reorder the report results.

All those options and more are possible in seconds without having to use the Customize button. In the following sections, we show you how to filter your reports with tools and enhanced drill-down and breakout options.

Using the Report Options section

When you open a report, it appears with a variety of filters in the Report Options section at the top of the page, as shown in Figure 23-7. By using the filters in the Report Options section, you can look at your data from multiple angles. The available standard filters depend on the type of report that you selected.

FIGURE 23-7: Identifying your report options.

To try out the standard filters in the Report Options section by using the Opportunity Pipeline report as an example, first go to the Reports home page and click the Opportunity Pipeline link. The report appears. From the report, you can do the following with the filters in the Report Options section:

>> **Summarize your report by a field.** From the Summarize Information By drop-down list, select a field that determines how your information is summarized. For example, if you want to look at your opportunities by rep, select Opportunity Owner.

>> **Choose a time frame.** From the Time Frame area, first select a date field, and then in the drop-down list to the right, select a standard range or create one of your own. For example, if you want to look at all opportunities created from 2015 to the present, you'd first select Created Date, and then define the interval.

>> **Choose a scope.** From the Show drop-down list, select the scope of records.

>> **Look at open or closed records.** Use the Opportunity Status drop-down list if you want open and/or closed records.

>> **Limit results.** Use the Probability drop-down list if you want to limit the results by probability.

At any particular time, click the Run Report button to apply your selected filters. The report reappears based on the filters you defined.

If you ultimately want to save the report, click the Save or Save As button, and then save the report as usual. (See the section "Building a report from scratch," earlier in this chapter, for details on saving.)

Hiding and showing details

To see a collapsed or expanded view of your report data, click the Hide/Show Details button in the Report Options section. For example, from the Reports home page, click the Sales by Account report under Sales Reports. When the report appears, click the Hide Details button. The report reappears in a collapsed view, and the Hide Details button morphs into the Show Details button. Now click the Show Details button, and the report expands again. By using Hide Details, you can easily view headings, subtotals, and totals, especially for matrix reports.

Filtering with the drill-down menu

Reports in Salesforce have a drill-down function that you can use to select rows within a report and instantly break them down by a different field. For example, if you're reviewing an Opportunity by Rep report, you may want to select a specific rep and then sort the rep's opportunities by stage. With enhanced drill-down and breakout options, you can do this in just a few quick clicks.

To use the drill-down and breakout options (using Sales by Rep as the example), follow these steps:

1. **From the Reports home page, click the Sales by Rep link under the Sales Reports folder.**

   The report appears.

2. **In the left column of the report, select check boxes for records you want to view.**

   If you don't see check boxes and you know you've closed opportunities in Salesforce, select an interval in the Report Options section to see all your historical opportunities and click Run Report to view more records.

3. **At the bottom of the page, select a field from the Check Rows to Filter, Then Drill Down By drop-down list to summarize the information, if desired, and then click the Drill Down button.**

The report reappears based on your selections. For example, if you chose the Close Month option from the Drill Down By drop-down list, your selected opportunities would be sorted by close month.

4. **If you want to use the report in the future, click Save As, and then follow the normal directions for saving reports.**

See the section "Building a report from scratch," earlier in this chapter, for saving details.

Clearing filters

If you have reports with advanced filters, you can easily view and clear the filters to expand the results. For example, if you created and saved the test report in the preceding section, you may want to clear the filter on the selected rep(s) to see all closed opportunities by close month for all reps. The advanced filters, if any, appear just below the Filtered By header on a report page.

To clear a filter, follow these steps:

1. **Click the link for a report to which you applied filters.**

The report appears, and your criteria filters are listed under the Filtered By header, as shown in Figure 23-8.

FIGURE 23-8: Clearing criteria filters in a drill-down report.

2. **Right below the Filtered By header, click the Clear link to remove a filter.**

   The report reappears, displaying a potentially wider universe of data.

3. **Be sure to click the Save or Save As button if you want to save this report.**

You can quickly modify advanced filters by clicking the Edit link next to the Filtered By header. The Report Builder page appears.

Exporting Reports to Excel

Ideally, you want to run your reports right out of the application, getting rid of that mad scramble of collecting data before your next big meeting. However, sometimes you'll want to generate a report and then export it to Excel. Maybe you need to run some complex spreadsheet calculations, or you need to plug numbers into an existing macro template. No problem. You can do that with the click of a button.

To export a report, click the Reports tab and follow these steps:

1. **Click the Name of the report you want to export.**

   The report appears.

   For some reports, you can skip this step by selecting the Export option in the Action drop-down menu next to the report name.

2. **Click the Export Details button.**

   A page appears to define your settings for exporting the file.

3. **Complete the fields and click the Export button.**

   A window appears, prompting you to open or save the file.

4. **Follow the steps, as desired.**

   When the file opens, the report data appears in Excel.

5. **Click Done to return to your Salesforce report.**

   The report page reappears.

Some companies get nervous about certain users having the ability to export company data. If this is a concern, and you have the Enterprise or Performance Edition, you can take one precaution by using custom profiles to eliminate the ability of some users to export to Excel. See Chapter 21 for more details on creating custom profiles.

Organizing Reports

TIP

A word to the wise: Reports start multiplying like rabbits as you become addicted to reporting in Salesforce. Do yourself a favor: Organize them from day one and lay out a process for maintaining and deleting reports.

Creating new folders

Nothing is worse than seeing a gazillion reports under the Unfiled Public Reports folder. You start wasting a ridiculous amount of time just identifying which report is the one you want. If you have permission to manage public folders, avoid the headache by creating new report folders.

To create a new report folder, click the Reports tab and follow these steps:

1. **Click the New Folder link to the right of the Find Folders search bar.**

   A New Report Folder page appears.

2. **Type a name for the folder in the Report Folder Label field.**

   For example, if you want a folder for operational reports, you might name it Sales Ops Reports.

3. **Use the Public Folder Access drop-down list to determine read versus read/write privileges to the folder.**

   If you select Read/Write, a user with access to the folder can save over the original report.

4. **Use the two list boxes and the Add/Remove buttons to select reports in the Unfiled Public Reports folder and move them to the new folder.**

5. **Use the radio buttons to select who should have access to the folder.**

   As with other Salesforce folder tools, your choices are All, None, and Selective.

6. **If you chose the Selective option in Step 5, use the two list boxes and Add/Remove buttons to highlight groups or roles and move them to the Shared To list box.**

7. **When you're done, click Save.**

   The Reports home page reappears, and your folder is added to the Folder menu.

Determining folder access

One of the great features of Salesforce reporting is the ability to determine who gets to access which reports easily and intuitively. Access to reports (and dashboards) is controlled via the settings on the folder in which they're stored.

When you've created some report folders, you can use them to determine who gets access to which folders. For example, if you don't want anyone to see a report you've created (or you're not ready to share it yet), just keep it in a personal folder that only you have access to. By default, any folder you create is only accessible to you and administrators until you decide to share it with others.

Salesforce has three different types of access levels to report folders:

>> **Viewer:** The viewer of a folder can view a report, refresh it, and run it. A user with this access level can't customize or save the report, unless he clones it into a new report.

>> **Editor:** An editor of a folder can view, refresh, and run a report, as well as edit, move, save, or delete it.

>> **Manager:** The manager of a folder can do everything a viewer and editor can do, plus she can share the report with others and rename it.

To add users with these privileges to a report, just hover over the folder in question, click the pin on the right side, and click Share.

Maintaining your report library

TIP

Actually, what's worse than a gazillion reports under Unfiled Public Reports is a universe of reports, some of which are valuable, others of which are useless. Creating public report folders is a good first step, but you may want to apply some of these additional hints on a periodic basis:

>> **Accurately name your reports.** You and your users can't know what's behind a report link unless you name it clearly and precisely.

>> **Consider using report numbers within your report names.** For instance, use standard file-naming conventions like 1.1 North America Pipeline. This way, managers can refer to report numbers so that everyone's looking at the same report.

>> **Delete unnecessary reports.** If multiple people in your company have permission to manage public reports, you may want to survey them before

accidentally deleting a report. Unnecessary or redundant reports just make it harder for everyone to find what he or she wants. And in case you mistakenly delete a report (you'll find out soon enough), you have up to 15 days to rescue it from the Recycle Bin.

» **Update existing reports as needs arise.** For example, if you created an Opportunity Product Report and used an advanced filter such as Product Family Equals Software, make sure that you manually update the report if the product family name changes. Otherwise, your reports will be off.

» **Use clear report questions.** For example, you might use the Report Question field to summarize certain filters to your report.

Mastering Reports

As Salesforce has matured over the years and more users have come to rely on it to house the bulk of their customer-touching information, users' reporting needs have also matured. Salesforce has done a great job of making potentially very complicated database queries still accessible to the business user.

In this section, we talk briefly about some of the more advanced functionality, in case you're feeling stuck about how to get information in your reports in a certain way. Most likely, you have a way to get you what you want, but you may need to dig a little deeper into Salesforce.

Building custom summary formulas

Salesforce provides prebuilt functionality that calculates the sum, average, highest value, and lowest value of certain fields that you select for your reports. However, you may need additional summary information based on calculations unique to your business. For example, your business may want to see win-rate percentages or coverage ratios in your reports. Salesforce allows the addition of custom formula calculations for your reports (and dashboards). This means that you can take summary information from other fields and lump them together to come up with a new calculation and corresponding result. It doesn't matter whether you know old math or new math, Salesforce can derive these values for you using Excel-like commands.

To create a new custom summary formula, follow these steps:

1. **Click a link for an existing report.**

   The report appears.

2. **Click the Customize button.**

   The Report Builder appears.

3. **In the Fields column in the left pane of the Report Builder, find the Formulas folder and click into that to drill down.**

4. **Select the Add Formula option, as shown in Figure 23-9, and drag it into the preview pane as its own column.**

   The Custom Summary Formula Wizard page pops up.

FIGURE 23-9:
Adding a custom
formula.

5. **Complete the fields, as required:**

   - *Enter a column name* as it will appear on the report in the Label field. Optionally, type a description. Ideally, this field helps explain the math formula in layman's terms.

   - *Select the type of format* that you want your results to be in from the Format drop-down list. For example, if you want to calculate the revenue per item of all your products in the pipeline this year, you'll want your result to be Currency.

   - *Select the number of decimal places to display* for your selected data type from the Decimal Places drop-down list.

   - *Choose where you want the summary calculations to be displayed in the report.* Reference the visual guide to assist you in determining if you want the output to appear at all summary levels or just specific ones.

6. **Build your formula in the Formula section, as shown in Figure 23-10:**

   a. *Select one of the fields listed in the Summary Fields drop-down list, and then choose the kind of summary type to use in your formula.*

      This field's value, and how it will be summarized, are automatically added into your formula. In our example, we select Amount and Average.

b. *Click the appropriate operator icons from the drop-down list with the same name.*

In our example, we select the / (Divide) option.

c. *Repeat these steps, as needed, to build your formula.*

If you need to know what functions to use for a particular operation, use the Functions picklist. Salesforce will also return some help text to give you an idea of how those functions should be formatted.

Custom Summary Formula   Help for this Page ⓘ ✕

Column Name: | Split Revenue | 🔲

Description: [   ]

Format: | Currency ▾ | Decimal Places: | 2 ▾ |

Where will this formula be displayed?

This formula calculation will be displayed in the report at the level you select.

● All summary levels
○ Grand summary only
○ **Grouping 1:** Stage

Formula   **Functions**   **Tips**

Summary Fields ▾ Operators ▾ [Check Syntax] | All ▾ | | ABS ▾ |

(AMOUNT:AVG)/ 1.12

ABS(number)

Returns the absolute value of a number, a number without its sign

[< Insert]   Help on this function

[OK]   [Cancel]

FIGURE 23-10:
Building your custom formula for your report.

7. **Click Check Syntax to check your formula.**

Syntax that contains errors is automatically highlighted.

8. **Click OK when you're finished.**

The pop-up window closes, and you're back at the Report Wizard. You should see the new column showing sample data in the Preview section.

REMEMBER

The custom summary formula isn't saved until you save the report. Clicking Done just includes it in this step of the Report Wizard. Make sure that you save the report.

9. **Click Run Report to see the new column showing real data.**

Understanding additional reporting options

You can do a lot more fun things with reports. Even many long-term users of Salesforce reports may not know about all these additional analytics capabilities. Here is a brief summary to get data detectives more excited about it:

» **Conditional highlighting:** You can apply conditional highlighting to summarize matrix reports and help you easily highlight values that may deserve more of your attention. You can use this with custom summary formulas to highlight high or low percentages, averages, and ratios. You see a lot of syllables in this feature, but conditional highlighting translates into setting thresholds for certain key numerical values and color-coding them to show whether a threshold has been surpassed. In an Opportunity Pipeline by Rep report, you can quickly get an understanding of how people are doing when each rep's total won opportunities are highlighted in red, green, or yellow.

» **Bucketing fields:** Bucketing a field lets you select a column in a report, define ranges for data in that field, and group them into "buckets" with names that you get to define. For example, the currency captured in an Amount field could be updated into three categories: small, medium, and large. You can define what currency ranges fall under the small bucket, what range falls under the medium bucket, and so on. You can identify columns in reports that are bucket fields by the little bucket icon to the left of the column name. To see an example of how a bucket field is created, refer to Figure 23-11.

FIGURE 23-11: Building bucket field ranges.

>> **Joined reports:** This is a powerful tool that allows you to create one report that consists of report "blocks," each of which is a separate report that may or may not be reporting off the same objects. So, if you were trying to run a report that showed both your closed won opportunities as well as the opportunity win rate, you could join two reports. One block would show the total of all your closed won opportunities for a time range, while a second block could be based off of all opportunities so that you can calculate that win ratio.

>> **Scheduled report runs:** If you have the fun job of providing the powers that be with the same type of report every Monday morning, or at the end of every month, you can automate the running and emailing of a report after you've customized it and made it just right for everyone.

For more in-depth information on each of these advanced analytics capabilities, click the Help & Training link in Salesforce and search using the appropriate keywords (conditional highlighting, bucketed fields, and joined reports) in the search bar.

Chapter 24

Seeing the Big Picture with Dashboards

D
ashboards are visual representations of custom reports that you create in Salesforce. For example, you can see data in a chart, a graph, or a gauge. You can use dashboards to illustrate key performance indicators (KPIs) and other metrics important to your business. A *metric* is simply something you want to measure (for example, sales by rep, leads by source, opportunities by partner, cases by agent, and so on).

What does this mean for you? If you're a sales or service rep, you can track your daily progress against attainment of goals. If you're a manager, you can easily see how reps stack up against each other and where you need to get involved to hit your numbers. And if you're on the executive team, you have dashboards with actionable charts and graphs for strategic decision making to improve the business.

In this chapter, we share tips on planning your metric reporting strategy. Then we show you how to create dashboards. We walk you through updating dashboard properties and components. We also explain how to organize dashboards and their related reports so that you know you're looking at the right information.

Figuring Out Dashboards

Dashboards are pages in Salesforce comprising tables and charts designed to help you understand important aspects of your business, such as opportunities per territory and leads by source. Dashboards are critical to being able to assess the health of your business and spot trends early. The following sections show you some basic concepts so that you can consider your strategies before you start unleashing them on your organization.

Breaking down basic elements

You can build a dashboard with as many as 20 individual charts, tables, metrics, gauges, or custom components; each item is a *dashboard component.* Similar to building charts with the Report Wizard (see Chapter 23), components are based on reports that you create. In fact, you can click a component on a dashboard to make the underlying report appear. Here's a quick summary of the components that are available to you:

» **Horizontal bar or vertical column charts** (see Figure 24-1) are great when you want to depict a simple measurement with an *x*-axis and a *y*-axis. For example, use bar charts if you want to create a component that displays pipeline by stage.

» **Horizontal bar or vertical column grouped charts** work well when you want to compare groups of bars with each other. For example, use grouped bar charts if you want to create a chart that displays pipeline by stage broken out for each month.

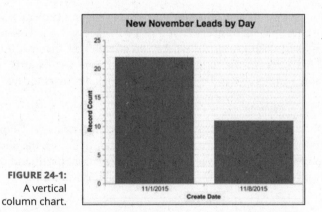

FIGURE 24-1:
A vertical
column chart.

>> **Horizontal bar or vertical column stacked charts** work well when you want grouping within a bar. For example, use stacked column charts if you want to create a chart that shows cases by status and then by type (such as problems versus feature requests).

>> **Horizontal bar or vertical column stacked-to-100% charts** are excellent when you're more interested in percentages than amounts. If you're comparing new versus existing business, stacked-to-100% charts can help you understand what percentage of each stage was new business versus existing business.

>> **Pie charts** (see Figure 24-2) work just like the standard bar charts, but the data is shown as a pie with the percentage and amount for each wedge.

FIGURE 24-2:
A pie chart.

>> **Donut charts** work just like pie charts but also show the total for the whole chart. (Goes great with coffee and morning meetings.)

>> **Funnel charts** add an additional visual element to the mix by changing the height of each grouping based on its proportion. For example, use a funnel chart if you want to easily see how much each stage in your pipeline is worth.

>> **Line charts** are helpful if you're trying to express trends, particularly when time is part of the measurement. For example, use a line chart if you want to analyze the number of newly created opportunities by month for your entire company.

>> **Grouped line charts** add a layer of complexity. For example, a line group chart could help you express the number of newly created opportunities by month broken out by region or unit.

>> **Cumulative line charts** allow you to track the progress of a single metric over time. For example, a line cumulative chart could help you see the number of closed cases by day over the course of an entire month.

>> **Grouped cumulative line charts** allow you to track progress over multiple metrics over time. For example, a line grouped cumulative chart could help you see the number of closed cases grouped by agent per day over the course of an entire month.

>> **Tables** create simple but powerful four-column tables. For example, use tables if you want your dashboard to show the top ten forecasted deals in the quarter in descending value.

TIP

You can create tables in dashboards but not in the charting tool of the Report Wizard.

>> **Metrics** insert the grand total of a report at the end of a dashboard label that you customize. Metrics are compelling when you want to tell a story that might require a bit more explanation. Metrics tend to work well in concert with other components. For example, if you use a pie chart to summarize opportunity by stage, you could add a metric to summarize total pipeline.

>> **Gauges** (see Figure 24-3) are useful when you have a specific measurable objective and you want to track your progress. A gauge applies the grand total of a report as a point on a scale that you define. For example, use a gauge if you want to measure actual quarterly new bookings against a quota that you define.

FIGURE 24-3:
A gauge.

>> **Scatter charts** aid in showing correlation between one to two groupings of data. For example, you can look at all closed-won opportunities last quarter, and group those by account owner. On your *x*-axis, you can measure the total amount of those closed-won deals (still grouped by the opportunity owner), and your *y*-axis can show the annual revenue for each account (which is a

standard field on that account record). Do your salespeople tend to close a higher value of deals when the customer itself generates more revenue? Let your scatter chart tell you.

>> **Visualforce Pages** allow you to create your own custom dashboard components (or download other people's). Even if you're just interested in a snazzier graphic element, go to www.appexchange.com and click the Components category to see what others have created.

If you're an administrator or a user with permission to manage dashboards, you can create, edit, and organize them. And even if you don't have such permissions, you can still view them by clicking the Dashboards tab on the home page.

Planning useful dashboards

We always say that the best way to build a system is to envision what you want to ultimately measure. Do you want to know who your top sales reps are? Would you like to understand what your best accounts are buying from you and how much? Do you wonder how long it takes to close a case? This method of starting with the business questions you want to answer applies to your building of reports and is true of dashboards.

TIP

If you're an administrator or part of the team responsible for deploying Salesforce, consider these tips as you develop your dashboards:

>> **Focus on your end-users.** Meet with sales, marketing, and support management and have them define their KPIs for their teams and business. Knowing this helps you customize Salesforce and construct useful dashboards.

>> **Create a common set of components to reflect a universal way to look at business health.** This is especially true if your company has multiple sales teams. For example, after you determine the key sales metrics for your company's overall dashboard, you can replicate the dashboard and then customize other dashboards for each sales team. By doing this, everyone in the company is speaking a common language.

Building Dashboards

To build a dashboard, you need to create your custom reports first. You also need to create public folders for your dashboard reports if you want dashboards to be viewable for other users. See Chapter 23 for all the details on creating custom reports and organizing them in folders.

Only system administrators and users with permission to manage dashboards can add, edit, and delete dashboards. See Chapter 21 for details on how to grant permissions.

In the following sections, we show you how to install a prebuilt dashboard and how to clone a dashboard. Then we cover the steps to build a dashboard from scratch.

Installing sample dashboards and reports

One of the best ways to get your feet wet with dashboards is to install sample dashboards from the AppExchange. Salesforce not only creates the dashboard for you but also builds the underlying sample reports to generate the components.

To install sample dashboards, follow these steps:

1. **In your web browser go to** www.appexchange.com.

   The AppExchange home page appears.

2. **Type** Dashboards **in the Search bar at the top and click the Magnifying Glass button.**

   A page full of AppExchange apps appears. The apps with the Salesforce or Salesforce Labs logos are made and provided for free by Salesforce.com.

3. **Click an app's listing to see more information about it.**

   The App Overview page appears with a description and images. If you find a set of dashboards that you'd like to download and install, check out Chapter 19 for more information on installing apps from the AppExchange.

If you're having trouble accessing dashboards, or installing them from the AppExchange, you may not have the proper permissions. In this circumstance, consult with your administrator.

Cloning a dashboard

To save time or repurpose useful features, you can generate a dashboard by cloning an existing one and then modifying it. For example, if you envision creating multiple dashboards for different sales units with common components, you can use this shortcut and then modify the associated reports.

REMEMBER

When you clone a dashboard, you don't clone another set of identical reports. Instead, the newly cloned dashboard *references* the same custom reports that the original dashboard references. If you want the new dashboard to refer to different reports, see the "Developing a dashboard from scratch" section, later in this chapter.

To clone a dashboard, follow these steps:

1. **Click the Dashboards tab.**

The last dashboard that you viewed appears.

2. **Type the name of a dashboard in the Find a Dashboard search bar to search for a dashboard, or browse and select an option from the Find a Dashboard drop-down list to select a dashboard that you want to clone.**

In this example, choose the sample dashboard entitled Company Performance Dashboard.

The dashboard appears.

3. **Click the Clone button.**

The Dashboard Builder page appears.

4. **Update any of the dashboard components as you see fit.**

5. **Click Save to leave the Dashboard Builder.**

The Save Dashboard dialog box appears.

6. **Change your new dashboard's settings, paying close attention to the following:**

- *Title:* Change the title of the dashboard.

- *Dashboard Unique Name:* This field is automatically populated for you with your title, but any spaces are replaced by underscores. The Dashboard Unique Name is used by Salesforce to distinguish dashboards from a database perspective.

- *Save To:* Select the folder in which to store this dashboard from this drop-down list.

- *Running User:* The *running user* is the user whose security settings will apply to the dashboard. So, any user who can view the dashboard will see what that running user sees.

REMEMBER

If the running user for a dashboard ever leaves the company or is made inactive for another reason, the dashboard won't show data. The same goes for any reports the dashboard references if that report is moved into a folder that the running user doesn't have access to.

7. **Click Save to view your new dashboard.**

Developing a dashboard from scratch

Now that you know the basics of dashboards, let's find out how to develop a dashboard from scratch.

To create a new dashboard, follow these steps:

1. **Click the Reports tab.**

   The Reports & Dashboards home page appears.

   You need to build your custom reports before you can develop a dashing new dashboard.

REMEMBER

2. **Build your custom reports and save them to a public folder.**

   See Chapter 23 to find out how to build custom reports.

   Dashboards that you want others to see can't use reports in your My Personal Reports folder. For purposes of this running example, find and click the Sales Reports folder (located in the left sidebar of the Reports & Dashboards folder navigation tree on the Reports & Dashboards home page) and click the following reports that show up in the main page:

   - *Sales by Rep:* Modify the Report Options to summarize information by Opportunity Owner and then Stage. Then save the report as Pipe by Rep and Stage to a public folder.

   - *Sales by Account:* Modify the Report Options to summarize information by Account Name. Then save the report as Top Revenue Customers to a public folder.

REMEMBER

   You must be an administrator or a user with permission to manage public reports if you want to add report folders.

3. **Click back on the Reports tab.**

   The Reports & Dashboards home page appears.

4. **Click the New Dashboard button.**

   The Dashboard Builder page appears.

5. **Drag the horizontal bar chart component from the Components tab on the left to one of the three available dashboard columns on the right.**

   A New Dashboard Component appears in Edit mode.

6. **Complete the fields, entering a header, footer, and/or title.**

   For this running example, name the header PIPELINE METRICS and enter the title **Pipe by Rep and Stage**. You could also add a footer at the stage, but don't bother for this example.

7. **Click the Data Sources tab on the left.**

   A list of reports grouped by folder appears.

8. **Find the appropriate report by expanding the folder you saved it in.**

   You can use the plus and minus signs to expand and collapse the report folders.

9. **Drag the report onto your dashboard component.**

   A preview of your dashboard component appears.

10. **Click Save.**

    The Save Dashboard dialog box appears.

11. **Enter a title and select a folder to save to.**

12. **Click the Save and Run Dashboard button to run the dashboard.**

    Your new dashboard appears with your dashboard component.

Modifying dashboard properties

Over time, you may have to make changes to your dashboards, whether for cosmetic reasons or to make substantive updates. We can come up with a dozen common edits, but the good news is that updating is easy.

If you need to change the basic settings of a dashboard — such as the title, folder, or running user — you need to edit the dashboard properties. To edit the properties, follow these steps:

1. **Click the Dashboards tab.**

   A dashboard appears.

2. **Select a desired dashboard from the Find a Dashboard search bar that also doubles as a drop-down list.**

   The dashboard you're trying to locate appears.

   You can also just start typing a portion of the name of one of your dashboards to be presented with a list of matching dashboards.

3. **Click the Edit button at the top of the dashboard page.**

   The Dashboard Builder appears.

4. **Click the Dashboard Properties button.**

   The Dashboard Properties dialog box appears.

5. **Modify the settings, as needed, and then click OK.**

When you click OK, the Dashboard Builder reappears, and your setting changes are applied.

Customizing components

You may want to add or change — *edit* — an existing component. To edit a component, follow these steps:

1. **Go to a dashboard and click the Edit button.**

The Dashboard Builder appears.

2. **Click the Wrench icon above a component that you want to modify.**

For example, you may want to change the chart type or display units.

The Component Editor dialog box appears, as shown in Figure 24-4.

FIGURE 24-4:
Modifying
component data.

3. **Modify the component data to adjust settings:**

- *For bar, column, or line charts:* From the Group By drop-down list, click a chart type to select the way multiple groups of values are displayed.

- *For unit of measurement:* Use the Display Units drop-down list.

- *Component type:* Click a chart image to select a component type. See the earlier section "Breaking down basic elements" for details on the components. In the example, select the vertical bar chart option. The steps will differ, depending on which component type you select.

4. **Click the Formatting tab to change the type and formatting of your dashboard component to best display your data:**

- *Table and chart components:* Use the Sort Rows By drop-down list to select the order of sorting. For example, if you want to rank the reps from biggest to smallest pipeline, choose Row Value Descending. You can also sort the row labels if you want to rank the reps by their names.

- *Maximum values displayed:* (Optional) If you want, enter a number under Maximum Values Displayed.

- *Bar, column, scatter, or line charts:* Select an option from the Axis Range drop-down list. If you select Manual, the next two fields (Chart Axis Range Minimum and Chart Axis Range Maximum) become available for input.

- *Legend position:* Select an option from the Legend Position drop-down list to display your graph's legend to the right of the chart or below the chart, or to not show it at all.

- *Chart labeling:* Adjust the chart labeling by selecting the Show Values and the Show Details on Hover check boxes.

- *Tables, metrics, and gauges:* Set up to two breakpoint values to separate different range colors from each other. Select Range Colors to represent a range of data, separated by the breakpoint values. (See Chapter 23 for more information on conditional highlighting.)

- *Gauges:* Set your Minimum and Maximum Values to represent the lowest and highest values on the gauge.

5. **Click OK.**

   The Dashboard Builder reappears with the changes you applied to the component.

6. **Click Save.**

   Your changes are saved, and your dashboard reappears.

Changing the layout

If you need to modify the dashboard layout, you can also perform this while in the Dashboard Builder.

Go to a dashboard, click the Edit button, and alter the layout. You can

>> **Modify a column size.** Select Narrow, Medium, or Wide from the drop-down list at the top of each dashboard component. All the components in the column change in size based on your setting.

>> **Add a component.** Drag a component or data source to a column and follow the steps in the section "Developing a dashboard from scratch," earlier in this chapter.

>> **Delete a component.** Click the X button located at the upper-right corner of a component. A pop-up window appears to confirm the deletion. When you click OK, the pop-up closes and the dashboard reappears, minus the deleted component.

>> **Add a column.** If you have fewer than three columns in your dashboard, you can click the plus button at the upper right or left of a column to insert a new column on that side, respectively.

>> **Delete a column.** Click the X button located at the top of a column. A pop-up window appears to confirm the deletion. When you click OK, the pop-up closes and the dashboard reappears, minus the deleted column.

>> **Rearrange components.** Drag and drop components in your dashboard to arrange them exactly as you see fit.

When you're satisfied with your changes, click the Done button. The dashboard reappears with your modifications.

TIP

You can add up to 20 components per Dashboard, but best practice is to keep your dashboards simple and easy to read. Your most important components should comprise the top row. The top row's components for a dashboard are displayed on the home pages of users who have chosen that dashboard as the one to view.

Setting a dashboard refresh schedule

Before you make decisions based on your dashboard, you'll want to make sure that those decisions are based on the latest data. Click any dashboard from your dashboard list. In the upper-right corner of the dashboard is a timestamp starting with *As Of.* You can use this to find out the last time your dashboard data was updated.

When you want to manually update your dashboard data, simply click the Refresh button at the top of the dashboard page. The components reappear one by one. When the refresh is completed, a new timestamp appears.

Enterprise and Unlimited Edition customers can schedule their dashboards to be automatically refreshed on a daily, weekly, or monthly basis. Just use the drop-down list next to the Refresh button.

To schedule a dashboard to automatically refresh, follow these steps:

1. **Click the Dashboards tab.**

A dashboard appears.

2. **Click the down arrow on the Refresh button.**

3. **Click the Schedule Refresh option.**

The Schedule Dashboard Refresh screen appears, as shown in Figure 24-5.

FIGURE 24-5:
Schedule a time
to refresh your
dashboard.

4. **(Optional) Select the To Me and/or the To Others check boxes to email a copy of the dashboard when it's refreshed.**

If you have regularly scheduled meetings, you can automatically email your dashboard to the meeting attendees prior to the meeting to give them a sneak peak of what will be discussed.

5. **Select the frequency that you want your dashboard to be refreshed.**

Each frequency option has additional options that allow you to specify exactly when the dashboard will be refreshed.

6. **Select a start and end date for the frequency that you want your dashboard to be refreshed.**

7. **Select a refresh time from the Preferred Start Time drop-down list.**

The dashboard reappears.

Organizing Your Dashboards

If you have the permissions necessary to manage dashboards, manage public reports, and view all data, you can organize your company's dashboards in folders and define the proper security access for users. By organizing dashboards, you can make sure that the right people are focusing on the right metrics to manage their business.

Viewing dashboard lists

Unlike most other tabs in Salesforce, clicking the Dashboard tab doesn't take you to its home page. Instead, the last dashboard that you viewed appears.

To access your viewable dashboards, follow these steps:

1. **Click the Go to Dashboard List link at the upper-left corner of any dashboard.**

A dashboard folder list page appears.

2. **Use the Folder drop-down list to select a desired folder.**

The Reports & Dashboards home page appears. The page for the selected folder appears in the main window with a list of available dashboards in the folder.

REMEMBER

From this list page, users with the permissions mentioned in the preceding section can perform a variety of functions:

- *Re-sort:* Click a column header to re-sort a dashboard list.

- *View:* Click a title name to view a dashboard.

- *Modify:* Click the downward-pointing triangle in the Action column of the row that matches the dashboard you want to edit. A drop-down list appears. The Edit link appears in the drop-down list for your selection.

- *Delete:* Click the downward-pointing triangle in the Action column of the row that matches the dashboard you want to delete. A drop-down list appears. The Delete link appears in the drop-down list for your selection. Select the Del link to delete the dashboard.

- *Build:* Click the New Dashboard that appears to the right of the Reports & Dashboards heading, or the folder icon to the right of the Find a Folder search bar.

Building dashboard folders

From the Reports tab, which takes you to the Reports & Dashboards home page, you can also create and edit folders. Editing a folder is easy when you understand how to create one.

To create a folder, follow these steps:

1. **On the Reports page, click the Folder icon to the right of the Find a Folder search bar and select the New Dashboard Folder option in the Folder drop-down list.**

   A New Dashboard Folder page appears.

2. **Type an intuitive name for the folder in the Dashboard Folder field.**

   For example, if you want a folder for only senior management, you might name it Executive Dashboards.

3. **Use the Public Folder Access field to determine read versus read/write privileges for the folder.**

4. **Use the radio buttons to select who should have access to the folder.**

   Your choices are All, None, and Selective.

5. **If you chose Selective in Step 4, highlight Groups or Roles in the Available for Sharing list box and add them to the Shared To list box.**

6. **Click Save.**

   The folder list page reappears. Now you can add dashboards or move existing dashboards to the new folder, which we explain in the section "Modifying dashboard properties," earlier in this chapter.

TIP

When naming folders, dashboards, and dashboard reports, consider using a standard numbering convention. For example, you could name the senior management folder 1.0 Executive Dashboards. Then the executive sales subordinate dashboard might be 1.1 and the executive marketing dashboard 1.2. By using a standard numbering methodology, you can more efficiently create, clone, and organize dashboards and dashboard reports.

The Part of Tens

IN THIS PART . . .

Use our top ten recommended Salesforce productivity enhancers.

Implement Salesforce right the first time.

Chapter 25

Ten Ways to Drive More Productivity

Salesforce.com drives much of its feature updates based on its existing road map and requests from customers just like you. A few times a year, Salesforce.com comes out with a new release of its award-winning service. That's the benefit of these cloud-based business applications, because the infrastructure isn't maintained by you. Unlike traditional software upgrades, these releases are immediately available to all customers, and most features can be activated or deactivated when you're ready to make the change.

Keeping track of all the cool new updates that Salesforce.com releases can get a little overwhelming. The speed with which it's able to roll out releases is often faster than our ability to write all about it and get it in your hands! On the flip side, perhaps you do keep track of the newest features but you've been struggling with an apparent feature limitation or you'd like more advice on how to best implement a particular feature.

Fortunately for us, both Salesforce.com and its community of users strongly believe in helping each other out to make every customer successful. Through a variety of channels, the Salesforce.com community shares best practices and offers suggestions and workarounds for even the toughest head-scratcher questions.

In this chapter, we introduce you to ten resources and tools that will help you get the most out of Salesforce. The first five sections cover essential resources that every user in your organization should know about. The last five sections fill you in on great productivity tools that you may have overlooked.

Salesforce Trailhead

Whether you're an administrator or end-user, bookmark Salesforce Trailhead (`https://developer.salesforce.com/trailhead`) *now*. Here you'll find interactive modules with real examples that help you learn various aspects of Salesforce. As you complete modules in various tracks, you'll earn badges that you can proudly share online.

Dreamforce Conference

Dreamforce (`www.salesforce.com/dreamforce`) is Salesforce.com's annual product conference that brings together developers, system administrators, and end-user business folks to learn from, network with, and party alongside product experts from Salesforce.com, as well as the ecosystem at large. Make the trek to San Francisco, and get inspired with all the great things Salesforce can do for your company.

Salesforce Success Community

Online within the Salesforce Success Community (`http://success.salesforce.com`), you can post or vote for new product ideas, see what other users are requesting, and ask and answer questions related to configuration or code. Not only do you get to see what the masses are clamoring for, but you also get to see Salesforce.com employees, partners, and customers joining together to provide feedback and assistance.

Salesforce.com Local User Groups

One of the best ways to regularly find out about upcoming features, hear about third-party vendor integrations, network with your peers, and provide product feedback is to join a local user group. You'll get to learn from and share tips with fellow customers in your vicinity. To find out if one exists near you, go to the Salesforce Success Community (`https://success.salesforce.com/featuredGroups`), and click the All User Groups by Region category in the left sidebar. If you don't see your city, think about starting your own group.

Salesforce.com Training

One of the best ways to become an expert and have an opportunity to ask an expert about your company's particular use of Salesforce is to be trained by Salesforce. com. Then you can be your company's expert and spearhead further ideas of using Salesforce to make your business processes run smoother. You find classes for every user role, and for every budget. If you'll be configuring and customizing Salesforce, you can find a series of certifications so that you can tell others just how special you are. Visit Salesforce University (`www.salesforce.com/services-training/training_certification/training.jsp`) and look for options that meet your budget and learning style.

Conga Composer

If you need to generate documents that include fields from Salesforce, as well as more static fields (like information on a quote, or legal contracts), the Conga Composer app (available on the AppExchange) helps you quickly build Microsoft document templates or Adobe Acrobat PDFs from within Salesforce. This eliminates the need to build complicated macros or forms (sometimes within Microsoft Excel or Word), while still taking advantage of the sophisticated text customization options within Microsoft products.

Field Trip

Fields in Salesforce remind us of barnacles on a boat. Over time, custom fields get created, some get abandoned, and they grow and grow over time. On a regular basis, you should slough off those unused fields, just like barnacles are scraped off a boat. Abandoned fields can clutter up your instance with redundant-sounding fields that also clog up the report-building experience, and make onboarding new hires tedious when people can't remember when a field is used or not.

Field Trip (available on the AppExchange) is a free app that does some analysis on fields in an object, and lets you know what percentage of those object records have data in that field. Of course, you need a sense as to what percentage an often-used field might have, so you can compare that to a less-used field. This tool gives you an initial start when it comes to cleaning up abandoned fields.

DupeCatcher

Salesforce has a native duplicate management feature, but DupeCatcher (an app available on the AppExchange) is a simpler option to help lower the chances of duplicate data making it into Salesforce. You'll have to know what specific fields need to match in order to determine that two records are a duplicate. You can create alerts that prevent users from saving potential duplicates. The alerts may be associated with any existing leads, contacts, or accounts with matching criteria, as well as leads with existing potential matches in the post-conversion world of contacts and accounts. Pretty nifty for something with a free price tag!

Rollup Helper

If you work with sales teams, you'll inevitably hear requests around accounts, their related parent accounts or child accounts, and how to best report on aggregate numbers across levels of accounts. For example, large multinational companies may be composed of several accounts linked together. Someone will want to analyze revenue from the ultimate parent level, or perhaps from the middle of the hierarchy to gauge regional revenue. Doing this out-of-the-box using Salesforce's parent account feature can be a challenge. Rollup Helper (an app available on the AppExchange) helps with that aggregation.

Mass Update and Mass Edit

Mass Update and Mass Edit (available on the AppExchange) allows two custom buttons to appear on a custom list view page, or on a related list. It allows you to do what the name implies — select a lot of records at once to either make the same change to one common field (that's the mass update), or select a bunch of records so they all display at multiple rows in edit mode, so you can change fields to whatever values you want to (that's the mass edit). You could use the app to perform a mass update of record owners to a single new sales user. And if you need to update the Next Steps field on your top-25 largest opportunities before the Monday morning meeting, you can use the app to select all those records and perform a mass edit. This allows you to type in each opportunity's unique next step, but without having to open up multiple tabs or use multiple mouse clicks to open each individual record.

Chapter 26

Ten Keys to a Successful Implementation

Several companies have rolled out customer relationship management (CRM) applications with the mistaken notion that you can buy the licenses, turn on the switch, and use the application as soon as you take it out of the box. Then these same companies look back months later and wonder why they're not experiencing the results they envisioned.

Nine times out of ten, the root cause is poor planning. No matter what size your implementation, building a strong plan and then executing the plan will substantially improve your chance of success.

Salesforce provides you with the tools and a platform to enhance your business effectiveness and productivity. If you're involved in the rollout of Salesforce, this chapter gives you ten tips to help you do it successfully. Check out the free webinars, answers, and more on the Salesforce Community site (http://success.salesforce.com) for more tips on leading a successful rollout.

Identifying Your Executive Sponsor

Rolling out or replacing a CRM solution is a big deal. For some managers and reps, this initiative can cause concerns for a variety of reasons: People get set in their ways, they think it's Big Brother, they assume that it's going to take a lot of their time, and so on. Sometimes other top priorities at work begin creeping in, and the importance of the CRM implementation falls along the wayside.

Every project needs a champion to help drive the CRM initiative in your company. That person is there to rally support, break logjams, and ensure that your team has the resources to get things done. We recommend that you identify an executive sponsor on day one and work with her so that she can communicate what's in it for the implementation team and set expectations for what's needed from all participants. This will go a long way toward calming fears, gaining support and commitment, and nudging the team toward a decision when the team members are at an impasse.

Building Your Project Team

CRM is less about technology and more about people, human processes, and your business. For your company to get the most out of Salesforce, you need to develop a team made up of critical stakeholders, Salesforce experts, and a cross section of end-users. If you're implementing Salesforce for sales and marketing, that might mean that the team includes managers from marketing, sales operations, and IT, some respected sales reps, and hopefully a member of your executive team. This team doesn't have to be huge, nor should members expect to be involved in this project full-time. But you must have people who can speak for the business, and you must have the resources you need to get the job done. Get every stakeholder to understand the team's objectives and to buy in from the first meeting.

Evaluating Your Processes

Conduct business process reviews as key elements to your planning process. Those meetings should include a key stakeholder (or stakeholders) who can speak for the business and to the CRM project team (for example, a channel sales session with the head of channel sales). By doing this, you gain further agreement to your plan and ensure that you're building a solution that meets existing or desired processes of managers and their teams.

Gathering Requirements

Think about why you're implementing Salesforce. Is it to increase sales, improve productivity, encourage collaboration, or all three? Because it's nearly impossible to implement anything correctly unless you know your goal, make your objectives measurable by applying specific success metrics to an objective. (A *success metric* is a numerical goal that you want to achieve, ideally within a specified time frame.) For example, it's one thing to say that you want to reduce customer service response time, and it's quite another to define that you want to reduce response time by 20 percent by the end of the year. It's important to choose the right metric to measure your company's progress.

Defining Your Scope and Prioritizing Initiatives

You can do a lot with Salesforce, but the more complex, the longer the implementation will likely take and the greater the chance you'll hit a snag. As you collect the requirements of key stakeholders, prioritize initiatives and determine what's in scope and out of scope for the initial implementation. Consider keeping the implementation limited by focusing on the major priorities. Then you can extend your initiatives by building on prior success.

Modeling Salesforce to Your Business

After you evaluate your company's business processes and gather scope requirements from your steering committee, you want to model Salesforce to your business. However, we realize that you're probably new to Salesforce and may have some questions as to what information should go where. For your company, what are leads, accounts, contacts, and opportunities? Make sure that you check out the various process maps on the Salesforce Success Community website (http://success.salesforce.com) before you start customizing Salesforce. If you still have questions, make sure to ask your peers on the community forums or contact your customer success manager for guidance.

Customizing for User Relevance

When designing records and layouts, keeping it simple isn't always appropriate. Some businesses do have complex needs. Just be aware that long, complicated records can affect end-user adoption, so don't build a field unless you think end-users will use it. Focus your customization on relevancy to your users. Standardize information as often as possible, using picklists rather than free text fields, which will help with more accurate reporting. For fields that have to be text fields (such as the Opportunity Name), work out a simple standard naming convention.

As you accomplish major milestones (such as customization of different records or layouts), validate your work with a representative of your end-users. By doing this, you can make sure at key points that you're building a solution that works for your internal customer.

Importing Clean Data

Identify your data sources that you want to bring over to Salesforce. Note where the information is coming from, what format it will be in, and how clean it'll be.

Armed with this information, you can discuss with your team the scope of your migration. Moving into Salesforce means that it's time for some spring cleaning. Work with your team to identify which data sources are the most valuable and whether your end-users will benefit from all that information coming over.

REMEMBER

Data that doesn't make it to Salesforce doesn't necessarily disappear. You can always archive it or keep it in the legacy system.

After you decide what data is going into Salesforce, you have to clean it. Scrubbing data isn't glamorous, but it has to be done. Reducing duplicates and ensuring consistency not only make Salesforce more valuable but also improve your users' adoption. If you don't have the resources to do this, check out the AppExchange (www.salesforce.com/appexchange) for partners that help with data cleansing.

Building a Comprehensive Training Plan

As early as you can in the implementation process, start building a training plan. Don't assume that users will know what to do. And don't just rely on the generic sales training offered by Salesforce.com — it may not be relevant enough to your customization. Blend prerequisite classes, custom sales training, and reinforcement training in your plan. The key is to make sure that enough relevant training is provided so that people effectively and correctly use the Salesforce application. Also, be sure that your end-users have personal copies of this book — just in case.

Connecting with Peers

After your teams are up and running with Salesforce, you should constantly gather feedback and track how adoption is faring. Also, get out there and meet your peers — others who have rolled out Salesforce and have advice and stories to share. Through online community discussion boards, local user group meetings, and Dreamforce (the Salesforce.com annual user conference), you have several channels where you can ask questions, seek guidance, and share information that can help you take your Salesforce implementation to the next level.

Index

Symbols

A

About the Authors

Liz Kao: Liz was an enthusiastic early adopter of the Software-as-a-Service (SaaS) model and has been using Salesforce for more than a decade. An early employee of Salesforce.com, she built Salesforce-centric solutions for both external clients and internal teams, including launching over one-third of the original applications on the AppExchange. Combined with a background in sales and marketing, she blends a hands-on perspective of business needs with using Salesforce (and now, other cloud products) to build solutions that scale. A veteran of the enterprise software industry, Liz lives in San Francisco. When she isn't busy keeping up with the latest enterprise software cloud products and features, she's enjoying all the culinary delights and Internet-signal-free natural surroundings of Northern California.

Jon Paz: Jon, a Salesforce consultant, has worked with enterprise clients to deliver world-class solutions to perplexing business challenges. Previously, he worked as an editor for a major international organization. After working with various clients and industries to implement cloud technologies, Jon has witnessed the transformative value of the product. He is an avid globetrotter, can talk to you about your business in five different languages, and is a staunch advocate for the legalization of unpasteurized cheeses!

Dedication

To friends, family, and former co-workers who have supported me in this journey since the first edition. Thank you for your wisdom, insights, patience, and laughter every step of the way.

—Liz Kao

To my family, friends, and those who blur the line between the two. Thanks for putting up with me through the writing process, all the way to the finish line.

—Jon Paz

Authors' Acknowledgments

Our most sincere thanks go out to family and friends, as well as anyone who has supported us throughout this not-so-insignificant endeavor. Thank you to Amy Fandrei and Elizabeth Kuball, as well as the greater Wiley team that helped make this idea a reality. We certainly could not have done any of it without your support, flexibility, and positive attitude. And finally, thanks to the innovators and evangelists at Salesforce.com. You made enterprise software applications fun to write about (we're serious!), and your continuous innovation over the years keeps us eager to spread the good news of your products to the rest of the world.

Publisher's Acknowledgments

Acquisitions Editor: Amy Fandrei

Project Editor: Elizabeth Kuball

Copy Editor: Elizabeth Kuball

Technical Editor: Michael Wicherski

Editorial Assistant: Matthew Lowe

Sr. Editorial Assistant: Cherie Case

Production Editor: Siddique Shaik

Cover Image: TCS Created/Wiley Owned

Apple & Mac

iPad For Dummies,
6th Edition
978-1-118-72306-7

iPhone For Dummies,
7th Edition
978-1-118-69083-3

Macs All-in-One
For Dummies, 4th Edition
978-1-118-82210-4

OS X Mavericks
For Dummies
978-1-118-69188-5

Blogging & Social Media

Facebook For Dummies,
5th Edition
978-1-118-63312-0

Social Media Engagement
For Dummies
978-1-118-53019-1

WordPress For Dummies,
6th Edition
978-1-118-79161-5

Business

Stock Investing
For Dummies, 4th Edition
978-1-118-37678-2

Investing For Dummies,
6th Edition
978-0-470-90545-6

Personal Finance
For Dummies, 7th Edition
978-1-118-11785-9

QuickBooks 2014
For Dummies
978-1-118-72005-9

Small Business Marketing
Kit For Dummies,
3rd Edition
978-1-118-31183-7

Careers

Job Interviews
For Dummies, 4th Edition
978-1-118-11290-8

Job Searching with Social
Media For Dummies,
2nd Edition
978-1-118-67856-5

Personal Branding
For Dummies
978-1-118-11792-7

Resumes For Dummies,
6th Edition
978-0-470-87361-8

Starting an Etsy Business
For Dummies, 2nd Edition
978-1-118-59024-9

Diet & Nutrition

Belly Fat Diet For Dummies
978-1-118-34585-6

Mediterranean Diet
For Dummies
978-1-118-71525-3

Nutrition For Dummies,
5th Edition
978-0-470-93231-5

Digital Photography

Digital SLR Photography
All-in-One For Dummies,
2nd Edition
978-1-118-59082-9

Digital SLR Video &
Filmmaking For Dummies
978-1-118-36598-4

Photoshop Elements 12
For Dummies
978-1-118-72714-0

Gardening

Herb Gardening
For Dummies, 2nd Edition
978-0-470-61778-6

Gardening with Free-Range
Chickens For Dummies
978-1-118-54754-0

Health

Boosting Your Immunity
For Dummies
978-1-118-40200-9

Diabetes For Dummies,
4th Edition
978-1-118-29447-5

Living Paleo For Dummies
978-1-118-29405-5

Big Data

Big Data For Dummies
978-1-118-50422-2

Data Visualization
For Dummies
978-1-118-50289-1

Hadoop For Dummies
978-1-118-60755-8

Language & Foreign Language

500 Spanish Verbs
For Dummies
978-1-118-02382-2

English Grammar
For Dummies, 2nd Edition
978-0-470-54664-2

French All-in-One
For Dummies
978-1-118-22815-9

German Essentials
For Dummies
978-1-118-18422-6

Italian For Dummies,
2nd Edition
978-1-118-00465-4

Available in print and e-book formats.

Available wherever books are sold. **For more information or to order direct visit www.dummies.com**

Math & Science

Algebra I For Dummies,
2nd Edition
978-0-470-55964-2

Anatomy and Physiology
For Dummies, 2nd Edition
978-0-470-92326-9

Astronomy For Dummies,
3rd Edition
978-1-118-37697-3

Biology For Dummies,
2nd Edition
978-0-470-59875-7

Chemistry For Dummies,
2nd Edition
978-1-118-00730-3

1001 Algebra II Practice
Problems For Dummies
978-1-118-44662-1

Microsoft Office

Excel 2013 For Dummies
978-1-118-51012-4

Office 2013 All-in-One
For Dummies
978-1-118-51636-2

PowerPoint 2013
For Dummies
978-1-118-50253-2

Word 2013 For Dummies
978-1-118-49123-2

Music

Blues Harmonica
For Dummies
978-1-118-25269-7

Guitar For Dummies,
3rd Edition
978-1-118-11554-1

iPod & iTunes
For Dummies, 10th Edition
978-1-118-50864-0

Programming

Beginning Programming
with C For Dummies
978-1-118-73763-7

Excel VBA Programming
For Dummies, 3rd Edition
978-1-118-49037-2

Java For Dummies,
6th Edition
978-1-118-40780-6

Religion & Inspiration

The Bible For Dummies
978-0-7645-5296-0

Buddhism For Dummies,
2nd Edition
978-1-118-02379-2

Catholicism For Dummies,
2nd Edition
978-1-118-07778-8

Self-Help & Relationships

Beating Sugar Addiction
For Dummies
978-1-118-54645-1

Meditation For Dummies,
3rd Edition
978-1-118-29144-3

Seniors

Laptops For Seniors
For Dummies, 3rd Edition
978-1-118-71105-7

Computers For Seniors
For Dummies, 3rd Edition
978-1-118-11553-4

iPad For Seniors
For Dummies, 6th Edition
978-1-118-72826-0

Social Security
For Dummies
978-1-118-20573-0

Smartphones & Tablets

Android Phones
For Dummies, 2nd Edition
978-1-118-72030-1

Nexus Tablets
For Dummies
978-1-118-77243-0

Samsung Galaxy S 4
For Dummies
978-1-118-64222-1

Samsung Galaxy Tabs
For Dummies
978-1-118-77294-2

Test Prep

ACT For Dummies,
5th Edition
978-1-118-01259-8

ASVAB For Dummies,
3rd Edition
978-0-470-63760-9

GRE For Dummies,
7th Edition
978-0-470-88921-3

Officer Candidate Tests
For Dummies
978-0-470-59876-4

Physician's Assistant Exam
For Dummies
978-1-118-11556-5

Series 7 Exam For Dummies
978-0-470-09932-2

Windows 8

Windows 8.1 All-in-One
For Dummies
978-1-118-82087-2

Windows 8.1 For Dummies
978-1-118-82121-3

Windows 8.1 For Dummies,
Book + DVD Bundle
978-1-118-82107-7

Available in print and e-book formats.

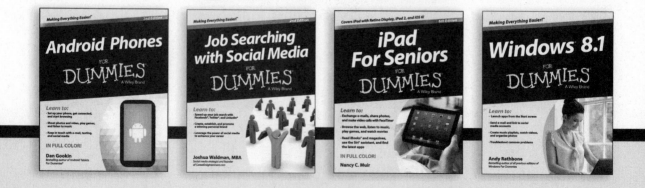

Available wherever books are sold. **For more information or to order direct visit www.dummies.com**